Reality Therapy *and* Self-Evaluation:

The Key to Client Change

Robert E. Wubbolding

AMERICAN COUNSELING
ASSOCIATION
6101 Stevenson Avenue, Suite 600
Alexandria, VA 22304
www.counseling.org

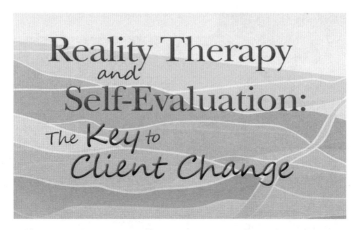

American Counseling Association

6101 Stevenson Avenue, Suite 600 • Alexandria, VA 22304

Associate Publisher • Carolyn C. Baker

Digital and Print Development Editor • Nancy Driver

Senior Production Manager • Bonny E. Gaston

Production Coordinator • Karen Thompson

Copy Editor • Kay Mikel

Cover and text design by Bonny E. Gaston.

Library of Congress Cataloging-in-Publication Data

Names: Wubbolding, Robert E., author.
Title: Reality therapy and self-evaluation : the key to client change /
  Robert E. Wubbolding.
Description: Alexandria, VA : American Counseling Association, [2017] |
  Includes bibliographical references and index.
Identifiers: LCCN 2016048750 | ISBN 9781556203701 (pbk. : alk. paper)
Subjects: LCSH: Reality therapy. | Psychotherapy. | Counseling psychology.
Classification: LCC RC489.R37 W8264 2017 | DDC 616.89/14–dc23 LC
  record available at https://lccn.loc.gov/2016048750

Dedication

*To the toughest editor I know, my dear wife Sandie,
who reviews and edits everything I write. We have been intimate partners
in writing this book, and we are the closest of friends. Together we have
made countless friends around the world as we travel to far off lands.
We are fortunate and grateful to have met and married 34 years ago.
Long live our marriage, our love, and our intimate friendship.*

Table of Contents

Chapter 9

Preface

"I have been impressed with the urgency of doing.
Knowing is not enough; we must apply.
Being willing is not enough; we must do. "

—Leonardo da Vinci

"Every person is the best judge of what relates to his own interests or concerns
. . . errors once discovered are more than half amended. "

—George Washington

• • •

In classes, training workshops, conferences, and during supervision, both experienced and neophyte counselors and therapists ask a personal question, "How do *I* help clients make meaningful changes in their actions, their thinking, and their feelings?" They also ask, "How and when do clients change?" "What motivates clients to alter their behavior?" "How can effective counselors elicit or instill in clients a desire or a motive for changing their behavior?" "How can clients better cope in the face of so many onslaughts from the world around them?"

The purpose of this brief and practical book is to provide answers to these questions as well as to help counselors formulate interventions that are useful in an age of short-term, brief counseling. The techniques presented are action centered, cognitive centered, and affective centered. "Self-evaluation" focuses on clients' explicit and controllable choices, self-talk derived from choice theory, and the emotional component of clients' total behavior. The neophyte counselor trainee and the seasoned professional can immediately implement the interventions described in this book. Moreover, if this book stimulates discussion and serves as a catalyst for conversation among professional people, it will, in my view, be successful. This hope does not minimize the value of the explanations. On the contrary, I believe the explanations add to the respect of choice theory/reality therapy (CT/RT) and place it where it belongs—in the mainstream of the profession of counseling and also in psychological theory and practice.

I am not a disinterested researcher who investigates phenomena as a detached neutral observer. Rather, I am an activist and an advocate for teaching CT/RT as a proven and practical system. In my opinion, a wealth of research provides ample support for the practice of reality therapy. Consequently, I am meticulous in my efforts to achieve both accuracy and precision in presenting both theory and practice.

Although these interventions are easily understood, experience has shown that their effective use requires thoughtful reflection and ongoing self-evaluation of their diverse applications by the user. Discerning counselors' habitual use of these skills over time reveals their subtlety and depth. In addition, I believe that these skills are compatible with cognitive counseling, motivational interviewing, narrative therapy, dialectical behavioral therapy, Adlerian counseling, and others. This integration does not diminish the fact that reality therapy is a stand-alone counseling system.

Utilizing the skills derived from this book, counselors are able to practice the art of counseling in a more spontaneous and elegant manner. By introducing advanced techniques based on reality therapy as action, cognition, and emotion centered, you can seamlessly integrate them into your own personal style and repertoire of skills. The counselor–client interactions described in this book will trigger additional questions and exploratory statements that fit individual personalities and enhance a wide range of styles. For instance, when implemented properly, the skill of helping clients self-evaluate becomes more than a formula or a cookbook recipe. Developing appropriate self-evaluation skills and interventions requires practice as well as a willingness to undertake a trial-and-error process.

The skills and techniques described in this book include both questions and explorations that appropriately and readily apply cross culturally. I have conducted training sessions in North America, Asia, Europe, the Middle East, and North Africa and trained instructors in countries around the world, encouraging them to make their own culturally appropriate adaptations. These ideas have been received with enthusiasm, and counselors have been willing to adapt them to their own traditions, customs, and language even though this may involve considerable modification. For example, when teaching in Germany, it became evident that the words *power* and *control* presented difficulties that needed detailed explanations as well as adaptations. Similarly, in cultures characterized by indirect communication (a communication style less assertive than that of many Western people), a softer mode of questioning and exploration is required. My friend and colleague Masaki Kakitani, professor emeritus and counselor at Rissyo University Tokyo, Japan, tells me that directly asking "What do you want?" can sound intrusive. His cultural adaptation—"What are you looking for?" or "What are you seeking?"—is more appropriate for Japanese clients. Rose Inza Kim, professor emeritus of Sogang University in Seoul, Korea, and known as the "Glasser of Korea," has expressed to me that the same holds true of the Korean adaptation of reality therapy. Many of my books have been translated into Japanese, Korean, Croatian, Hebrew, and Arabic, which further illustrates that indigenous peoples find the concepts useful and appealing to counselors as well as being beneficial for their clients.

Of increasing relevance to the use of reality therapy around the world is the need for the practitioner to be aware of various styles of communication and thus to understand how to adapt reality therapy to individual clients. Michio Kaku (2011) presents a far-reaching observation:

> In the West, there is an expression "the squeaky wheel gets the grease." But in the East there is another expression: "The nail that sticks out gets hammered down." These two expressions are diametrically opposed to each other, but they capture some of the essential features of Western and Eastern thought. (p. 374)

You are invited to interpret this statement and apply it to the theory and practice of reality therapy as you implement the ideas presented in this book.

Chapters 1 and 2 address human motivation: why people do what they do. Human beings possess five genetic, universal needs that are the source of behavior. More specifically, we develop pictures, or specific wants, related to the needs that are unique to each person. Human behavior consists of actions, thinking, feelings, and physiology that spring from our inner world of wants and is an attempt to influence the world for the purpose of achieving need-satisfying perceptions. This statement is clarified in Chapters 1 and 2.

Chapter 3 summarizes specific interventions made by practitioners of reality therapy for the purpose of establishing a safe, warm, and empathic relationship. Chapter 4 constitutes the heart and soul of reality therapy, the WDEP system. This acronym summarizes many direct as well as subtle interventions that are explained and illustrated throughout the book.

Chapters 5, 6, and 7 present specific hypothetical dialogues. Chapter 5 includes the application of reality therapy to two adults: an employee who is unmotivated and drinks excessively, and a culture-specific lonely client seeking a promotion at work.

Chapter 6 introduces four cross-cultural cases, beginning with a troubled adolescent student, followed by a cultural exploration of wants or goals underlying those initially expressed by the client. The third case describes an adult female with a record of arrests for drug dealing who is living in a halfway house and feels lonely, powerless, and unattractive. The final case is of a young male probationer whose ethnicity is not described, which demonstrates the applicability of reality therapy to all clients regardless of ethnicity.

Chapter 7 contains seven case studies. The first case illustrates the use of reality therapy with an adult couple experiencing tension in their relationship. Subsequent to this case is one of a self-referred woman suffering the loss of her husband. The third case focuses on the posttraumatic stress of a 12-year army veteran. The final four cases illustrate applications to an adult female with multiple diagnoses living in poverty with a history of self-injury and child neglect; an adult male who demonstrates a discrepancy between his stated values and his behavior; an adult female who fears that her career might be in jeopardy because of anxiety that is rooted in a serious loss; and, finally, we revisit a teenage client who is dealing with feelings of fear and anger.

Chapter 8 provides answers to questions about spirituality, the value of expressing reality therapy as the WDEP system, the place of feelings and emotions in reality therapy, and the connection between reality therapy and ethics principles. It also provides the answer to the question, "What is the evidence for the effective use of reality therapy?" The chapter ends with a self-evaluation applied to the professional, with questions for your consideration and criticisms of reality therapy.

Chapter 9 summarizes the central place of self-evaluation in reality therapy as described by its founder, psychiatrist William Glasser (1925–2013).

Specific dialogues illustrate many kinds of direct self-evaluations. For example, the interchange between the counselor and Simon in Chapter 5 includes asking Simon whether he believes that his current work habits are helpful or hurtful in keeping his job. Also, Dr. Phil's famous question, "How's that working for you?", exemplifies a direct inquiry focusing on clients' self-evaluations. Furthermore, the advanced use of self-evaluation skills includes subtle and indirect techniques. Implicit or indirect self-evaluation such as the use of metaphors and stories offers additional pathways for utilizing these keys to client change.

I offer four suggestions for your consideration. First, due to the fact that many graduates of counseling programs and licensed counselors work in agencies that identify them as therapists, in this book I use the terms *counseling* and *therapy* interchangeably. However, please note that counseling is not merely an activity; it is an independent profession. Although there are differences between the activities of counseling and psychotherapy, I do not differentiate between the two processes because reality therapy has found a home among a wide variety of mental health workers: counselors, corrections workers, nurses, psychologists, addictions specialists, school counselors, classroom teachers, managers, supervisors, and administrators, to name a few. According to Patterson (1973), "there are no essential differences between counseling and psychotherapy in the nature of the relationship, in the process, in the methods or techniques, in goals or outcomes, or even in the kinds of clients involved" (p. xiv). Nystul (2011) states that "the counseling literature has not made a clear distinction between these concepts, perhaps because the two processes are more similar than different" (p. 6). Nevertheless, if you wish to differentiate between the two, I will not argue the point. Whether you identify yourself as a counselor or a therapist, I believe you will find that you can use the ideas described in this book. In describing the interaction between the professional person and the client, I will, for the most part, refer to the professional person as a "counselor."

Second, as you read the book, look for surprises and the unexpected, such as the client washing dishes with his mother. Some of the interventions will undoubtedly seem familiar, but others might seem unusual or even startling. There might even be one that dazzles you! When you employ these tactics, you will notice that clients begin to think about their lives in a different way. Frequently, they demonstrate their change of thinking nonverbally. They tend to look up and adopt a hesitating and thoughtful facial expression. If the technique is familiar to you, remember the admonition of the famous British writer Samuel Johnson who observed that we need to be reminded more than we need to be taught. In a like manner, Oliver Wendell Holmes said, "We need education in the obvious more than investigation of the obscure" (as cited in Sowell, 2015, p. 46). In an overstatement, President Harry Truman observed that the only thing new is the history you do not know. If the technique is new, enjoy it, use it as soon as possible, and don't fret about whether it is old or new.

Third, this is not a book merely about concepts. Included are many examples of dialogues and interactions between counselor and client illustrating a variety of self-evaluations and specific usable interventions. I encourage you to utilize the questions and other interventions in your professional relationships. They may feel awkward at first, but with continued use they will become spontaneous and natural. An important extension of reality therapy counseling is my suggestion that at the end of each session you ask the client, "What was the most useful idea discussed today?" Implementing this simple idea, a question and an answer, requires no more than a few seconds, but it provides the opportunity for clients to evaluate the process and to provide helpful feedback to the counselor. To emphasize the importance of this intervention, I include a question such as, "What was most useful to you in our session today?"

Fourth, be aware that the use of easily understood language is intentional. I have written about self-evaluation with a purposeful focus on the language of everyday living. Very few technical words and phrases are required to explain and learn the powerful interventions defined as "self-evaluation." Similarly, I hope you will teach these principles to colleagues, clients, families, parent groups, and the public. They are indeed life-changing ideas that, because of down-to-earth language, can be learned not only by licensed professionals but also by people from virtually every background.

Finally, I invite you to contact me with questions, difficulties encountered, and, especially, success stories at wubsrt@fuse.net.

Acknowledgments

I am forever indebted to the founder of reality therapy, William Glasser. My mentor died August 23, 2013. I miss his wisdom, his wit, and his unbounded enthusiasm for teaching. Naomi, his first wife, died in December 1992. She was a friend and an enthusiastic supporter of Bill and of the members of the William Glasser Institute. Within a few years, Bill married Carleen Floyd, my wife's best friend, and Carleen Glasser remains committed to keeping Bill's voice alive. During his life, Jon Carlson showed a unique commitment to counseling theory and practice. He assisted many young professionals and pointed the way toward excellence in the world of publishing and counseling. My good friends Jerry and Marianne Corey have always provided encouragement and enthusiasm.

My adaptation of reality therapy to many cultures around the world has been made easy by partnering with John Brickell from the United Kingdom, Leon Lojk from Slovenia, Rose In-Za Kim from South Korea, Masaki Kakitani and Aoki Satoshi from Japan, Kwee Ong, Sister Liz Than, and Evelyn Koh from Singapore, Farida Dias from India, Ali Sahebi from Iran and Australia, Ivan Honey from Australia, as well as students from many continents.

I wish to extend a special acknowledgment to the faculty and students of Xavier University for their support and encouragement. Al Anderson, a professor at Xavier, was a special mentor and friend during my years there; may he rest in peace.

Finally, I cannot pay enough compliments or express my gratitude sufficiently to Carolyn Baker and Nancy Driver whose patience and gentleness are written in the book of life. Working with the entire staff at the American Counseling Association has been a most enjoyable experience.

To those who have died, I say rest in peace. To my many living friends, "Live long and prosper."

About the Author

Robert E. Wubbolding, EdD, LPCC, NCC, BCC, IABMCP, internationally known teacher, author, and practitioner of reality therapy, has taught choice theory and reality therapy in the United States, Europe, Asia, the Middle East, and North Africa (Morocco). His contributions to the theory and practice include the ideas of *Positive Symptoms, The Cycle of Counseling, Five Levels of Commitment,* and others. He has also significantly expanded the *Procedure of Evaluation.* He has written more than 150 articles and essays, 35 chapters in textbooks, 15 books, and published many DVDs on reality therapy. His books include *Using Reality Therapy, Understanding Reality Therapy, Reality Therapy for the 21st Century, A Set of Directions for Putting and Keeping Yourself Together,* and *Reality Therapy: Theories of Psychotherapy Series* (published by the American Psychological Association), and he is coeditor for *Contemporary Issues in Couples Counseling* and coauthor of *Counselling With Reality Therapy* (2nd ed., Speechmark, London, UK).

He is professor emeritus at Xavier University in Cincinnati, Ohio. His busy professional life includes being director of the Center for Reality Therapy and senior faculty for William Glasser International. He was personally appointed by William Glasser to be the first Director of Training for the institute. In this position he coordinated and monitored the Certification, Supervisor, and Instructor Training programs (1988–2011). Currently, he is also faculty associate at Johns Hopkins University and is a board-certified coach.

Formerly, he consulted with the drug and alcohol abuse programs of the U.S. Army and Air Force. He was a group counselor at a halfway house for women, an elementary and secondary school counselor, a high school teacher, and a teacher of adult basic education. For 2 years he taught for the University of Southern California in their overseas programs in Japan, South Korea, and Germany.

Professional memberships include Professional Clinical Counselor, Psychologist, member of the American Counseling Association, the American Psychological Association, the American Mental Health Counseling Association, and many other national and state psychological and counseling associations.

His personal mission is to "Keep the flag flying." His goal is to maintain and expand the system of reality therapy founded by William Glasser, who wrote an introduction to his book and stated, "He is one of my closest and most trusted associates. I couldn't recommend anyone more highly."

Whenever he writes, he depends on his wife of more than three decades, Sandie, whom he describes as his best friend, "finicky" editor, and who he says challenges him every day to be the best person he can be.

Awards include the Marvin Rammelsberg Award, presented to a person in a helping profession best exemplifying qualities of friendship, brotherhood, and humanitarianism, displaying exemplary leadership qualities, and making outstanding contributions to professional organizations; the Herman J. Peters Award for exemplary leadership to promote the profession of counseling; the Greater Cincinnati Counseling Association unique Recognition of Merit Award; the Mary Corre Foster Award for exemplifying qualities of leadership within the counseling profession and promoting the standards of excellence within the profession; Distinguished Alumnus Award, College of Education, University of Cincinnati, 2002; Distinguished Counseling Graduate of the 1970s decade, Counseling Department, College of Education, University of Cincinnati, 2005. In 2009 he was given the Gratitude Award for Initiating Reality Therapy in the United Kingdom from the Institute for Reality Therapy United Kingdom. Also in 2009 he was awarded the Certificate of Reality Therapy Psychotherapist by the European Association for Psychotherapy. In 2014 he was honored as a "Living Legend in Counseling" at the American Counseling Association Conference in Honolulu, Hawaii. In 2015, the Malta Reality Therapy Association made him an honorary member because of his work in introducing reality therapy to their country. In 2015, he was invited to deliver the keynote address at the 25th anniversary of the founding of the Japan Reality Therapy Association, Tokyo, Japan. In 2016, he received the title "Friend of William Glasser Institute Singapore," in Singapore. In

2016, he was invited to deliver the keynote address to the first international William Glasser Institute Conference held in Asia, in Seoul, South Korea.

Currently he spends his time teaching reality therapy around the world with his wife, Sandie, and introducing reality therapy to new audiences, cultures, and professions.

Chapter 1

Human Motivation: "In General Why Do People Do What They Do?"

The origins of reality therapy are rooted in the experience of psychiatrist William Glasser. He was formed by the conventional psychiatric training of the 1950s and 1960s, but Glasser came to believe that helping clients gain insight and study their early childhood conflicts did not necessarily cause behavioral change. He also noted that the successful therapy given to mental patients included holding them responsible for their behavior without blaming the world around them, their childhood, their parents, or their culture. He discussed this apparent anomaly with his supervisor, whom he referred to throughout his life as "my teacher, Dr. Harrington." In a well-known and oft quoted gesture, Dr. Harrington reached across his desk and said, "Welcome to the club." Thus reality therapy was given birth (Roy, 2014).

Reality Therapy Develops

As Glasser became a public figure lecturing throughout North America and Canada, his audiences consisted of counselors and therapists as well as educators at every level. After publishing *Reality Therapy* (1965), he crystalized his ideas as they applied to schools in his book *Schools Without Failure* (1968).

The Anchor and Mainstay of Reality Therapy

Why did counselors, therapists, and teachers find reality therapy appealing and effective? This is the key question answered throughout this book. In general, the counseling intervention known as *self-evaluation*—the core and cornerstone of reality therapy—is usable with virtually any client and adaptable to every known culture. The latter part of this statement might seem grandiose and simplistic; however, I have personally seen indigenous instructors adapt this principle to non-Western cultures. For example, when teaching in Singapore, I learned that helping clients self-evaluate means encouraging them to disclose how their parents and even grandparents would see their behavior and asking, "Is it helpful or unhelpful?" Glasser (1972) described self-evaluation as the *basis for change*. It can be very helpful to counselors regardless of their theoretical orientation. Glasser even extended its application to organizational development where it serves as an essential component of the Glasser Quality School. Qualifying as a Glasser Quality School results from thoroughly and comprehensively implementing the principles of choice theory/reality therapy (CT/RT) for several years and attaining goals of increased student achievement and behavioral improvement. Then, with administrative, staff, and parental involvement, through self-evaluation based on criteria established by the William Glasser Institute (now known as William Glasser International), the school declares itself a Glasser Quality School (Glasser, 1990; Wubbolding, 2007).

Reality Therapy Finds a Validating Theory

Choice theory, along with its application through reality therapy, provides the bedrock principles for self-evaluation. For the sake of brevity and because this book focuses on self-evaluation within the context of counseling, I refer to this complete system (theory and application) with the term *reality therapy*. This is the standard practice represented in many textbooks such as Capuzzi and Stauffer (2016), Corey (2017), Tinsley, Lease, and Wiersma (2016), and many others.

Glasser (1981, 1984) at first accepted the terms *control theory* or *control system theory* for validating the delivery system of reality therapy. The theoretical principles date to the 1940s. Even before that, John von Neumann, an associate of Albert Einstein, foreshadowed the use of analog and digital computers as an explanation for the human nervous system (Powers, 1973). More proximately, the influential writer Norbert Wiener (1948, 1952) described the brain as a negative input control system whose behavior is purposeful. When it is not achieving its purpose, it receives negative input that it is not on target; then it corrects its trajectory to align itself with its targeted goal, much like a torpedo or a rocket.

Similarly, according to control theory, the human brain functions analogously to a thermostat that reads the temperature in the room and signals its heating or air conditioning system to correct what might be called its behavior. It cools or heats the room for the purpose of achieving its goal, which is maintaining the room's preset or desired temperature.

With the emphasis on human choice and its corollary personal responsibility, Glasser (1998) significantly altered control theory. Consequently, he renamed this new version "choice theory." A detailed rationale for this change is described in Glasser's book *Choice Theory* (1998), my book *Reality Therapy for the 21st Century* (Wubbolding, 2000b), and William Glasser's biography, *William Glasser: Champion of Choice* (Roy, 2014).

Principles of Human Motivation

Describing both the connection and the distinction between choice theory and its delivery system, Glasser and Glasser (2008) state, "Choice theory is the track and reality therapy is the train" (p. 1). CT/RT interface with each other and yet are separable. They are like two hands folded together: interdependent and yet independent.

Choice theory, the foundation for reality therapy procedures, especially self-evaluation, is summarized in the following principles.

The first principle is that human motivation originates within the human person. This means that human behavior cannot be completely coerced. The world outside the human mind does not force people to behave in a predetermined manner. The external world has a major influence on how people live, and it is quite evident that other people can be very persuasive. Al Capone once remarked that he could get what he wanted with a kind word and a gun more efficiently than with only a kind word. Nevertheless, people always retain at least *some* control over their actions. History is filled with examples of people refusing to alter their beliefs even to the point of suffering; such martyrs realized that they had choices.

From the point of view of choice theory, people generate behaviors for the purpose of satisfying five universal needs or genetic instructions. I prefer to describe these five motivators as *somewhat hierarchical*. The need for survival or self-preservation is more basic than the four psychological needs: belonging, inner control, freedom, and fun. Starving individuals often ignore the other needs in order to preserve their lives. Also, the need for belonging, although not as basic as survival, nevertheless occupies a central place in choice theory and therefore in the practice of reality therapy. Human service workers who work with the poorest of the poor are often faced with client problems that appear to have no solution. Their problems are many and their intensity is both extreme and fierce. The workers are at a loss, and they themselves feel helpless. Yet they can provide at least a modicum of assistance by helping their clients improve at least one human relationship. The five universal human needs are discussed in the following sections.

Belonging or Involvement With People

A counselor would find it impossible to identify a problem that does not *at least* contain a relationship issue. Consequently, counselors utilizing reality therapy often explore the interpersonal relationships of their clients. In his lectures, Glasser emphasized his belief that most long-term psychological problems are, in fact, relationship problems. I prefer to temper this principle by teaching that regardless of the presenting issue, improving human relationships helps to alleviate pain and suffering. The need for belonging can be made more concrete by recognizing three kinds of belonging: family belonging, work belonging, and social belonging. This need expresses itself primarily in the family. Children need to feel safe, nurtured, and appreciated, and as they grow, they need to feel valued. Children are born with a need to connect with the people around them. When I teach choice theory and reality therapy, I ask participants what they like about their jobs. A high percentage invariably answer, "The people I work with." When workers feel appreciated and connected with their peers, their productivity increases, and, even more important, they satisfy their need for belonging on the job. Homeless individuals lack employment but often satisfy their need for belonging by associating with other homeless people. Social belonging means friendship. This is especially evident at times of transition, such as transferring from one school to another, changing jobs, or changing residences. In working with military families, a counselor needs to assist the children to adapt to frequently changing schools and making new friends to building support systems ("Understanding Military Culture," 2016). Helping clients satisfy the multifaceted need for belonging constitutes a major focus for the practitioner of reality therapy. The need for belonging is often unfulfilled and even assaulted by the use of toxic behaviors such as arguing, blaming, and criticizing.

Discussion Questions
1. What additional aspects of the need for belonging can you describe?
2. In what ways can you apply the need for belonging in your counseling?
3. What role does belonging play in your life?

Power or Inner Control, Including Competence and Achievement
In addition to belonging, counselors often help clients satisfy their need for power. Like belonging, this source of human motivation expresses itself in a variety of ways. The satisfaction of power often means that one individual wins at the expense of another. Athletes, politicians, people seeking jobs or promotions, even rivalries in love relationships often involve the satisfaction or the frustration of the need for power. One person feels rewarded or fulfilled and the other person feels deprived or unfulfilled. In short, the drive for power often involves winning and losing.

The word *power* derives from the French word *pouvoir*, meaning to be able or capable without reference to the deprivation of another person. Upon receiving good news from a surgeon, a patient feels a sense of inner satisfaction, a feeling of inner control, without the thought that someone else is deprived of good health. This aspect of power underlies many human behaviors. When driving to a specific destination in an unfamiliar city, a sense of achievement or accomplishment often follows arrival at the journey's end. Some airline passengers feel a much higher degree of inner control when the plane's wheels touch the ground after a turbulent flight. These illustrations point to the undeniable fact that human behavior springing from power need not be competitive.

Though it is connected with belonging, the satisfaction of the power need also involves gaining recognition. This story is told about the New York Yankees baseball star Mickey Mantle. After his retirement, he was attending a party on an upper floor in a hotel during a heavy rainstorm, and he was standing with his ear close to the window. Someone asked him about this, and his comment was that the rain sounded like applause. Evidently he missed the accustomed recognition he received while on the baseball field. Incidentally, he also holds the record for the longest homerun ever hit in baseball: 734 feet, May 22, 1963, at Yankee Stadium against Kansas City off pitcher Bill Fischer. This achievement, discussed among baseball fans even today, represents the satisfaction of the power need. The question is, "Could Bill Fischer also feel a sense of recognition?"

Discussion Questions
1. In what other ways do people seek and gain recognition?
2. How do the following satisfy the need for power or recognition or inner self-satisfaction: salary or compensation for work, medals for achievement or bravery, awards, verbal compliments, "pats on the back"?
3. How does this description of power apply to you? Is your need for power centered on inner control or recognition fulfilled as much as you desire?

Freedom or Independence

Human beings are born with the need for freedom. This need becomes more obvious as the child grows and matures. Freedom relates to the urge to make choices. For a child this need is often expressed by the response, "No." Growth and maturity bring its own developmental tasks and expressions of the need for freedom. Every parent and teacher has experienced children who seek freedom from the restraints, rules, and expectations of authorities. Independence is closely related to freedom and implies the need expressed popularly by the phrase, "Standing on my own two feet." Many individuals seek a wide latitude for making choices, whereas others paradoxically feel free when they live in a more externally structured world. The need for freedom is expressed in many ways. Viktor Frankl's experience, described in his classic book *Man's Search for Meaning* (1963), illustrates that freedom can exist in the midst of unspeakable external restraints. A prisoner in a Nazi concentration camp during World War II, he described how he retained a deep sense of freedom. He had the choice of how he would perceive the diabolical world around him. He chose to see his experience as having purpose and meaning and was able to satisfy at least to some extent his need for freedom. I will later refer to this heroic man several times.

Discussion Questions
1. How can people meet their need for freedom and independence at various stages of development, such as in late adulthood (people over 70 years of age)?
2. How would you assist a client who feels rejected and oppressed by society, such as an ex-prisoner, an ethnic minority person, or an individual with Tourette's syndrome?
3. How do you experience freedom or independence in your own life, and do you see any overlap between freedom and power? If so, in what ways?

Fun or Enjoyment

To state that fun is a basic human need at first might appear to be a superficial concept. However, even a superficial reading of the fifth edition of the *Diagnostic and Statistical Manual of Mental Disorders* (APA, 2013) reveals that individuals with mental disorders lack skill in satisfying their need for fun. The following words are not listed in the index: fun, enjoyment, laughter, endorphins. More specifically, a random selection of the diagnostic criteria for specific disorders describes behaviors that are the opposite of fun. Among the criteria describing Intermittent Explosive Disorder are outbursts accompanied by distress, verbal aggression such as temper tantrums and tirades, and other behaviors devoid of fun (p. 466 ff). Similarly, the diagnostic criteria for Persistent Depressive Disorder (Dysthymia) include poor appetite, insomnia, low energy, low self-esteem, poor concentration, and feelings of hopelessness (p. 168 ff). These are hardly characteristics of fun or enjoyment.

Laughter and humor have many benefits, including medical healing qualities. Bernie Siegel (2011) states, "Studies show that cancer patients who laugh several times a day for no other reason live longer than those who do not laugh. So every few hours treat yourself to a laugh and those around you will thank you too because laughter is contagious and he who laughs, lasts."

Glasser (2005b) asserts that satisfying the need for fun facilitates learning. Through play children learn mathematics, develop reading skills, and enhance their socialization abilities. John Cleese, the British comedian and writer, states that he who laughs most learns best. Maria Montessori's frequently quoted philosophy included, "What is learned through play is there to stay."

Discussion Questions
  1. Why do you think fun and enjoyment are not emphasized in the literature on mental health?
  2. How can you help clients more effectively fulfill their need for fun and enjoyment as you counsel them?
  3. Are you having fun yet? Please justify your answer.

Survival or Self-Preservation

The most basic human need or motivator is staying alive. The many functions of the human body work to preserve health and maintain life. For instance, the very fact that it is called the circulatory system implies that blood moves about the body and brings nutrients to its organs and helps to dispose of waste. When a human being feels a severe threat or excitement, the body secretes the hormone adrenaline, which constricts the blood vessels of the belly and skin, making more blood available for the heart, lungs, and voluntary muscles. It provides an emergency preparation for the stress reaction "fight or flight or freeze."

In a sense, the human body sends signals to which we are well advised to listen. Pain and many other signals communicate that all is not well and that some action is required. Although counselors do not practice medicine, they can ask clients how their total behavior (action, thinking, and feelings) has affected their health and survival behaviors. Loss of sleep, poor diet, stressful lifestyle, and many other health-related behaviors influence the satisfaction of the psychological needs: belonging, power/inner control, freedom/independence, and fun/enjoyment. Even Freud recognized that the survival needs and their derivatives are basic to effective living; he once stated that a man with a toothache cannot be in love.

Discussion Questions
1. How have you dealt with a client whose presenting issue is clearly the need for survival?
2. How do you see yourself connecting the need for survival with the psychological needs?
3. What does your own self-evaluation look like regarding your need for survival, more specifically addressing diet, exercise, and recreation?

The five individual human needs constitute a system of human motivation that Glasser (2003) described as genetic instructions. In this view of human motivation, human beings possess innate drives from which their behavior springs, especially their choices. The individual needs overlap with each other. For example, frequently we choose to have fun with other people, satisfying both fun and belonging needs. Choosing an exciting activity such as skiing, bungee jumping, sky diving, or playing a successful game of golf on a sunny day results in the satisfaction of inner control, fun, freedom, and, especially, belonging.

The individual needs are not only genetic; they are also generic. They are general, not specific. They are analogous to empty salad bowls that are functional only when they contain specifics. These specifics are precise pictures of what is desirable. An individual has a need for belonging and satisfies it by inserting a specific image of a partner or a pet.

The needs can vary in levels of intensity. For some individuals, a high need for belonging is more prominent and intense than the need for power or independence. Comedians have a high need for fun and have converted it into a career, thus combining it with the need for power or achievement and survival.

Central to understanding the significance of the need system is the realization that it functions in the here and now, or in the present. Behavioral choices spring from current motivations. This controversial principle means that everything people do is done to satisfy current motivations. The controversial corollary is that past behavior, such as early childhood experiences, though influential, do not dictate current behavior choices. A person suffering from childhood trauma or from a near death experience during wartime or any other time need not be permanently imprisoned by these memories. Such a client can learn to satisfy current needs more effectively by learning the principles of choice theory and the components of reality therapy. The case of Vivian in Chapter 7 illustrates this principle.

In making choice theory operational through the use of reality therapy, counselors can use the five needs as a diagnostic schema to help clients identify deficits that will lead to effective treatment planning (Fulkerson, 2014).

Finally, choice theory is best viewed as an open system, flexible enough to incorporate additions. Some counselors add the need for faith or for a higher power. Frankl (1963) saved his own life with the belief that the most fundamental human need is a sense of meaning and purpose. This principle is congruent with, but additional to, the basic theory taught by William Glasser: choice theory.

Chapter 2

Human Motivation:
"Specifically Why Do People
Do What They Do?"

The second principle of human motivation is an extension of the principle described in Chapter 1. The human needs are general, universal motivators. Additional specific motivators spring from the five human needs described in Chapter 1.

Quality World:
Mental Picture Album, Wants and Desires

As people interact with the world around them, they develop specific wants, or pictures, related to each need. This collection of wants is referred to as their *quality world*, a world that resulted from evaluating their experiences (that is, their interactions with the world around them). Contrasted with human needs that are general and innate, pictures in the quality world are unique to each individual. Each of us has specific desires related to the five-need system. Some people find satisfaction in a relationship with one person but not with another person. They satisfy the power/in control need with a specific activity, such as a job. Skydivers report that jumping out of an airplane provides a unique sense of freedom. The wide diversity of hobbies and sports and enjoyable activities illustrates the unlimited range of satisfying fun pictures. Some people enjoy collecting coins, others enjoy collecting butterflies, running, or watching baseball or soccer. In some cultures, cheering and gambling at the brutal competition between a snake and a mongoose provides a fun picture.

These pictures are sometimes blurred. For example, a person may desire a relationship with someone but has yet to clarify the precise qualities of the other person. The counselor's responsibility often is to help clients clarify their blurred pictures. Clients wants are frequently in conflict. The desire for fun, such as getting high on drugs, almost invariably conflicts with a desire for a lasting relationship. Even more significant from a counseling point of view, wants or desires, though satisfying to one person, can create conflicts with the wants and desires of another person. It is not unusual for marriages to end because of intense differences and commitments to opposing political candidates. Counselors often focus on helping clients establish a sense of priority among wants or desires. This effort is itself a high priority in counseling people or families with addiction issues because they often have difficulty clarifying appropriate priorities. The case of Morgan and Simon described in Chapter 5 exemplifies the application of reality therapy to this aspect of the quality world.

From a developmental point of view, the effective use of reality therapy and, in fact, the effective practice of any counseling system, rests on evidence regarding the appropriate satisfaction of clients' needs and wants. Kaku (2011) described the significance of delayed gratification, and his own words are significant:

> We judge other humans, in fact, by their ability to predict evolving situations and formulate concrete strategies. An important part of leadership is to anticipate future situations, weigh possible outcomes, and set concrete goals accordingly. In other words, this form of consciousness involves predicting the future, that is, creating multiple models that approximate future events. This requires a very sophisticated understanding of common sense and the rules of nature. It means that you ask yourself, "what if" repeatedly. Whether planning to rob a bank or run for president, this kind of planning means being able to run multiple simulations of possible realities in your head. All indications are that only humans have mastered this art in nature.
>
> We also see this when psychological profiles of test subjects are analyzed. Psychologists often compare the psychological profiles of adults to their profiles when they were children. Then one asks the question: What is the one quality that predicted their success in marriage, careers, wealth, etc.? When one compensates for socioeconomic factors, one finds that one characteristic sometimes stands out from all the others: the ability to delay gratification. According to the long-term studies of Walter

Mischel of Columbia University, and many others, children who were able to refrain from immediate gratification (e.g., eating a marshmallow given to them) and held out for greater long-term rewards (getting two marshmallows instead of one) consistently scored higher on almost every measure of future success, in SATs, life, love and career.

But being able to defer gratification also refers to a higher level of awareness and consciousness. These children were able to simulate the future and realize that future rewards were greater. So being able to see the future consequences of our actions requires a higher level of awareness. (pp. 113–114)

From the point of view of the reality therapist, future consequences can serve as a standard for effective self-evaluation. The standard or possibility of positive or negative consequences can be explicitly presented to clients or implied. When counselors ask, "Do your choices help or hurt you?", clients sometimes conclude that consequences often follow their choices.

Specific Characteristics of Wants

Wants are desires and goals unique and specific to each person. Keep in mind that the basic characteristic of wants is that they represent pictures related to each general and universal need.

- *Need fulfilling*: Wants desired intensely; genuine quality world pictures are more than whims or wishes.
- *Related to each need*: The counselor's work often aims at assisting clients to formulate wants and goals connected with their need for belonging, power, freedom, and fun.
- *Prioritized*: A self-actualizing person has developed the ability to distinguish between what is important and what is unimportant. Individuals growing up in a chemically dependent family and substance abusers themselves as well as clients from attention-deficit families often need special help in establishing a sense of helpful and constructive priorities. Counseling clients in the early stages of addiction recovery often includes helping them evaluate the usefulness of 12-step programs as well as their efforts to benefit from them. Similarly, when a counselor discusses schoolwork with an underachieving student, emphasis is placed on establishing a study schedule in which the student determines for him- or herself the value of studying at a specific time of day. In both cases, the work of the counselor is not to impose values or judgments but to assist clients in learn-

ing the art of evaluating the appropriateness of the hierarchy of their wants, that is, their sense of priorities.

- *Changeable and changing*: Wants, goals, and desires are not static. As a person matures, develops, and grows in experience, wants change. Eric Erikson described eight psychosocial stages of development that provide background for this characteristic. For instance, in his third stage of development—preschool, ages 3 to 5 years, exploration (initiative vs. guilt)—"children need to begin asserting power and control over the environment." In the context of the quality world, children incorporate specific age-appropriate ways to gain control, thereby satisfying their need for achievement or power. In his eighth stage of development—maturity, age 65 to death, reflection on life (ego integrity vs. despair)—"older adults need to look back on life and feel a sense of fulfillment." This is the opposite of regret and despair (Cherry, 2016; Harder, 2012). Clearly, adults at this stage of development have a fulfilled quality world or mental picture album that is quite different from a child's. Marriage and family counselors understand that couples change their pictures. They remove the picture of their partner and insert a picture of another person. The divorce courts are filled with individuals whose quality worlds are in flux. In his lectures, Glasser was fond of facetiously saying that in *Gone With the Wind* Rhett Butler, in fact, said "Frankly, my dear, I am taking you out of my quality world" rather than "I don't give a damn."

- *Specific and unique*: Individual human needs are general and non-specific, but wants are specific. Just as a camera records particular events, the quality world contains specific and confined wants, such as a child inserting a picture of his or her mother as a need-satisfying person. Wants are also unique to each individual or, more accurately, the collection of wants is unique. Even though an individual's desires can be similar to those of others, the sum total is still diverse. Human conflict occurs when two individuals have a specific picture of a person or a thing that each person chooses to pursue. Hence, pain and disappointment accompany the rejection by a lover who chooses another person. Frustration results when the bid for an intensely desired house that is for sale is lost to a higher bidder. Moreover, because of the singularity of each person's interaction with the world around him or her, the individual totality of each person's quality world is different from that of every other person's. This helps to explain human diversity. In other words, each person's quality world is circumscribed by experience. How human beings interact with others, how and whether they achieve a degree of success, their range of perceived choices, and their manner of experiencing fun or enjoyment provide a wealth of material and a foundation for effective counseling. Hence, empathy can be a challenge and yet a necessity for effective counseling. In some cultures, the game of cricket is an occasion for satisfying wants related to belonging, achievement, and fun. For others, the game is unintelligible. A British friend of mine sat through three innings of a pitcher's duel in a professional baseball game, known as the American pastime, and said, "When is something going to happen?" To him the game did not satisfy his world of wants. Likewise, an adolescent growing up in Afghanistan often enjoys "kite running," an activity that is rarely part of life for a resident of Omaha, Nebraska; Sydney, Australia; or Valletta, Malta.

- *Can be blurred*: Images contained in the quality world are specific and yet sometimes vaguely defined. The counselor's role is to assist clients in clarifying what they want from the world around them and from themselves. Adolescents often state, "I want to be left alone," without being able to spell out exactly what their desired freedom or independence would look like. The skilled counselor helps clients clarify their picture of being left alone. These specific descriptions can be a prerequisite for their self-evaluations.

- *May be in conflict*: Wants are often in conflict with each other. A client (we'll call him Simon) once stated that what he wanted more than anything else was to drive his truck 250 miles, cross a specific bridge, sit beside a lake, and enjoy his freedom from responsibilities. When he felt himself approaching his destination, he shouted out loud in his car, "Free at last, free at last, thank God I'm free at last." The conflict, however, was that he was employed and such trips interfered with his desire for the salary he needed to support himself. He had clearly defined his wants, yet he believed they were mutually exclusive.

- *May be in conflict with those of other people*: Simon also discussed the conflict with his employer's expectations, which Simon described as follows: "I want you on the job five days a week, not four days, or three and a half days." On the surface these diverse quality world wants appeared to be irreconcilable.

- *Realistic and unrealistic*: A college student has a clear picture of graduating and has survived his freshman year. During his sophomore year, however, he skips class, parties excessively, and is in danger of flunking and losing his financial aid. The skilled counselor refrains from lecturing the student or imposing judgments on him and helps the student come to a judgment about the attainability of his goal. Counselors also assist such students to make the connection between their wants and their behavior. A commonsense illustration is a person who wants to win a lottery. This is at least made more possible by taking the first step: buying a ticket.

- *Personal:* Specific wants are sometimes easily expressed and at other times are withheld from other people. But all desires are the personal possessions of clients and of all human beings. A practitioner need not pressure clients to disclose their embarrassing desires. When a trusting counseling relationship is developed, clients are more inclined to share their hopes and dreams, their wants and desires.

- *Linked with each other:* In some recovery programs, clients learn that they can help themselves by separating their comingled wants. For example, a counselor helps a client avoid listening to the music that the client associates with drug or alcohol use. By attending 12-step meetings, people in recovery often replace pictures of their old friends with pictures of new ones, old activities with new activities, old music with new music.

- *Remote and immediate:* Through self-evaluation, clients decide whether immediate gratification overrides the long-term satisfaction of quality world pictures. Simon ultimately decides whether being "free at last" is more advantageous than earning a living, thereby enabling him to achieve a higher degree of freedom during an earned vacation or at some point in the near or distant future.

- *Overlapping:* Quality world pictures sometimes interconnect with each other. Partners enjoying a meal together exemplifies the satisfaction of their desires for fun and belonging. Glasser, an avid tennis player, frequently stated in his lectures that he always played tennis with another person because "it is very difficult to play tennis alone unless the individual is very fast."

- *Reminiscent:* A pleasant experience results in the development of specific wants surrounding the experience. In the summertime, I remember my father, a wiry, energetic person, walking with me as a child to a grocery store to buy ice cream. He resembled the actor and dancer Fred Astaire. To this day, I still associate my love for ice cream and Fred Astaire movies with my father's love and interest in me.

Counselors can implement the principles of the quality world not only with clients but also on a systemic level. For instance, a school counselor can intervene to help students appreciate the many expressions of diversity by facilitating group activities where students learn to interact with and trust others that they formerly might have mistrusted or even felt hostile toward. They learn to appreciate similarities of wants and to understand that individuals different from them have legitimate wants and goals that might be quite different from theirs.

It is clear that the concepts of wants, desires, hopes, dreams, and goals—the quality world—are much more intricate than they first appear. Understanding casts new light on the wide diversity of our institutions in our ever-changing world. Appreciating the significance of the quality world, and more specifically its content, provides a wealth of material for facilitating the counselor–client relationship, establishing trust, assisting counselors in developing and expressing empathy, and finally in developing skills for collaborating with clients as they conduct fearless and searching self-evaluations.

The counselor using reality therapy assists clients in evaluating the merits of delaying the satisfaction of immediate wants, such as the intense pleasures often involved in acting on wants that focus on immediate gratification. In some instances, clients' choices are obvious: to "hang out" with friends or to study; to sleep late and wait for a job to knock on the door or to pursue employment opportunities; to overpromise the benefits of a product or service or to cultivate satisfied long-term customers for repeat business. The conflict between immediate and delayed gratification of wants takes many forms from the cradle to the grave.

Some wants or desires (the pictures in the quality world) are realistically attainable and some are unattainable. This book focuses on the myriad ways you can help clients conduct self-evaluations. Counselors ask clients to examine whether their wants are attainable or beyond their current reach. This effort to help clients evaluate is far removed from the imposition of values. Rather, self-evaluation rightfully belongs to the client even when the counselor provides information. The 16-year-old student can better evaluate his own actions after understanding that to become a rock star musician requires years of learning and mastering the trade, networking, and capitalizing on opportunities. An informed self-evaluation by an employee desiring a promotion is the result of understanding the work habits of others who have been promoted and the necessity of adopting these productive habits. The counselor provides information, and the client provides the energy or the cognitive behavior to conduct a genuine and searching self-evaluation.

Comparing Place: Scales

Human beings experience a state of homeostasis when they perceive that what they want synchronizes or is congruent with what they are getting. When a gap or discrepancy exists between what individuals want and what they perceive they are gaining from the world around them, they generate behaviors to try to close the gap. Many of these behaviors are consciously chosen, but some are automatic and not chosen. The discrepancy is analogous to a mental scale that is out of balance. The metaphorical location for this comparison is called the *comparing place* (Glasser & Glasser, 2005). For example, Fran is attracted to Lee and wishes to have a relationship with Lee, but Lee rejects Fran. As a result, Fran experiences an out-of-balance mental scale and chooses behaviors to rebalance the scale. Some behaviors may be effective, and others may be ineffective. Out-of-balance scales provide the immediate trigger for behavior. People perceiving that they do not have what they want at a given moment generate behaviors. These out-of-balance scales can be slight or major. When we are at home and feeling thirsty, we want a drink of water and experience a mildly out-of-balance scale. Someone wanting a sense of safety and security and faced with possible death or a serious threat, such as a soldier on the battlefield or someone in a hospital or a victim of domestic violence, experiences a major out-of-balance scale. Such out-of-balance scales cause human behaviors such as flight, fight, or freeze.

The work of the counselor regarding the quality world and out-of-balance scales is twofold. The counselor works to become part of the client's quality world so that the client sees the counselor as competent, ethical, and empathic. The counselor also assists the client in determining whether the scales are permanently out of balance or whether there is the possibility of rebalancing them through effective action.

Behavior as Chosen

In Figure 1, a jagged arrow connects the out-of-balance scale with behavior. This arrow indicates that behavior is a choice. That people choose their behavior is a controversial principle with many distinctions. I suggest that counselors treat behavior with the "as if" qualification. Even though people do not have complete control over every aspect of their behavior, counselors can help clients learn that they have more control than they at first accepted or acknowledged. Us-

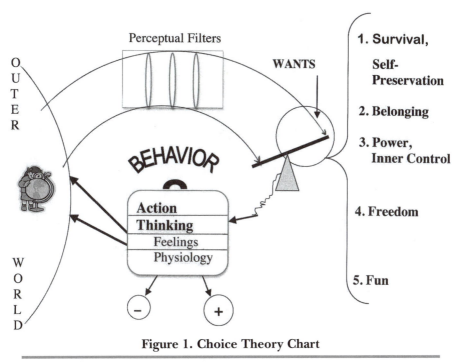

Figure 1. Choice Theory Chart

Note. Adapted by Robert E. Wubbolding, EdD, from a diagram of *How the Brain Works*, Glasser (2005a). Adapted with permission.

ing reality therapy, counselors respond to the most obvious part of the behavior system, for example, the feeling level, and connect the affective component to the action component of the behavior system. By taking action, clients gain a sense of hope and experience a change in how they feel. Reality therapy is an empowering system for clients. When clients learn that they have choices, they feel more self-confident and more in control of their lives, and thus they gain a sense of self-mastery. Chapter 6 contains a sample dialogue illustrating how to use reality therapy with a person who feels put upon or oppressed by society.

Total Human Behavior: Four Components

Human behavior, seen as "total behavior" in choice theory, has four components: action, thinking, feeling, and physiology (Glasser, 1998). All behavior consists of these four inseparable elements. In teaching and learning choice theory and reality therapy (CT/RT), it is useful to think of total behavior as analogous to a suitcase with four layers of behavior (Figure 2). The handle of the suitcase is at-

19

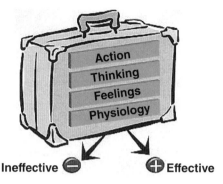

Figure 2. The Suitcase of Behavior

tached to the action, which illustrates that it is the most controllable and directly changeable component of total behavior. Yet when someone lifts the suitcase by its handle, the entire suitcase follows. Thus changing actions also brings about a change in thinking, feeling, and often in physiology (Wubbolding, 2016).

As we develop from childhood to adulthood, we put into our suitcases the behaviors that we observe in our environment. The collective result is the wide diversity of behavior among cultures of the world. An assertive behavior used effectively by a person from North America might be seen as ineffective and even counterproductive in an Asian country. People from vastly different cultures have learned different ways of expressing themselves, and a behavior that might be acceptable in one culture may be quite unacceptable, or at least confusing, to someone from a different culture.

To better understand how behavior functions as a unit, we can think of total behavior as being similar to how a car moves. The front wheels symbolize action and thinking, and the back wheels represent feelings and physiology. When the driver turns the front wheels, the entire car follows (Glasser, 2005a). This illustrates that the most direct way to change total behavior is by altering actions as a first choice and secondarily altering thinking or self-talk.

The car and suitcase analogies are limited in their application. An immediate change in actions might *not* suddenly alter the other components of total behavior. There is often a time lag between changing what we do and feeling better. Depressed people initiating exercise programs do not always sense an instant change in thoughts, feelings, and physiology. However, more than likely, tagging along behind the change in actions will be at least some positive alteration in thinking, feelings, and physiology.

Purposes of Human Behavior

Similar to Adlerian psychology (Alfred Adler.org, 2016), choice theory states that all behavior is purposeful or goal oriented. It aims at satisfying the five internal motivators, even though the chosen behaviors often appear haphazard or aimless to other people. To the untrained eye, the shimmying up and down and back and forth of a tightrope walker's pole might appear purposeless, but even the slightest movement has a definite purpose. Although the purposes of behavior might be obscure to an observer, the person generating the behavior is at least marginally aware that the behavior is purposeful. In Figure 1, the arrows to the left of the suitcase symbolize two behavioral purposes. The tightrope walker seeks to maneuver in a way that affects the exterior world and satisfies a purpose. In this case, perhaps the quality world picture is the feeling of excitement or of being in control under death defying circumstances. Michelangelo was accustomed to saying that his purposeful sculpturing served to liberate the statue within the marble. In reality, the statue was in his quality world, and the purpose of his behavior was to mold or shape the external world so that it matched the image he wanted. From a choice theory standpoint, we are all sculptors. A parent imposes rules on a child with the hope that the child learns inner discipline. Glasser (1998) spoke of depression as purposeful. It allows a person to ask for help, gain attention, and suppress anger. Oftentimes, the explicit purpose of specific behaviors is unclear to the client. The practitioner of reality therapy asks such clients, "What did you have in mind when you made that choice?" "What was the purpose of that specific behavior?" Understanding the purposeful nature of behavior opens a rich area for assisting others in self-evaluation.

Wubbolding (2015b, 2015c, 2016) describes a second purpose of human behavior. It not only affects the external world but also sends out a signal or a message to the environment. For example, in paying compliments to Lee, Fran sends a message of interest and desire toward Lee through both verbal and nonverbal behavior. This second purpose of behavior, sending a signal to the world, provides an opportunity for counselors to reframe behavior and to deal with clients from a different point of view, especially those who demonstrate hostility and resistance. The user of reality therapy, for instance, asks the manager at a company, "What message does shouting and raising your voice send to the employees about your attitude toward them?" Or to the tardy and truant employee, "What message does your sarcasm and perceived indifference send to your manager and other employees about your commitment to do quality work?"

People seek the perception that they are fulfilling a want and its related need through purposeful behaviors and messages that they send to the world around them. In other words, even though we teach that individuals aim to satisfy their wants and fulfill their needs, it is more precise to say that they seek the *perception* of such satisfaction and fulfillment. For instance, if Lee responds favorably to Fran's outreach, Fran gains the perception that a want is satisfied in addition to balancing Fran's previously out-of-balance scales connected with the need for belonging. The perceptual system functions like a camera with three lenses, or filters. The lowest level of perception picks up images without labeling them as want or need satisfying. The middle level of perception picks up images and connects them with another perception. The highest level of perception places a value, either positive or negative, on the image. For example, when Fran first meets Lee, Fran's lowest level of perception acknowledges Lee as a human being. Fran's middle level of perception labels Lee as perhaps a neighbor living close by. Fran's highest level of perception labels Lee as an attractive and appealing person. This process can happen instantaneously or gradually over a period of time.

Choice theory is an internal control system that explains human behavior as being motivated by five human needs. Each component of the theory serves as the basis for procedures that counselors can use to help clients apply the technique of self-evaluation to their lives. The counselor helps clients evaluate their wants, each component of their behavior, the purpose of their behavior, and their perceptions. A counselor would help Fran conduct a searching self-evaluation regarding the realistic attainability of achieving a relationship with Lee and evaluate the effectiveness of behaviors chosen to bring about the desired relationship. The principle of self-evaluation is analogous to the keystone of an arch. It holds the reality therapy process together and is inseparable from other interventions of the WDEP system of reality therapy, which are described in Chapter 4.

Cognitive Behavioral Therapy

This book focuses on reality therapy as a cognitive behavior therapy, but the rational emotive behavior therapy (REBT) of Albert Ellis and the cognitive therapy of Aaron Beck serve as a blueprint for developing further self-evaluation interventions. Ellis described three basic *musts* as the sources leading to emotional disturbance (Ellis & Harper, 1997). In essence they are:

- I *must* be perfect in order to be good.
- Other people *must* always treat me the way I want to be treated.
- I *must* always get what I want.

This irrational self-talk often results in "catastrophic thinking" and in a sense of debilitation and powerlessness. The counselor's role is to dispute such absolutist thinking (D. Ellis, 2012). Within the context of self-evaluation, counselors help clients evaluate the effectiveness of this inner discourse and assist them in replacing it with more helpful cognitions.

Similarly, Aaron Beck provides additional areas for counselors to help clients evaluate their "logical errors," such as overgeneralization. Corey (2017) describes this logical error as "a process of holding extreme beliefs on the basis of a single incident and applying them inappropriately to dissimilar events or settings" (p. 283). Other logical errors include magnification and minimization, dichotomous thinking, and labeling/mislabeling. Christine Padesky, coauthor with Dennis Greenberger of *The Clinician's Guide to Mind Over Mood* (2012), states that the more structured the therapy the better the result. Utilizing this principle and extending Beck's theoretical principles, she describes how Socratic dialogue utilizes four steps for empowering clients. These steps are congruent with standard counseling practice and therefore with the principles of reality therapy. They are (1) asking informational questions: eliciting evidence that supports the client's belief system; (2) listening and reflecting on the client's responses but not presenting explanations to the client, such as why the client experiences panic attacks; (3) summarizing: this is the most important part of the Socratic dialogue and should be done in the client's own exact language; (4) conducting analytical synthesizing: asking clients to describe their perceptions of their experience and their thinking, helping them connect one with the other, and assisting them in determining how they can use these ideas to help themselves.

In general, irrational thinking or illogical cognition adds a dimension to self-evaluation that can be integrated into the general practice of counseling and clearly is congruent with the reality therapy–based procedures. The reality therapist adds questions such as, "Does your self-talk help you or hinder you in any way?"

Based on the information provided, list three possible self-evaluation interventions you could use with clients.

1. _____
2. _____
3. _____

Chapter 3

The Counseling Environment: "How Do I Set the Stage for Self-Evaluation?"

This book describes self-evaluation techniques that spring from choice theory and reality therapy. There are also adaptations derived from rational emotive behavior therapy (REBT), Adlerian therapy, and Ericksonian concepts (see the Milton H. Erickson Foundation website). These systems, as well as others, are sometimes described as *internal control systems*. Common to these theories is the underlying principle that human behavior is composed of action, cognition, and emotions that originate from internal sources of motivation. This chapter summarizes the limitations and constraints we all face in making changes in our own lives and in helping others do the same. It also presents ideas that reality therapists use to create a counseling environment in which the therapeutic alliance can flourish.

Societal Limitations

Certainly society, culture, personal history, and many other external influences circumscribe human behavior and limit our choices. For example, some people born into a loving family that values education, that possesses more than minimal wealth, and that is free of drug abuse are able to concern themselves with more than basic survival needs. If they also have a quality education system available, they clearly have more choices open to them than a person born into a chaotic family, extreme poverty, personal isolation, cultural oppression, or societal rejection because of physical or mental abilities. More specifically, a person born into a stable and affluent society has more options than a person born in war-torn Darfur. Yet despite their external circumstances, people always retain some ability to choose their actions and to some extent their perceptions. For example, Ben Carson (2012) describes how his single mother with a third-grade education raised him and his brother. Because she wanted her sons to have more opportunities than she had, she was determined to provide an atmosphere of discipline and loving guidance as well as educational opportunities. She instilled in them self-confidence and a love of science, art, and education in general. Ben went on to become a world-renowned neurosurgeon and chair of the department of neurosurgery at Johns Hopkins Medical Institutions at the age of 33. In 2016, he was a candidate for the presidency of the United States. In spite of seemingly overwhelming barriers and obstacles to human self-actualization, many people demonstrate the ability to rise above their situations. The counselor's responsibility is often to help clients climb mountains, navigate treacherous waters, circumvent opposing forces, discover new strategies, strengthen their level of commitment, and make the journey easier. In the more abstract theoretical language of the counseling profession, the following principle provides the groundwork for this book:

Counselors empower clients to identify and make more effective choices.

• • •

Many slogans and affirmations designed to inspire people to take charge of their lives are based on the assumption that people have choices. I am a member of a health center that focuses on cardiac rehabilitation. As people walk or run around the track, they are greeted with the opportunity to think about statements such as these:

- "A man who wants something will find a way; a man who doesn't will find an excuse." (Stephen Dolley Jr.)
- "A journey of 1,000 miles begins with a single step." (Lao-tzu)
- "It's not whether you get knocked down, it's whether you get up." (Vince Lombardi)
- "No one has ever drowned in sweat." (Lou Holtz)
- "Believe you can and you're half way there." (Theodore Roosevelt)

Such slogans are more than empty clichés. They serve to reprogram the subconscious, to counter irrational thinking, or, from the perspective of choice theory, to replace ineffective external control ideas with more effective in-control self-talk leading to more satisfying action behaviors, that is, choices.

In describing the significance of effective choices, Jon Carlson (2012), Distinguished Professor of Adlerian Psychology, Adler University, Chicago, states, "In life as well as marriage we make choices that lead to happiness or misery. No one else can make these choices" (p. 231). Michael Berman and David Brown (2000) add, "We can regard ourselves as victims of circumstances, or learn how to take control of our lives—the choice is ours" (p. 65). In speaking of the dangers of denying personal responsibility due to an overemphasis on faulty conclusions based on neuroscience, Satel and Lilienfeld (2013) state, "The daily work of recovery, whether or not it is abetted by medication, is a human process that is most effectively pursued in the idiom of purposeful action, meaning, choice, and consequence" (p. 70).

Empathy and Trust

A genuine counseling relationship with the client precedes the application of any skill or the use of the wide range of techniques available to counselors, including self-evaluation interventions. Without a mutual attitude of trust and confidence, the skill of self-evaluation is rendered less effective if not completely useless.

Clients need to feel that counselors have their best interests at heart. They need to be convinced that the counselor is competent and ethical, empathic, and mentally healthy. Reality therapy interventions build on establishing a safe and empathic atmosphere called the "counseling environment" (Glasser, 2005a; Wubbolding, 2015c, 2017), which is described later in this chapter. Glasser (2000) emphasized the importance of the relationship with clients as a prerequisite for helping them "connect with others in their lives" (p. 227). Not only does the counseling relationship provide a foundation for successful counseling and the formulation of better human relationships, it is also a tool for helping clients evaluate the effectiveness of their choices.

In summary, human relationships are the outgrowth of individuals asking themselves the following three questions:

- Can I trust this person?
- Does this person know what he or she is talking about?
- Does this person care about me?

These three questions can be asked in almost any human relationship: a dating relationship, a sales relationship, a negotiating relationship, and most emphatically in a counseling relationship.

Assisting clients in self-evaluation is rooted in the quality of the counseling relationship. This relationship has the characteristics described by Rogers (1957)—empathy, congruence, and positive regard—that he states are the necessary and sufficient conditions for change. The counselor attempts to see the world as the client sees it and is emotionally well grounded and respects the client as a unique and valued person.

In describing the effectiveness of cognitive behavior therapy, Kalodner (2011) states that "counselors and therapists cannot become so reliant on techniques that they forget that clients require a warm and supportive environment in the therapeutic process" (p. 198). She adds that in Beck's cognitive therapy empathy is "necessary but not sufficient" (p. 198). Similarly, rational emotive behavior therapy builds on the counselor–client relationship. Vernon (2011) states that "REBT counselors or therapists are empathic both affectively and philosophically, communicating that they understand how clients feel and also showing clients that they understand the beliefs underlying their feelings" (p. 245). Marsha Linehan's dialectical behavioral therapy (DBT) emphasizes interventions aimed at client change. It also stresses "the importance of the psychotherapeutic relationship, validation of the client, the impact of having been raised in an invalidating environment and confrontation of resistance" (as cited in Simpson, 2011, p. 231). Linehan adds that "a warm communication style and a use of validation will balance the focus on change-oriented strategies" (p. 233). Siang-Yang Tan (2011) states that the expression of accurate empathy "is an integral part of effective therapy" (p. 141) regardless of differences among the schools of counseling. I have attended many Ericksonian conferences and find most Ericksonian principles congruent with choice theory/reality therapy. Jeffrey Zeig (2006), president of the Milton H. Erickson Foundation, states, "Clinicians are supplicants. We entreat entry into the patient's world . . . the essential purpose of offering an induction of hypnosis is to knock at the door of the patient's inner world and request entry" (p. 14). He adds, "When the patient responds it is as if the patient indicates 'Come in. You are welcome into my living room'" (p. 14).

This sampling of the place of empathy in the counseling relationship illustrates that the practice of counseling, or therapy, *at least* includes the therapeutic relationship as a foundational component for implementing various theories. Each system describes counselor qualities as they pertain to the counselor–client relationship. Parenthetically speaking, the inclusion of empathy, congruence, and positive regard points to the monumental and pervasive contribution of Carl Rogers to the helping professions.

Therapeutic Alliance: What Is It?

Emerging from an empathic counseling relationship is the formulation of counseling goals and strategies mutually agreed on by client and counselor. This threefold system of relationship, goals, and strategies serves as the foundation for change. It is the basis for effective self-evaluation and is technically referred to as the *therapeutic alliance*. Effective outcomes achieved through the use of reality therapy and its cornerstone intervention of self-evaluation require a strong yet flexible foundation. "Regardless of the presenting issue, the effective use of reality therapy includes a therapeutic alliance as a foundation for assisting clients to improve their interpersonal relationships" (Wubbolding, 2014, p. 310).

Using the information just discussed, list three ways you can establish a therapeutic alliance with your clients.

1. _____
2. _____
3. _____

In summary, societal limitations impede human choice. Nevertheless, with empathy and by extending the therapeutic alliance, a counselor can avoid toxic behaviors and utilize tonic behaviors to establish a therapeutic alliance and create an environment of trust.

Establishing the Environment: Helpful Behaviors—Tonics

Some reality therapy skills and attitudes effective for building and maintaining counseling relationships are common to other counseling modalities. Other components are more characteristic of reality therapy (see Figure 3). I invite you to identify and discuss with colleagues this distinction as it applies to the principles presented in the following sections.

CYCLE OF COUNSELING, COACHING, MANAGING, SUPERVISING, & PARENTING

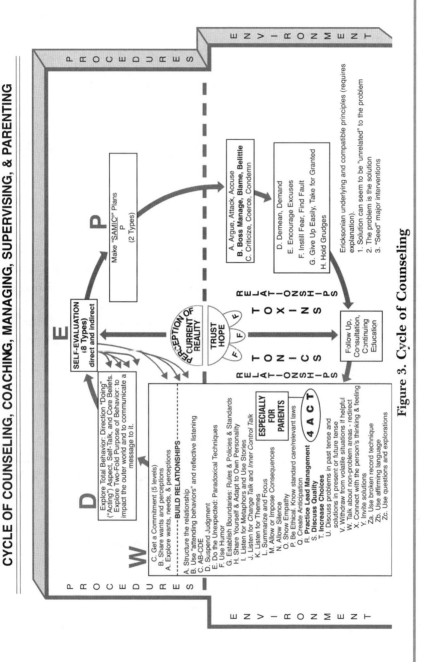

Figure 3. Cycle of Counseling

Note. Developed by Robert E. Wubbolding, EdD, from the works of William Glasser, MD, founder of choice theory/reality therapy. Copyright 1986 by Robert E. Wubbolding, EdD (20th rev., 2017). Reprinted with permission.

SUMMARY DESCRIPTION OF THE
"CYCLE OF COUNSELING, COACHING, MANAGING, SUPERVISING, & PARENTING"

The Cycle is explained in detail in books by Robert E. Wubbolding: *Reality Therapy for the 21st Century, 2000*
A Set of Directions for Putting and Keeping Yourself Together, 2001
Reality Therapy In APA's *Theories of Psychotherapy Series, 2011*

Introduction:

The Cycle consists of two general concepts: Environment conducive to change and Procedures more explicitly designed to facilitate change. This chart is intended to be a **brief** summary. The ideas are designed to be used with employees, students, clients as well as in other human relationships.

Relationship between Environment & Procedures:

1. As indicated in the chart, the Environment is the foundation upon which the effective use of Procedures is based.

2. Though it is **usually** necessary to establish a safe, friendly Environment before change can occur, the "Cycle" can be entered at any point. Thus, the use of the cycle does **not** occur in lockstep fashion.

3. Building a relationship implies establishing and maintaining a professional relationship. Methods for accomplishing this comprise some efforts on the part of the helper that are Environmental and others that are Procedural.

ENVIRONMENT:

Relationship Tonics: a close relationship is built on TRUST and HOPE through friendliness, firmness and fairness. **Cf. Caring Habits: Glasser**
A. Structure the relationship.
B. Using Attending Behaviors: Eye contact, posture, effective listening skills.
C. AB = "Always **B**e . . ." **C**onsistent, **C**ourteous & **C**alm, **D**etermined that there is hope for improvement, **E**nthusiastic (Think Positively).
D. Suspend Judgment: View behaviors from a low level of perception, i.e., acceptance is crucial.
E. Do the Unexpected: Use paradoxical techniques as appropriate; Reframing and Prescribing.
F. Use Humor: Help them fulfill need for fun within reasonable boundaries.
G. Establish boundaries: the relationship is professional.

4 ACT
• Affirm feelings
• Accept
• Show affection
• Action consequences
• Conversation (WDEP)
• Time together

H. Share Self: Self-disclosure within limits is helpful; adapt to own personal style.
I. Listen for Metaphors: Use their figures of speech and provide other ones. Use stories.
J. Listen for *Change Talk* and *Inner Control Talk.*
K. Listen to Themes: Listen for behaviors that have helped, value judgements, etc.
L. Summarize & Focus: Tie together what they say and focus on them rather than on "Real World."
M. Allow or Impose Consequences: Within reason, they should be responsible for their own behavior.
N. Allow Silence: This allows them to think, as well as to take responsibility.
O. Show Empathy: Perceive as does the person being helped.
P. Be Ethical: Study Codes of Ethics and their applications, e.g., how to handle suicide threats or violent tendencies.
Q. Create anticipation and communication hope. People should be taught that something good will happen if they are willing to work.
R. **Practice lead management, e.g., democracy in determining rules.**
S. **Discuss quality.**
T. **Increases choices.**
U. Discuss problems in the past tense, solutions in present or future tense.
V. Withdraw from volatile situations if helpful.
W. Talk about non-problem areas - redirect.
X. Connect with the person's thinking and feeling.
Y. Invite solutions.
Za. Use broken record technique.
Zb. Use affirming language.
Zc. Use questions and explorations.

Relationship Toxins: Cf. Deadly Habits: Glasser

Argue, **Boss Manage,** or Blame, Criticize or Coerce, Demean, Encourage Excuses, Instill Fear, or Give up easily, Hold Grudges.

Rather, stress what they **can** control, accept them as they are, and keep the confidence that they can develop more effective behaviors. Also, continue to us "WDEP" system without giving up.

Follow Up, Consult, and Continue Education:

Determine a way for them to report back, talk to another professional person when necessary, and maintain ongoing program of professional growth.

PROCEDURES:

WDEP

Build Relationships:

A. Explore **W**ants, Needs & Perceptions: Discuss picture album or quality world, i.e., set goals, fulfilled & unfulfilled pictures, needs, viewpoints and "locus of control."

B. Share Wants & Perceptions: Tell what you want from them and how you view their situations, behaviors, wants, etc. This procedure is secondary to A above.

C. Get a Commitment: Help them solidify their desire to find more effective behaviors.

Explore Total Behavior:

Help them examine the **D**irection of their lives, as well as specifics of how they spend their time. Discuss core beliefs and ineffective et effective self-talk. Explore two-fold purpose of behavior: to impact the outer world and to communicate a message to it.

Evaluation – The Cornerstone of Procedures:

Help them evaluate their behavioral direction, specific behaviors as well as wants, perceptions and commitments. Evaluate own behavior through follow-up, consultation and continued education.

Make **P**lans: Help them change direction of their lives.

Effective plans are **S**imple, **A**ttainable, **M**easurable, **I**mmediate, **I**nvolved, **C**onsistent, **C**ontrolled by the planner, and **C**ommitted to. The helper is **P**ersistent. Plans can be linear or paradoxical.

Note: The "Cycle" describes specific guidelines & skills. Effective implementation requires the artful integration of the guidelines & skills contained under Environment & Procedures in a spontaneous & natural manner geared to the personality of the helper. This requires training, practices & supervision. Also, the word "client" is used for anyone receiving help: student, employee, family member, etc.

For more information contact:

Robert E. Wubbolding, EdD, Director

Center for Reality Therapy
5490 Windridge Court
Cincinnati, Ohio 45243

(513) 561-1911 • FAX (513) 561-3568
E-mail: wubsrt@fuse.net • www.realitytherapywub.com

The Center for Reality Therapy provides counseling, consultation, training and supervision including applications to schools, agencies, companies and other institutions. The Center is a provider for many organizations which award continuing education units.

This material is copyrighted. Reproduction is prohibited without permission of Robert E. Wubbolding. If you wish to copy, please call.

Figure 3. Cycle of Counseling Summary *(Continued)*

Note. Developed by Robert E. Wubbolding, EdD, from the works of William Glasser, MD, founder of choice theory/reality therapy. Copyright 1986 by Robert E. Wubbolding, EdD (20th rev., 2017). Reprinted with permission.

Initial Establishment of Trust

- *Structure the relationship*: The counselor provides information regarding professional disclosure and counselor expectations congruent with professional ethics such as those outlined in the *ACA Code of Ethics* (American Counseling Association [ACA], 2014, A.2.a; Herlihy & Corey, 2015). More specifically, counselors describe what they will do for clients and what they will not do. As a counselor in a correctional halfway house for women, I communicated that I would work to the best of my ability to help clients but would not socialize with them, lend them money, or facilitate breaking the rules of the house or the law. Within these boundaries, clients evaluated their relationship with me and with all staff members.

- *Evaluate attending behaviors*: Pay attention to nonverbal behaviors such as eye contact, physical posture, tone of voice, gestures, and many others. Counselors need to consider cultural practices as they relate to attending behaviors (Ivey, D'Andrea, & Ivey, 2012). For instance, in some cultures lack of eye contact is more prevalent when a client is speaking to a person in authority, such as a counselor, teacher, or supervisor. When visiting India and teaching corporate managers, I observed many participants in the audience shaking their heads from side to side. At first I thought they were indicating their disagreement with the concepts I was presenting. But then I noticed the movement of their heads was not the same as that of a person from North America. Rather, the shaking was more of a slight rocking to and fro, which signifies agreement. It can be very confusing to a Westerner who asks a question of an individual from the Indian subcontinent and he or she responds "Yes" while rocking his or her head back and forth. This "yes" accompanied by the nonverbal head movement means "yes, I agree." More generally, the reality therapist can respond to nonverbal behaviors by translating them into an implied evaluation. For instance, at times a counselor may suggest a plan of action but realize the client is resistant: "Judging from your response, you don't think the plan would work. Can you think of a better plan for you?"

- *Promote AB-CDE*: Counselors deal with and teach clients "*a*lways *b*e *c*ourteous, *d*etermined to work out the problems, and *e*nthusiastic." Enthusiasm suggests more than cheerleading. It means looking for something positive in the client's presentation. In teaching reality therapy, I utilize the phrase "We cannot build on what is not there. We can only build on something that already exists."

- *Suspend judgment:* Counselors attempt to be nonjudgmental as much as is reasonable. They accept clients as worthwhile human beings regardless of the presenting problem. However, counselors retain their values and intervene when required, such as when there is a threat of serious danger or when the counselor suspects child abuse.

- *Do the unexpected:* To maintain a relationship with a client, the counselor must be able to see the world through the eyes of the client, but the counselor also sees the world from a different perspective, which can surprise the client. Some clients coerced into receiving counseling may feel imposed upon and believe they ought to be able to help themselves without the assistance of an outsider. Seeing the situation from a different point of view, the counselor can surprise the client with an unanticipated comment such as this: "Congratulations on your decision to seek help. You have already taken a big step forward. How do you think this process might help you?" The counselor sees the decision to seek counseling, even forced counseling, as a strength and not as weakness.

  Part of doing the unexpected is the use of paradoxical techniques, especially reframing negative actions, perceptions, or feelings to positives. For instance, a counselor might state the following to a parent who is hypercritical of his or her 15-year-old child: "You obviously want the best for your child. You're very observant and watch carefully what he does. He sees you as impatient and critical, and you feel guilty about how you act toward him. And yet I see you as eager and willing to say what's on your mind. You said you feel 'guilty.' It could be that you are therefore motivated to deal with him more effectively." The parent receives this information and can self-evaluate his or her intentions.

- *Incorporate humor:* Because fun is a basic human need, the practitioner of reality therapy infuses appropriate and well-timed humor into the counseling relationship. Victor Borge, the great comedian, once remarked that the shortest distance between two people is a laugh. The use of humor in counseling can be misunderstood as superficial or shallow, but in choice theory the need for fun is central to healthy living. A counselor can help the client reflect on a brief humorous interaction by asking, "How did you feel when you were laughing just now?"

After the client's response, the counselor adds, "If you can feel better for a brief instant, you have evidence that you can feel better for longer periods of time. It is clear that you need not imprison yourself or feel imprisoned by how other people treat you." The value of humor reinforces a basic principle in reality therapy: It provides an alternative to behavioral symptoms that indicate mental disorders. For example, the *DSM-5* (American Psychiatric Association, 2013, p. 184) description of symptoms for depressive disorders includes these characteristics: feelings of tenseness, restlessness, worry, fear that something awful may happen, fear of loss of control. These are symptoms devoid of joy and humor. The Mayo Clinic Staff (n.d.) describes the value of humor as stimulating organs, relieving stress, improving the immune system, relieving pain, increasing personal satisfaction, and improving mood.

Practitioners using reality therapy often stress discussions of healthy behaviors rather than consuming precious time persistently reviewing symptoms of mental disorders. The following principle is central to the practice of reality therapy:

Reality therapy is a mental health system, not a mental disorder system.

● ● ●

- *Communicate boundaries, ethical principles, and agency policies*: The reality therapy counselor works within the standard professional practice, providing the appropriate structure for the counseling relationship. This includes relationship boundaries, confidentiality and its limitations, duty to warn, and possibility of referral, as well as the policies of the agency, school, or university, such as supervision issues outlined in the *ACA Code of Ethics* (ACA, 2014; Herlihy & Corey, 2015).
- *Share yourself*: Counselors expect clients to self-disclose, and the practitioner of reality therapy reciprocates when it is timed appropriately and enhances the counseling process. With training, supervision, consultation, and especially with experience, self-disclosure becomes more than a technique. It is an intuitive and spontaneous tool for complementing the relationship. The Swedish proverb applies: "A sorrow shared is half a sorrow, a joy shared is twice a joy." By observing the counselor's modeling behavior, clients can judge the effectiveness of doing the same.
- *Listen for metaphors and use stories*: Clients frequently use figures of speech rather than psychological language in describing

their actions, thinking, and feelings: "I'm down in the dumps" can be the equivalent of "I'm depressed." "I feel like a floor mat" can be another way of saying "I have low self-esteem." Paraphrasing clients' comments can be valuable, and using their metaphors provides a communication tool for invigorating the counseling relationship. A counselor might say, "Would you like to lift yourself out of the dumps?" or "Would you like to stand tall instead of being a floor mat?" "What would help you accomplish your goal?" Client-initiated stories as well as counselor-initiated stories serve as extended metaphors and aids in engaging clients. They also serve as tools to communicate the universality of the client's situation. For example, a counselor may state, "Your situation reminds me of a similar problem faced by one of my clients several years ago. She made many choices that subsequently alleviated her distress." The counselor can elaborate on as many details as would be helpful. Stories and metaphors also serve as tools for assisting clients in evaluating their total behavior. This method of self-evaluation is illustrated later in the text.

- *Listen for change-talk and in-control talk*: Reality therapy embraces the principle expressed in motivational interviewing: listening carefully and eliciting language that indicates a desire to change "by asking open ended questions, the answers to which involve the client's own desire, ability, reasons, and need for change" (Arkowitz, Westra, Miller, & Rollnick, 2008, p. 331). Clients enter the counseling process because of a decision. This decision takes many forms. Some clients are highly motivated to alter their own behavior. Others seek ways to motivate their children, their spouses, or their friends to make changes. Still others merely "show up" because of external coercion. They are sent to a counselor by a person or persons in authority such as teachers, judges, parents, administrators, and a multitude of other individuals who believe the client needs to make major or minor behavioral changes. From the beginning of reality therapy, a key principle has been that change occurs when clients decide that a better alternative is available to them (Glasser, 1965). They express a desire to change when they feel an inner motivation that the totality of their life or a relatively minor part of their life is not advantageous to them. This expression is made concrete by means of language. Therefore, practicing reality therapy means listening for language that indicates even a slight hint that clients wish to change.

Counselors then assist clients to increase and extend their language as it relates to future behavioral change. This technique of listening for change-talk constitutes a significant contribution to any counselor's ability. Miller and Rollnick define change-talk as "any client's speech that favors a client's movement toward a particular change goal" (as cited in Jones-Smith, 2016, p. 343). The manifestation of desired change is closely allied with the level of commitment, which is discussed in Chapter 4. Counselors practicing reality therapy not only demonstrate empathy for the plight of clients and the pain associated with it but also listen for the language of change. Wubbolding and Brickell (2005a) state that "firm levels of commitment or the intensity of expression during conferences point toward learning a new language and making effective choices" (p. 39). Counselors also listen for current in-control language. Clients often state, for example, "I felt like saying . . . but I held back." "I knew I should not have . . . but I chose to do it anyway." Such statements indicate at least some willingness to accept responsibility.

- *Listen for themes:* Self-evaluation centers on the components of the motivational system such as actions, self-talk including core beliefs, perceptions, and so forth. Motivations can be more easily accessed when the counselor helps the client articulate a series of wants, behaviors that have been effective or ineffective, positive or negative perceptions, and inner self-verbalizations. For example, with the help of a counselor, a client can list what he or she wants from parents, children, career, or school. The counselor might then elicit from the client a description of recent action steps aimed at fulfilling his or her wants and divide them into "those that have worked" and "those that have not worked." Listing perceptions could include a description of a partner's perceptions of the other person. In response to the question "What do you see when you look at your son?", a parent responded, "I see a lazy bum, a kid who's going nowhere and who will probably end up in a lot of trouble." The parent can then evaluate whether such negative perceptions enhance or diminish the parent–child relationship.

- *Summarize and focus:* In the DVD *Reality Therapy: Psychotherapy With the Experts Series* (Wubbolding, 1997), the counselor works with a challenging client who wants to discuss the world in general; Juan wants to discuss everything except his own controllable behaviors. The majority of reality therapy interventions provided by the counselor strike a balance between listening and helping the client focus on choices needed to complete his master's degree thesis. Effective focusing means leading the client in such a way that he or she takes more effective inner control, examining options and makings plans. As illustrated in the DVD, focusing often requires patience balanced with a relentless determination to pinpoint an issue that can be realistically dealt with in a limited amount of time (Burdenski & Wubbolding, 2011).

Deepening the Relationship

- *Allow or impose consequences:* Part of structuring the relationship includes both positive and negative consequences resulting from the client's behavioral choices. The counselor is not a psychological rescuer preventing the occurrence of *reasonable* consequences. Application of this principle is always in line with the standard of care and ethical principles. Furthermore, the possibility or likelihood of positive or negative consequences serves as a standard for self-evaluating choices.

- *Allow silence:* It has been said that silence is often misinterpreted, but it is never misquoted. Mark Twain once remarked that he would rather remain silent and have people *think* he is a fool than open his mouth and remove all doubt. More relevant to counseling, however, is the fact that silence is an appropriate way to put responsibility on the client. One of the limitations of reality therapy is that the counselor often feels the necessity of filling the silences and feels the responsibility to say something insightful, brilliant, and wondrous, thereby inducing a rapid positive change in behavior. Often it is helpful for counselors to remain silent for a brief amount of time, especially when they are at a loss for a "proper" intervention. The silence provides a moment for inner self-evaluation for both client and counselor.

- *Show empathy:* As in other methodologies, the counselor attempts to see the world from the perspective of the client. But empathy can mean more. I wish to extend the concept of empathy to the ability to see the world not only as clients currently see it but also as they *could* see it in the future (Wubbolding, 2016). The counselor needs to perceive clients as potentially more self-actualizing and successful in the future. This kind of perception leads to more effective self-evaluation interventions presented by the counselor. The counselor might ask, "If your life were to be better than it is now, what helpful positive choices would you be making this afternoon after you leave this office?" Clients then reflect on such self-evaluation interventions, leading them to motivate themselves to make more satisfying choices aimed at achieving more self-actualizing behaviors.

- *Be ethical:* In helping clients self-evaluate, counselors function within the boundaries of standard practice and the standard of care. For instance, counselors communicate the need for confidentiality, its limitations, and the duty to warn. They provide a structure for informed consent, shun dual relationships, and seek consultation and supervision when necessary. They aim at achieving a high level of cultural competence. They are aware of and implement the codes of ethics of their respective professional organizations and conduct their own self-evaluation based on professional standards.

- *Create anticipation:* Clients learn that counseling is more than idle talk. With both verbal and nonverbal behaviors, counselors communicate that change is possible and likely as a result of the counseling process.

- *Practice lead management:* Practitioners using reality therapy sometimes function as probation officers, managers, and coaches by assisting clients in developing job skills, career goals, and more effective work habits. Wubbolding (2015c) states that by employing the WDEP system they avoid authoritarian behaviors. For example, boss management mottos are "It's my way or the highway." and "I will evaluate *your* behavior." The lead manager or democratic manager motto is "Together we will work it out" (p. 14). Reality therapy is an excellent system for life coaching. As a board-certified coach, I can verify the statement of Williams and Davis (2007) that reality therapy, along with many other therapies, is adaptable to strategies used in coaching.

- *Discuss quality:* Among the many characteristics of the quality movement as expressed by W. Edwards Deming (1986, 1993) is the fundamental principle of continuous improvement or *kaizen*. This was first incorporated in Japanese industry after World War II and later adopted by institutions in the United States and elsewhere. Clients whose companies are familiar with *kaizen* sometimes seek the help of counselors. In discussing total quality management (TQM), Daft and Marcic (2015) state, "Four significant elements of quality management are employee involvement, focus on the customer, benchmarking and continuous improvement often referred to as *kaizen*" (p. 42). Counseling with reality therapy means focusing on the client and establishing a range of achievable and measurable goals (benchmarking), with the underlying assumption that the entire process embraces the principle of continuous improvement or hope for a better future. Therefore, it is advantageous for counselors to be familiar with the principles of continuous improvement. Effective counselors communicate that clients can feel need satisfaction when they *begin* their journey toward improvement. They also realize that they can legitimately feel a sense of satisfaction at achieving success in taking small steps toward their goals. The cornerstone of such achievement is an assessment and an ongoing self-evaluation of their current behaviors with quality as a standard. Counselors adapt the following question to the multitude of client situations: "Is your current behavior increasing or decreasing the quality of your relationships, your work, your sense of inner control, as well as your role in society?" A thread running through the counseling dialogues contained in this book and a theme in the practice of reality therapy is *kaizen*. The possibility of improved mental health and resolution of problems are the implicit and sometimes explicit messages received by clients. They learn the value of telling themselves, "I can improve. There is hope for me." In fact, the entire profession of counseling and supervision, and more specifically practitioners of reality therapy, hold in high esteem the principle that their clients can continually improve. In a world of turmoil and with constant bombardment through the media reporting a turbulent and dangerous world, achieving peace of mind is a continuous uphill struggle. It has been said that maintaining mental health is similar to going up a down escalator or rowing a canoe upstream. Reality therapy provides a GPS for navigating the turbulent waters faced by people living in the 21st century.

- *Increase choices*: In teaching and in practicing the concepts of counseling, it is useful to converse about choices and to convey a sense of accomplishment that results from effective decision making. A small success often results in a general feeling of well-being. When clients choose small but effective plans, they can reflect on them and feel the positive result of their choices. If you wish to apply this to your own life, make a plan to do one thing that you have been procrastinating about. See it through to its completion, and then spend a few minutes reflecting on how you feel.

Advancing and Widening the Relationship

- *Discuss problems in the past tense and solutions in the present and future tenses*: This Ericksonian technique is a form of metacommunication that implies the attainability of success in the near future or as a long-term and realistically achievable goal.

- *Withdraw from volatile situations if helpful:* Many agencies have policies and procedures regarding potential violence, but not all counselors feel qualified or have had training for dealing with extreme crises. When faced with physical violence, counselors are well advised to seek help with out-of-control clients. Counselors conscious of the need for systemic interventions can assist their schools or agencies in establishing policies and plans as well as initiating training programs for staff who would implement appropriate procedures in crises.

- *Talk about problem-free areas:* Effective self-evaluation includes redirecting the conversation to past or current successes. Sometimes the best way to deal with problems is indirectly. Many problems are not "overcome"; they are left aside. A slogan in 12-step programs is "drop the rock." There is no need to pulverize the problem, to attack it; just leave it behind by cutting it loose.

- *Connect with the client's thinking and feeling:* Even though we speak of action choices and positive plans for specific behavioral change, counselors need to explore self-talk and emotions as part of self-evaluation: "Is what you are telling yourself helping or hurting you?" One of the misconceptions about reality therapy is that the counselor ignores the feelings or the emotional state of clients. As clarified and explained in the dialogues, this omission would indicate an incomplete knowledge of and skill in practicing reality therapy.

- *Invite solutions:* Part of the exploration of cognition is helping clients verbally evaluate their own thoughts about possible ways to address problems and to make improvements in their behavior.

- *Use the broken record technique:* With clients who are out of control and who continually and emotionally repeat their feelings of upset in a threatening manner, the counselor asks them in a multitude of ways, "Is this helping you solve your problems and improve your well-being?" This intervention is not used in isolation nor in a mechanistic manner. It is most effective when counselors combine it with empathic reflections on the current emotional state of the client.

- *Use affirming language:* Whenever possible, counselors look for ways to reinforce success, identify a willingness to take responsibility, and encourage effective planning. This helps clients realize that they are already making positive choices.

- *Use questions and explorations:* In self-evaluation, a key question is, "How does your current behavior improve your life?" But the effective use of counseling interventions involves more than relentless inquiry. "Tell me what would happen if you tried something different, such as . . ." Based on the mindful technique—"name it to tame it"—described by Daniel Siegel (2010, 2015), the counselor can use the following interventions: "Tell me what thoughts went through your mind when you did such and such." "Describe your gut feeling when you made that choice." "What label most appropriately fits the turmoil you felt inside: anger, resentment, rage, revenge, shame, guilt, worthlessness, stupidity, incompetence?" Clearly, reality therapy is not merely a softer form of interrogation. Rather, the phrase "warm, accepting, empathic relationship" characterizes the effective use of the WDEP system of reality therapy.

The suggestions presented here facilitate clients' self-evaluation by building a trusting relationship that is professionally sound, empathic, supportive, and focused on positive improvement and goal achievement. These eclectic, comprehensive, and widely used techniques are congruent with counseling theory and standard counseling practice. They also form the foundation for current and future self-evaluation. The skillful use of reality therapy strikes a balance between the endless deliberation of feelings and the hasty and incautious effort to solve problems.

Establishing the Environment: Unhelpful Behaviors—Toxins

Several patterns of behavior create a toxic atmosphere in a counseling relationship and can be a threat to the therapeutic alliance. Most counselors are skillful enough to avoid harsh or harmful behaviors, but many clients employ unhelpful and even vicious behaviors in their interpersonal relationships. Consequently, counselors who utilize reality therapy ask clients to evaluate their behavioral choices based on the fundamental evaluative standard: "Is what you are doing helping you to become more connected, less connected, or even disconnected with the people around you: your spouse, your children, your parents, your teachers, your friends, your employer, your neighbors, your acquaintances, and all the people you meet?" "Are you getting closer to or farther away from the people around you?" "Are you satisfied or unsatisfied with your manner of dealing with other people?" Counselors can explain or teach the following toxic behaviors and ask clients to evaluate whether they wish to continue using them in their interactions with others. They are listed below in alphabetical order. When teaching these toxic behaviors, I suggest that counselors stress A, B, and C because it is easier to remember a list of three items. In other words, KIS—keep it simple.

A. *Arguing:* This toxic behavior does not refer to intellectual debates. Rather, it pertains to behavioral arguments, often accompanied by accusations and attacks. Through self-evaluation, parents who argue with their teenager come to the conclusion that arguing only stiffens resistance and poisons the relationship. When consulting with parents about a rebellious adolescent, my first question is, "Do you argue with him or her?" I then apply the principles of reality therapy, especially the questions, "Is arguing healing or poisoning the relationship?" and "Does arguing result in agreement between you and the adolescent?"

B. *Blaming:* Pointing the finger, bossing, and belittling often worsen an already damaged relationship. The tonic behavior, silence, serves as an effective antidote to this toxic behavior. Clients can evaluate whether to follow their first instinct or impulse when dealing with people close to them.

C. *Criticizing:* "Explain how useful it is to criticize your children, spouse, partner, employee, friend, or in fact anyone." This intervention serves as a gentle but jarring self-evaluation technique for parents. Additional self-evaluation questions and interventions include the following: "Describe whether you are satisfied with coercive methods for bringing about a desired change in behavior." "Has condemning your children's friends convinced them to find new friends who meet your approval?"

D. *Demeaning and demanding:* This toxic behavior is an intense form of belittling and criticizing. Also, making excessive demands poisons a relationship and creates resistance.

E. *Encouraging excuses:* Although accepting and encouraging excuses at first appears to be a humane and empathic choice, its habitual use communicates an underlying message of weakness and powerlessness for both the sender and the receiver. A possible implied message is, "I am too faint hearted and frail to believe that you are capable of taking responsibility for your own behavior. And you are too pathetic and delicate to take charge of and accept the consequences of your choices." Clients can determine whether the constant and ingrained use of making excuses facilitates cooperative and secure relationships with the people in their environment.

Because of the significance of excuse making, I suggest that you make a brief list of excuses you have heard for avoiding responsibility for one's own actions. Be sure that these are as controversial as you can make them. However, keep in mind that a good excuse is one that the client *believes* is a good excuse.

1. _____

2. _____

3. _____

4. _____

Reality therapy is sometimes critiqued as a system that underestimates the impact of an external world that excessively restricts the choices of individuals and groups (Corey, 2017). However, the skilled practitioner of reality therapy does not practice toxic behaviors that can include discarding and minimizing social conditions. Rather, the artful application of reality therapy principles means that the counselor focuses on clients' strengths and their power to make choices. Counselors do not see clients as frail, impotent, or feeble and therefore condemned to a life of victimhood. The practitioner of reality therapy helps clients believe that they are capable people and assists them in finding the wide range of opportunities available to them. A dialogue in Chapter 6 between a counselor and a high school student who believes he is victimized illustrates how to empathize with the client, help him capitalize on his strengths, and avoid colluding with his view of himself as oppressed.

F. *Instilling fear.* Although some fear is helpful and necessary for safe living, relationships whose essential connection is characterized by fear are unsatisfying and violate the need for belonging. For instance, the counselor asks the father of a family, "If your core connection with your adolescent children is fear, what will happen when they become less dependent on you?"

G. *Giving up easily.* After listening to a parent remark about his son, "I can't stand to be around that 17-year-old," the counselor responds, "If you tell that to your son, will you get what you want from him?" So rather than ask for a direct and explicit self-evaluation judgment built around the relationship, the counselor can focus on whether the parent is achieving his or her goal separate from the relationship. In human relationships, the ongoing failure to give recognition or to express affection, gratitude, appreciation, or regard equates with taking the other person for granted and creates a noxious atmosphere in the relationship.

H. *Holding a grudge.* Forgiveness and reconciliation provide the antidote to hurt feelings and angry attitudes. Clients often evaluate whether nursing resentments and spitefulness helps them or hinders them from feeling in control of their lives. They are asked whether indulging their indignation improves their worldview and even whether they would feel physically better and more emotionally serene by letting go of some of their misery and distress. A person practicing reality therapy might respond in a variety of ways. One comment could be, "I can help you with your pain and frustration. But first I want to ask you if you would be willing to do an activity that on the surface has nothing to do with your pain. Would you be willing to do something enjoyable that absorbs your attention and requires effort? I would like to help you formulate a choice to do something each day for a limited amount of time, for example 30 minutes."

The counseling environment serves as the basis for counseling interventions that more specifically represent reality therapy. These tonics and toxins apply to most human relationships. They can be taught to clients for implementation in their own lives, and they provide a basis for assisting clients in their self-evaluation. When individuals or families choose to avoid the toxic behaviors, they can replace them with behaviors summarized in the WDEP formulation of reality therapy procedures. Rather than arguing, blaming, and criticizing, their communication becomes characterized by discussions focusing on what they want, how they perceive the world, their current behavior, its effectiveness for building better relationships, and, finally, their future plans.

Glasser (2005b) has formulated helpful and harmful behaviors that he calls the seven caring habits and the seven deadly habits. Characteristics of efforts to control other people and that destroy relationships are criticizing, blaming, complaining, nagging, threatening, punishing and bribing, or rewarding to control. He suggests that these be replaced with supporting, encouraging, listening, accepting, trusting, respecting, and negotiating differences.

Chapter 4

What Is the WDEP System?

William Glasser (1965) founded and developed reality therapy through his work as a psychiatrist in a mental hospital and a correctional institution. In his biography of Glasser, Roy (2014) states, "His ability to question his teachers, as well as his desire to share his beliefs, began early on to cause some difficulty for him with psychiatrists from UCLA" (p. 59). Since its early application to the profession of counseling and therapy, reality therapy has now been adapted to a wider range of human relationships. Its use is no longer limited to mental health. Reality therapy techniques have expanded to schools, addictions, corrections, and other mental health relationships, as well as to parenting, management, and supervision. Wubbolding (1991, 2011, 2016) has formulated and extended practical ways of implementing, teaching, and learning reality therapy. He calls these additions the WDEP system: wants, doing, evaluation, and planning. Each of the letters in the acronym represents a cluster of ideas and possible interventions that operationalize the underlying theory: choice theory (Glasser, 1998, 2011).

The formulation of the procedures is intended to provide a flexible structure. The procedures serve as an outline that effective counselors use in an imaginative and pliable manner. They are not steps followed mechanically one after another. Rather, they should be seen as components of an adjustable and elastic delivery system. Combined with a working knowledge of choice theory, they open vistas previously unseen by the untrained eye. Implementing the WDEP system helps people become more aware of their wants, their behaviors, the effectiveness of their behaviors, and their perceptions of the world around them. The system is congruent with the current state of neuroscience. Daniel Siegel (2012) states

> Because of this now established fact that the brain changes in response to our focus of attention, we can realize that mind, brain and relationships are profoundly interwoven with each other. Recurring patterns can alter the way we connect with each other, how we experience our subjective inner lives, and even how we come to shape the architecture of our own brains. . . . We can embrace the now proven truth that how we focus our attention can transform the brain's structure. (p. 3–6)

These profound truths make reality therapy a system with far-reaching effects much deeper than previously understood, even by skillful practitioners. Describing the relationship between theory and practice, Heinz Kohut once remarked that without theory and ordering principles we see nothing. But with theory alone, we are closed to new experience. Choice theory provides the ordering principles, and the WDEP system provides a path to new experiences for client and counselor. This will become clearer as you read the cases and dialogues.

Choice Theory and Reality Therapy: What Is the Difference?

There has been much discussion in the reality therapy organization known as William Glasser International about "doing choice theory" and the difference between theory and practice. From my perspective, practitioners implement a theory by means of a method. The theory is choice theory; the method is reality therapy. Hence, counselors and others *practice* reality therapy. Glasser has stated that choice theory is an explanation of how the human brain functions. More specifically, it clarifies human motivation by its explanation of why people generate behaviors that include actions, thinking, feeling, and physiology. It is an attempt to make understandable how the mind works. Because it is a theory, that is, an explanation, it requires a delivery system. Reality therapy provides the vehicle that activates, energizes, and makes concrete the application of the theory to all human relationships. In the *William Glasser Institute Newsletter*, Dr. and Mrs. Glasser (2008) stated, "We now wish to state publicly that teaching the procedures, the WDEP system, continues to be an integral part of training participants wishing to learn choice theory and reality therapy and is particularly effective in our training programs" (p. 1). Because this distinction and explanation is so important to mastering theory and practice, I repeat this analogy several times in the book. Moreover, the theory and practice described in this book are congruent with recent research in neuroscience that describes the human mind as "the embodied and relational process that regulates the flow of energy and information" (D. Siegel, 2012, p. xxvi). From the point of view of choice theory, the flow of energy can be seen as behavior, the output chosen to meet human needs. The information can be seen as data or input received from the external world as a person seeks to influence the external world and maneuver it through behavioral choices.

Use of Reality Therapy: The WDEP System Overview

The summary of the delivery system described here illustrates the evolving nature of reality therapy. An expanded description of each component is presented and illustrated by dialogues in subsequent chapters. The dialogues also illustrate an advanced usage and application of reality therapy.

As you deepen your skill in using reality therapy, it is acceptable to implement these skills even if they feel awkward and mechanical. The spontaneous use and ease in applying any skill requires practice, even though the practice may feel clumsy and unnatural at first. The dialogues provide a development and an extension of the basic procedures. Someone learning reality therapy for the first time can extract questions and reflections and apply them to a wide range of clients in counseling, in supervision, and in management. As you read the dialogues, think about what *you* would say that would be different from the counselor's interventions. Your own creative system and your experiences will help you formulate your own responses. The counselor's responses illustrated here do not represent the only ones acceptable in practicing the WDEP system of reality therapy.

Using Acronyms

Using acronyms to summarize the names of companies, services, organizations, and psychological concepts provides a memory peg as well as a way to identify a brand. Widely known acronyms include NFL, ESPN, PGA, FIFA, JAL, KAL, WGI, KART (Korea Association for Reality Therapy), EART (European Association for Reality Therapy), and IAR (Iranian Association for Reality Therapy).

To acquire a working knowledge of mindfulness and neuroscience, especially the work of Daniel Siegel (2007), a lover of acronyms, it helps to be aware of COAL. Each letter represents a concept congruent with reality therapy: being *c*urious about what is happening, being *o*pen to what is going on, *a*ccepting that at the present moment it is necessary to let go of judgments, and having a *l*oving stance toward the experience and yourself. D. Siegel (2015) states, "This is the COAL that warms the experience of time-in" (p. 121). He states that focusing on SIFT—sensations, images, feelings, and thoughts—can provide effective help to self and others. To achieve the desired outcome, he suggests that the helper be flexible, adaptive, connected, energized, and stable (FACES).

Many counseling systems identify themselves or at least their significant methodologies with acronyms, such as the ABCs of rational emotive behavior therapy (activating circumstances, belief system, consequences), solution-focused brief therapy (SFBT), the BASIC I.D. of multimodal therapy (behavior, affect, sensation, imagery cognition, interpersonal, and drugs/biology).

The WDEP formulation represents the standard acronym for counselors learning and practicing reality therapy (Wubbolding, 2015a). For instance, I have written 34 chapters in textbooks and other books that allude to this formulation. Each letter represents not a single counseling intervention but a cluster of ideas to be learned, skills to be studied, and techniques to be practiced. Studying the concepts contained in this formulation might appear simple at first, and the initial practice of the WDEP system of reality therapy often seems mechanical or simplistic. Delving deeper into the practice of reality therapy, however, reveals a more subtle and complex system. Some of this depth is reflected in the dialogues contained in this book. Like riding a bicycle, the skill of reality therapy becomes more comprehensive and intricate as the user encounters hills and valleys and bumps in the road, that is, the wide range of clients from the mildly upset to the addicted or psychotic. When the external world changes, the cyclist and the counselor make creative adjustments. WDEP helps counselors stay curious, open, accepting, and loving. The goal is to assist clients to effectively evaluate the specifics of their lives and to satisfy their needs more effectively.

Practicing Reality Therapy

Chapters 1 and 2 contained a summary of choice theory with illustrations and applications to the everyday world outside the work of the counselor. The WDEP system discussed and illustrated in the remainder of the book focuses on how to implement various skills and techniques contained in and derived from this formulation. The components of the WDEP system are not steps to be followed one after another; they are not like the rungs of a ladder that a person climbs sequentially. They are more closely analogous to a fishing net or a geodesic dome, in which each component depends on the other components. It is commonplace for counselors to follow a sequence, and counselors often begin establishing the therapeutic alliance by asking about the clients' wants. Other counselors may begin the process by exploring the actions of the client or how the client is spending time. From a pedagogical point of view, it is useful to discuss each component as it is formulated: W-D-E-P.

Exploring the Quality World: W

Exploring the quality world offers the counselor a wide range of possibilities such as helping clients become aware of and explore what they want from the world around them: parents, children, family, employer, employees, society, religion, government, friends, school, and neighborhood. Clients discuss the wants that they are fulfilling as well as the wants that are unfulfilled. I have outlined and discussed 132 possible interventions related to wants and perceptions (Wubbolding, 2000b, 2015c).

The exploration of the world of wants includes helping clients identify and develop their level of commitment. After clients formulate a goal or decide to work on satisfying a want, it is helpful for a counselor to ask, "How hard do you want to work at achieving your goal?" Clients' desires for living more effectively take many forms. Some demonstrate a whimsical wish. Others are willing to exert a 100% effort. The skilled reality therapist helps clients decide and reflect on their level of commitment (LOC). Experience shows that clients describe five levels of commitment:

1. "I don't want to be here. Leave me alone." This level of commitment is often seen in the involuntary client. A client coerced into attending counseling sessions sometimes responds in this way.
2. "I would like to have the outcome, but I don't want to make any effort." These clients show a minimal desire to take charge of their lives; making behavioral changes appears to require too much effort.
3. "I'll try." "I might." "I could." This middle level of commitment indicates a willingness to exert some effort. A reality therapy counselor might respond, "I know you'll try, but will you do it?"

4. "I will do my best." Clients willing to do their best show a fairly firm commitment to take action and to assume responsibility.
5. "I will do whatever it takes." This is the highest level of commitment.

Discussion Questions

1. What practical techniques can you think of that you could use to help clients identify and clarify their wants? _____
   _____
   _____
   _____

2. What level of commitment to the completion of a task would you want from the following? Why?

   Your family surgeon _____
   The airline pilot as the plane lands _____
   Your clients _____

After helping clients identify their LOC, the counselor may ask questions like these: "Will that specific level of commitment make a difference for you?" "Will it get the job done satisfactorily?" Part of exploring the W is a discussion about how much energy clients are willing to expend and their willingness to work at making behavioral changes aimed at more satisfying and productive living. These levels are so important that we will revisit them later.

Exploring Perceptions: W

Exploring perceptions includes understanding whether clients perceive themselves as worthy, as valuable human beings, and especially whether they believe they are in control of their lives or are victims of their past history, society, or their environment. Used properly, this procedure helps clients move from an awareness of themselves as victims to an awareness of themselves as self-empowering agents.

The principle that people choose their behavior and are responsible for it opens reality therapy to the criticism that reality therapy blames the victim. Nothing could be further from the truth. Victims abound in the world, but reality therapy incorporates the principle that people have at least some control over their lives regardless of external circumstances. Other professionals have reached a different conclusion. Erik Helzer (2012) asserts that there is a widespread bias that human behavior is intentional or willful. He states that much behavior "arises from a number of causes, most of which have nothing to do with the person's intentions or goals. . . . Behavior comes from a much richer web of causes some of which are intentional but most of which are not" (p. 21). He then seems to agree with the principle of choice theory that people are responsible for their behavior and that his position does not exonerate people from being accountable. Similarly, in warning about possible excesses in the application of recent brain research, Satel and Lilienfeld (2013) warn of the possibility of removing personal responsibility from the courtroom with the excuse "my amygdala made me do it" (p. 97ff). The implication is that emotions can be so strong that they eliminate human choice from behavior.

The astute reality therapist treats behavior "as if" the client has choices, but no hint of blame or criticism is directed toward the client. Once again, from the perspective of choice theory and reality therapy, clients have more control over their lives than they believe they have. This is not to say that choices are easily carried out or that there are not societal restrictions on personal opportunities.

Exploring Total Behavior: D

Exploring total behavior embraces four levels of behavior: physiology, feelings, thinking, and actions (see Figures 1 and 2). Some clients express their problems and issues by presenting their symptomatic awareness: sleeplessness, loss of appetite, headaches, and many other physical signs. Emotions also signal the need for help: anger, resentment, shame, and many others. Depression is an umbrella term for a wide range of debilitating or energy draining emotions. A significant difference between cognitive therapies and reality therapy is that the following self-talk accompanies and underlies rather than causes actions. Also, the content of the self-talk is more focused on choice theory.

- "I can't. I have no control over what I do. I have no choices."
- "No one is going to tell me what to do."
- "Even though what I'm doing is not working, I will continue doing it."

Implementing the WDEP system means focusing on actions, the part of the suitcase most proximately attached to the handle (see Figure 2). Consequently, counselors ask clients to explore what they are doing, but counselors also ask what clients are thinking and feeling. Becoming more self-aware, clients reflect on their current actions and how they are spending their time. Reality therapists ask clients to describe their actions in detail because we are more aware of our feelings and our thoughts than we are of our actions. Yet we have more immediate control over our actions and can change our actions more readily, which leads to changes in our thoughts and feelings. Consequently, efficient and effective reality therapy emphasizes the discussion of actions. But this emphasis does not diminish the necessity of exploring clients' self-talk about their thoughts and what their gut feelings are about their current situation. Regarding the labeling of emotions, contemporary advanced reality therapy embraces the mindfulness injunction "name it to tame it" (D. Siegel, 2010, 2015). If made explicit, this awareness adds to the efficiency and the effectiveness of the next component: self-evaluation.

Lifting the suitcase by the handle and thereby altering thinking and feeling converges with the injunction used in 12-step programs: "It is easier to act your way to a new way of thinking than to think your way to a new way of acting." In these and other support groups, participants are surrounded by other people wishing to provide guidance and friendship. The result of these tangible relationships is more than feeling good for the moment. If they continue to be part of such groups and to implement their new awareness, they actually restructure the architecture of their brain, making new and different neuronal connections. This occurs by taking action, by choosing to do something different from what they had previously done. Arden (2014) quotes a study describing how adults who juggled three balls for three months "increased the gray matter in . . . the areas that are associated with making the movements to juggle" (p. 31). Elsewhere he adds that he often tells his patients, "You're going to have to do things that you don't feel like doing to rewire your brain so that you will feel better" (p. 239). It is indisputable that changing actions plays a significant role, not merely as a handy technique but as an efficacious life-changing intervention on a previously undreamed of level.

In discussing how choice theory is validated by recent brain research, Marlatt (2014) discusses the value of directly altering the thinking process. She states, "From the time an individual is born until his/her time of death the brain has the ability to create new neuronal connections and also to fine-tune existing connections. Neurogenesis occurs every time an individual has a significant new thought and new neuronal connections are forged" (p. 19). We can change the biology of our brains by changing our actions and our cognitions.

Exploring the Core Principle of Reality Therapy: E

George Washington once stated that "every person is the best judge of what relates to his own interests and concerns. . . . Errors once discovered are more than half amended" (as cited in Wubbolding, 2015c, p. 20). Before behavioral change occurs, there is either the explicit self-evaluation by the client or an implicit assessment in which the client looks inward and ultimately formulates a better course of action. Ask yourself, "Have I ever misplaced my car key, important papers, cell phone, eyeglasses, or a to-do list?" Did you ever continue to frantically look for them in the same place over and over again? At some point you probably said to yourself, explicitly or implicitly, "This behavior is not helping. It is not achieving the goal. It is not getting me what I want." When you reached this conclusion, you decided to try another tactic, that is, to make a new and different plan. You made the new plan based on your inner self-evaluation, more specifically the evaluation of the effectiveness of your actions.

Types of Self-Evaluation

The crucial component in the practice of reality therapy—the keystone in the arch of procedures—consists of clients' judgments about various components of the choice theory system. Clients decide, for instance, that their current actions are effective or ineffective. They judge their wants to be attainable or unattainable. They make a decision about whether their perceptions of themselves and the world around them are working to their advantage or to the benefit of others. Glasser (1990) described self-evaluation as the core of reality therapy. The most important and most often used kinds of self-evaluation implemented by counselors, therapists, school personnel, and others are listed here. These forms of self-evaluation extend the principle summarized as, "Is _____ helping or hurting you?"

1. Helping clients decide whether and to what degree their current *actions* are helping or hindering them. Counselors assist clients in deciding whether their actions constitute a "plus or minus" for them. Similarly, clients make a decision about whether their actions facilitate the satisfaction of their quality world and their need system or whether their actions prevent them from getting what they are seeking.
2. Counselors facilitate an examination of whether clients' current *behaviors are congruent* or opposed to civil law, school or company policies, family rules, or other external explicit societal prescriptions. Spiritual leaders using reality therapy assist their congregations or their followers to examine whether their current actions match or violate God's laws.

3. Some self-evaluations focus on the effectiveness of actions that have little to do with written rules or policies. A counselor assists clients in examining whether *their behavior is acceptable or unacceptable* to their parents, family, or society's norms, even if there is no written rule forbidding it.

4. A therapist or counselor helps clients make judgments about their *inner self-talk,* or their core beliefs. Clients often explicitly but more often implicitly tell themselves internal statements that are unhelpful, such as "I have no choices." "I can control other people," and "Even though what I'm doing is not working, I am going to continue to do it." These statements refer to the fact that this inner discourse differs from the self-verbalizations of rational emotive behavioral therapy developed by Albert Ellis (2008). "This is the inner language of many people who have minor problems as well as individuals and families who are more seriously disturbed or dysfunctional" (Wubbolding, 2000a, p. 270).

   In addition to evaluating their actions and cognition, or self-talk, clients can improve their lives when a counselor helps them describe and evaluate their quality world. Counselors ask clients about the realistic attainability of their strivings or goals. Such evaluations occur when counselors ask, "How realistic is it for you to satisfy or to attain what you are seeking from the world around you?" or "Tell me about the realistic possibility of satisfying your desires."

5. Sometimes clients insert in their quality world pictures or specific hopes that are self-destructive or ruinous to others. Although these may *appear* desirable at first glance, some clients are able to determine that achieving a short-term goal could be harmful to them or to their families in the long term. For example, stealing or getting drunk might seem appealing for immediate gratification, but looking into the distant future can reveal more accurately the benefit or the damage that this quality world picture could generate.

6. A counselor utilizing the principles of reality therapy helps clients evaluate the amount of energy they wish to exert to improve their life. Another way of stating this is that clients express either explicitly or implicitly a level of commitment or an intensity of desire to make things different for themselves. Previously, I described several levels of commitment expressed by clients, students, and employees. A more usable summary and one that can be explicitly taught to clients contains these

options: "I won't do anything to change." "I might make changes." "I will definitely choose a new behavior." Even more simply stated, they are "I won't," "I might," "I will."

7. A counselor helps clients evaluate whether their level of commitment has a reasonable chance of triggering behaviors that will fulfill their quality world and thus satisfy their needs.

8. A form of self-evaluation that incorporates many principles of reality therapy relates to the impact of clients' behavior on their families and on people around them. Counselors ask clients to examine whether their behavior helps the people surrounding them or brings them shame and embarrassment. The individual situations of clients and their choices determine the nature of the counseling interventions. In general, clients are asked to respond to statements such as, "Please describe how your current behavior has helped or wounded your family and the people around you." Because of the unique significance of human relationships, this self-evaluation occupies a central place in the practice of reality therapy.

Example of Behavioral Change

Several years ago, I was asked to conduct a training session in Albuquerque, New Mexico. I arrived a day early to enjoy the magnificence of the area. I drove 63 miles to Santa Fe to view the landscape, visit the shops, and appreciate the local artistic pottery. At dusk, I began my journey back to the Albuquerque motel. The road zigzagged, and I was completely caught up in the magnificent scenery, realizing why New Mexico is referred to as "the land of enchantment." After driving for approximately 45 minutes, I suddenly realized that I had seen no signs indicating the distance to Albuquerque. On the contrary, the signs indicated the distance to cities that were in the opposite direction of my intended destination. I could almost hear my inner voice shouting, "Is my current behavioral direction taking me where I want to go?" My answer could only be a resounding "No." Abruptly evaluating my behavior, I realized that continuing to choose my current behavior and direction would not result in attaining my goal.

In the space below, give two examples of choices you have made in the past: how you self-evaluated them and then how you altered them.

1. _____
   _____
   _____

2. _____
   _____
   _____

This brief exercise illustrates the pivotal nature of the cornerstone and necessary prerequisite for behavioral change: self-evaluation.

The detailed types of self-evaluation described in this book can be integrated into virtually any counseling system. They are congruent with solution-focused therapy, impact therapy (Jacobs & Schimmel, 2013), motivational interviewing (Arkowitz et al., 2008), Adlerian therapy, and others.

The central place or efficacy of client self-evaluation cannot be overestimated. I would like to restate two examples presented earlier by asking you the following questions: Did you ever misplace your car keys and look for them in the same place over and over again? Did you ever drive from Santa Fe to Albuquerque the wrong way round? Have you ever repeatedly told your own children any of the following without achieving the desired result?

- Be careful.
- Don't hang around with those kids.
- Don't run.
- If you fall out of that tree and break your leg, don't come running to me!
- Be home before 11 o'clock.
- Don't look at me that way. Look at me when I'm talking to you.

Did you ever repeat the bumper sticker slogan, "Get in, sit down, shut up, and buckle up"? If these injunctions did not work, did you repeat them louder and more often? These are behaviors that are repeated in cultures from Singapore to Kuwait, from Seattle to Stockholm. I can unabashedly make the unscientific assertion that repeatedly choosing ineffective actions is a multicultural choice. The reason people continue to make such choices is very simple: We are human beings and subject to human idiosyncrasies, and we often adopt the motto, "If it's not working, do more of it." Clients who seek counseling frequently adopt this ineffective self-talk. Therefore, the work of the counselor consists in helping clients become their own best judges of their behavior, examine it more carefully, and alter or amend it. The skill of self-evaluation is rendered more difficult for individuals and families who abuse drugs or are members of families subject to attention deficit disorders. Children praised for a behavior on Monday and criticized for the same behavior on Tuesday insert conflicting data into their minds and experience difficulty when making self-evaluations as they grow from one developmental stage to the next. Nevertheless, assisting clients' self-evaluation can be successful *if* the counselor maintains an empathic relationship and *if* clients are willing to change. Clients are able to restructure the architecture of their brains and make new neural connections by means of self-evaluation. Consequently, counselors have the twofold task of connecting with clients and helping them select wants or goals that will motivate them to achieve a higher level of inner satisfaction and overall well-being.

Self-evaluation consists primarily as a judgment made by clients about their quality world: perceptions, actions, thinking, and feeling. Sometimes self-evaluation is erroneously mistaken for self-criticizing, self-blaming, self-reproaching, or self-disparaging. On the contrary, self-evaluation enables clients to view their lives through new lenses. Rather than a debilitating process damaging self-esteem, self-evaluation empowers clients by enhancing their awareness that a happier and better life is possible. Self-evaluation signals the beginning of subsequent behavioral change because it facilitates innovative neural connections. Self-evaluation, whether explicit or implicit, is a necessary foundation for change. In fact, when it occurs, it is itself a change. In the interchange between client and counselor, the client initiates a different thinking process that constitutes an alteration in behavior and thus predisposes the client toward more improvements in his or her actions, thinking, and feelings that occur outside the counseling session.

Self-Evaluation Regarding Actions and Purpose of Behavior

The second purpose of behavior is to communicate with the world around us, to send a signal. In this context, behavior is a metaphorical language. A teacher's tone of voice, thoroughness of preparation, gestures, body language, and many other aspects of behavior in themselves communicate a message. The message could be one of excitement about the students and the subject matter. It could be a message of love for the course content and for the students. It could be boredom and even dislike for the material or for the students. The teacher's behavior might even communicate a love for teaching in general or a disdain for it. I recall an incident as a new teacher. I walked into the faculty room where several teachers were discussing various topics. There was a moment of silence. Another teacher sitting outside the group made the unprompted comment, "Today is bad but tomorrow is going to be worse." The entire teachers' lounge burst into laughter. They had never labeled this teacher as a positive thinker, and this statement confirmed their perception of him. Similarly, television personalities make an attempt to sound excited about their reporting or analysis. It appears that they are coached not merely to read a script but to enliven it with animation and even melodrama at times. They hope to dazzle the audience so that viewers keep their hands away from the channel changer button on the remote control. Human behavior sends a message to the world around us that indicates our attitude is negative, positive, excited, anxious, fearful, hopeful, interested, or something else. Eye contact and many other forms of behavior signal interest in another person, which leads to acquaintanceship, friendship, and romance. Other forms of self-evaluation include determining the attainability of wants or goals, the efficacy of clients' level of commitment, and the congruence between values expressed and actions.

Planning for Change: P

Counseling sessions that include self-evaluation aim at the formulation of a plan of action. There is a saying, "To fail to plan is to plan to fail." Some clients merely think about the content of the session. Others focus on change characterized by the following elements of an effective plan (SAMIC³ plan):

S = *Simple.* The plan is uncomplicated and clearly understood.
A = *Attainable.* It is realistically achievable.
M = *Measurable.* It answers the question, "When will you do it?"
I = *Immediate.* It is not delayed but rather carried out as soon as possible.
C = *Controlled* by the planner or minimally dependent on the behavior of others.
C = *Committed to.* The plan is made firm by writing it down, a handshake, or other means.
C = *Consistent.* The most efficacious plan is repetitive.

Evaluating the Action Plan as Effective or Ineffective

The following exercise will help you assist clients in formulating efficacious plans. Each of these statements violates at least one characteristic of effective planning. On the lines provided, mark the *first letter* of the characteristic or characteristics of effective planning that are lacking. (Answers are at the end of the chapter.)

_____ 1. With the help of the counselor, the seventh-grader plans to study each night for 2 hours, ride his bicycle to a friend's house, help with the dishes, sweep the sidewalk, and complete a jigsaw puzzle.

_____ 2. "From now on I will do better."

_____ 3. "I'll try."

_____ 4. "I'll look for a job if the staff (at the halfway house) wakes me at 8:00 a.m."

_____ 5. "Next week I will begin an exercise program."

Preliminary Comments About the Dialogues

The purpose of the dialogues is to illustrate the wide range of counseling interventions available to assist clients in conducting their self-evaluations. I wish to re-emphasize that a genuine self-evaluation, either implicit or explicit, constitutes a necessary prerequisite for behavioral change. Therefore, I suggest that you keep the following in mind when reading the dialogues:

1. Because the dialogues are written, the absence of tone of voice, eye contact, facial expression, and other forms of body language or nonverbal communications limits the full impact of the counselor's interventions and the many subtleties of the client's total behavior. Placing specific emphasis on self-evaluative procedures and interventions has necessitated the omission of many side comments and relationship building interchanges and conversations characteristic of counseling relationships.

2. Throughout the dialogues, counselors listen carefully for hints indicating that clients have developed or are developing a lesser or greater sense of inner control. For instance, when a client says "I've worked very hard to get other people to change," a counselor can perceive that the client is taking some responsibility in that he uses the phrase "worked very hard." This response differs from the expected, "You can't change other people." The latter comment reflects a central principle of choice theory but fails to reflect an advanced use of the principles of reality therapy. Very often the use of counseling procedures can reflect genuine theory but are misused and directed at changing clients rather than helping them make their own changes.

3. Choice theory and reality therapy provide many opportunities to implement the Ericksonian principle of utilization, that is, to utilize all the material, even the problems presented by

clients (Short, Erickson, & Klein, 2005; Zeig, 2006). Jacobs and Schimmel (2013) suggest incorporating props and objects in the counseling room as aids to help clients conduct self-evaluations. The most valuable elements in the room are the counselors themselves who can use gestures and body language to enhance the counseling process. Examples of this include illustrating an out-of-balance scale with your arms and hands, turning the steering wheel on a car, creating a wall between the client and other people, leaning forward or backward from the client, and picking up the suitcase of behavior by the handle. Such intentional gestures illustrate and teach the principles of choice theory and reality therapy. They are not like the random and meaningless gestures often witnessed in speeches by public figures, in the movies, or on television. When conducting family counseling sessions, I often hand a simple 2-foot-long wicker spoon to an argumentative participant with the observation, "It looks like it's your turn to stir the pot today." This intervention, based on the impact therapy of Jacobs and Schimmel (2013), helps the family evaluate their behaviors in a rather humorous and indirect manner and see that they are ineffective in bringing the family closer together. Unfortunately, these effective aids cannot be shown in a written transcript.

4. I suggest that you read the dialogues out loud and utilize your own tone of voice, formulate gestures, observe your own body language, and utilize peer consultation for feedback.

5. The dialogues between the hypothetical clients and counselors constitute the epicenter of the message contained in this book. A brief background is provided for each dialogue as well as a commentary at the end of each session and a space for you to add your personal interventions to the dialogues. I have omitted many details that emerge in counseling interchanges and have concentrated on the specifics of client self-evaluation. Zeig (2006) speaks of "seeding the plan" or engaging in a preparatory dialogue leading up to a plan of action. The same concept of seeding applies to preliminary interchanges that lay the groundwork for effective client self-evaluation. Counselors assist clients in formulating and clarifying their wants, their behavior, and their perceptions. Following this process are inquiries and requests: "Are your wants realistically attainable?" "Describe how your current actions or choices are helping or hurting you." "If you see yourself as an incapable victim, how will you be able to take better charge of your future?"

The dialogues offer the opportunity for you to use your creative behavioral system to develop your own responses within the framework of the WDEP system of reality therapy and to apply them to your own clients. In fact, my intent in writing this book, especially the dialogues, is to trigger innovative and creative applications for you to use with your clients.

Finally, the dialogues can serve as topics for class discussions, focus groups, skill building sessions, and consultation meetings. I invite you to read this book and critique the dialogues while asking yourself these questions: "What can I learn about reality therapy from this dialogue, and how can I personalize and use it?" "There are many counseling methodologies. How is Adlerian counseling, brief solution-focused therapy, impact therapy, cognitive therapy, psychoanalytic therapy, REBT, feminist therapy, existential therapy, multicultural counseling, or my own eclectic applications of counseling theory and practice congruent or incongruent with reality therapy?"

Case Example:
Self-Evaluation of Behavior as Language

This first example of a dialogue focuses on one aspect of reality therapy: behavior as a method of communication. When practitioners of reality therapy perceive behavior as a communication system, they open a new dimension to the practice of counseling. The counselor speaks with a troubled female adolescent client who places blame for her plight on the world outside herself. (We visit Lynn again later in the book.) Notice the use of tonic behaviors and the avoidance of toxic behaviors by the counselor.

Lynn, 17, is referred for counseling because of ongoing conflict with her mother, with whom she lives, and with her teachers. Currently, she is flunking her high school classes, breaking her home curfew, uttering obscenities to her mother when asked to perform simple chores, associating with friends her mother disapproves of, and, at times, returning home high on drugs. Lynn desperately wants to move away from her mother and live elsewhere with her father. After establishing a solid working counseling relationship, the counselor focuses on the W, D, and, especially, on the E of reality therapy.

Counselor: Lynn, you've told me very frankly about what's going on in your life, and your description is pretty much the same as what your mother told me. I'm curious about what you think she wants from you.

Lynn: She wants to run my life for me, tell me what to do every minute. She doesn't want me to have any friends. She's always on my back. I'm 17, and I ought to be able to do what I want to do. I can never do anything right. She hates my friends and always tells me to stay away from them.

Counselor: It seems that your mother has gotten her message across to you. You clearly understand what she is saying. In fact, it seems to me she keeps making it clear to you over and over again and relentlessly hammers on you. But you *really* don't like what she's saying.

Lynn: Yeah, all she does is hassle me, nag me. She's always dogging on me about something. She keeps ragging on me all day, and I hate it.

Counselor: It must be hard for you to walk in the house every day.

Lynn: I stay away from the house as much as possible.

Counselor: And you're getting sick of hearing the same old message, and you would like her to make some changes.

Lynn: Like I said, she nags me constantly. I told her she's like a repeating decimal. It gets boring listening to her.

Counselor: What is your gut feeling about all of these things?

Lynn: I hate her.

Counselor: Hate. That's a pretty strong word. You must feel pretty upset about the way your life is going.

Lynn: Hate. That pretty much describes it.

Counselor: That's your first feeling. Any others?

Lynn: I don't know.

Counselor: I wonder if it isn't a feeling of hurt?

Lynn: (*Long pause and tears.*) Yes, I am hurt. One of my girlfriends called it "wounded."

Counselor: And after the feeling of hurt comes anger. How does she hurt you?

Lynn: She tells me I'm worthless and no good.

Counselor: I can't help wondering if you're afraid too.

Lynn: I guess so.

Counselor: Fearful? It's really no fun to be hurt, afraid, maybe even rejected. I wonder what those feelings are really all about. What are you afraid of?

Lynn: I'm afraid she might be right.

Counselor: It's hard to reject a message when you hear it over and over. And you've just told me what you hear, even if she doesn't use those exact words. Lynn, I have a very important question to ask you. Is what you're feeling in any way helpful to you?

Lynn: (*Responds almost inaudibly.*) No.

Counselor: It's painful to talk about this. I imagine it weighs heavy on your heart.

Lynn: Very much so. I've never talked this way about my situation.

Counselor: (*Speaks in a slow, deliberative manner and demonstrates empathy in tone of voice and body posture.*) I have found that when people talk as deeply as you are right now, they feel better, both in their heart and even in their mind. They often feel relief. That's what I hope you would feel as a result of talking about this with me.

Lynn: (*Long pause.*) I think you are reading me right.

Counselor: I wonder if the pain you feel could be a motivation for you? Would you like to see your situation change?

Lynn: Definitely.

Counselor: I believe I can help you. Are you willing to work at it in ways different than in the past?

Lynn: But like I said, she yells at me constantly and never has a nice thing to say to me. And to be honest, I yell back at her. It's a constant f____ fight.

Counselor: So what you want is for her to stop yelling and leave you alone. Furthermore, you want to move in with your father.

Lynn: Yeah, I want to get away from that s____.

Counselor: It seems to me that you have worked very hard and held nothing back to try to get your message across to her. You've been very clear about what you want from her.

Lynn: I sure have.

Counselor: It also is quite clear that she wants a number of things from you that she's not getting, and she tells you repeatedly what they are. On the other hand, you've listed the things that you have been doing and described your current choices. Tell me if I'm right. Your current *actions* seem to be your way of getting a message across to her.

Lynn: Yeah. I can't stand to be around her, and I can't get through to her.

Counselor: Lynn, there was a time when I taught history, and your situation reminds me of two countries fighting over a piece of land that both of them claim as their own. They can't agree on whose it is because neither side is willing to admit defeat to the other side. They keep sending messages back and forth that are hostile and really make the other side even more angry.

Lynn: That's about right.

Counselor: So, you're trying to get a message across to her, and you're doing things to motivate her to change what she's doing, which is refusing to let you move out. And yet she clings to that decision to say "no" to you about moving in with your father. You seem to be using a lot of energy and working hard at getting this message across so that you can get what you want from her, and, as you said, you "can't get through to her." So these two countries stand facing each other in a stalemate. What would you tell these two countries?

Lynn: I don't know. I guess they should sit down and talk things over and try to come to an agreement.

Counselor: Would you recommend that they go to war?

Lynn: No. I don't think they should go to war. But they should try to get their message across to each other.

Counselor: And you have definitely tried to get your message across so that you can get what you want from your mother.

Lynn: That's for sure. I try and try, and after all that I can't get through to her at all.

Counselor: I have a very important question to ask you. It's what we call a self-evaluation question. In other words, I'd like you to make a judgment and say it out loud. Is the way you've been communicating with your mother working to your satisfaction?

Lynn: I never thought of it that way.

Counselor: Here's another way I'd like to ask you the same question. Is what you're doing helping you or hurting you?

Lynn: (*In a quiet tone of voice.*) I guess it's not helping me.

Counselor: And you said that you are hurt and even fearful. And so I want to add another request. Would you think about whether what you're doing is helping you remove the feelings of hurt, of fear, and maybe even fear of rejection by her? As I said before, I believe I can help you if you are willing to think in a different way and take a different kind of action regarding your situation.

Commentary: In this dialogue, the counselor prepares a self-evaluation question by helping Lynn articulate her current actions. He helps her connect her actions with her wants. She is stunned as she comes to the realization that her actions are linked to her wants and that her behavior is purposeful. She has indeed increased her awareness about the messages she sends to her mother. The counselor artfully helps her realize that in order to satisfy her quality world and get what she wants, she will need to connect her specific wants with her specific actions and do this more explicitly and more effectively. Lynn has already made a change in her total behavior, especially her thinking. This abbreviated dialogue is a prelude to effective planning and a change in direction for Lynn. Central to the effective use of interventions that focus on self-evaluation is the expression of accurate empathy. The counselor helps Lynn to look at her emotions and name the surface and deeper feelings. The counselor helps Lynn "name it to tame it" by at least labeling her gut feelings of hurt and fear. The counselor reflects on Lynn's marginal but not explicitly stated fear of rejection by her mother. Because Lynn trusts the counselor, she is willing to accept the counselor's suggestion that the fear is focused on an unwanted future event, that is, possible rejection by her mother.

The session continues.

Counselor: Let's come back to the idea of sending messages back and forth. Tell me about the people at school, the teachers.

Lynn: They're so stupid. They're always yelling at me.

Counselor: How often would you say you actually went to school and stayed all day in the last month?

Lynn: About half the time.

Counselor: And when you do show up, they nag you like your mother?

Lynn: It's kind of nagging.

Counselor: They keep telling you what to do: be on time, do your work, come to class, be respectful, stay all day, pay attention, and on and on and on. It's the same old song isn't it?

Lynn: That's exactly right.

Counselor: So they've made their message clear about what they want from you. There's no doubt in your mind what they stand for and what their expectations are.

Lynn: Yeah, they're good at preaching, yelling, picking at me.

Counselor: I'm wondering, Lynn, do you ever do things just to aggravate them?

Lynn: Oh, it's easy. I don't even have to think about it, and I can really get them going. Some are easier than others.

Counselor: Let me get this straight now. You show up about half the time, and you're flunking several subjects, not doing the assignments. Do you ever talk back to them?

Lynn: Oh yes. All I have to do is open my mouth, and they get upset with me.

Counselor: So, you have tried your best to get your message across to them, "Leave me alone!" It sounds like you have put in a lot of energy at times, as you have with your mother, to get them to respect your wishes. What about your probation officer and the juvenile court judge?

Lynn: Well, they're on my back every chance they get. The probation officer said if I don't shape up he'd send me to detention and then to the girls' state reformatory.

Counselor: I know it well. I heard all about the food there.

Lynn: What did you hear?

Counselor: The same that you probably heard. Let's just say that it's not very good. By the way, how's your mother's cooking?

Lynn: She cooks good meals.

Counselor: Oh! (*Expresses surprise and shows it in his facial expression.*) So there is something you like about living with her.

Lynn: Yes, the food's pretty good.

Counselor: Let's get back to school. Everybody that meets you at school seems to show some kind of disapproval of you. Then there's the court and the probation officer. Same thing, they're on your back giving you a message.

Lynn: Yes, they are all telling me the same thing. And as you said, I work hard to get my message across to them.

Counselor: It's almost like they don't understand the language you're using. You're speaking one language, but it's a language they don't comprehend.

Lynn: They're so stupid.

Counselor: And yet these "stupid" people are running your life! (*Long pause; client has startled look on her face.*) Unfortunately, they don't understand what you're trying to get across to them.

Lynn: They sure don't.

Counselor: This must be very frustrating, aggravating, annoying. And generally, you get angry with them. Even feeling rage at them.

Lynn: Yes, that's for sure. It's the same s____ I get at home.

Counselor: Would you like to have this situation change for you?

Lynn: You bet I would.

Counselor: Now I have a very important question for you, Lynn. Do you want to continue to use the same language in dealing with them?

Lynn: What do you mean?

Counselor: Let's put it this way. If you were to visit a foreign country and they didn't understand English, would they understand it if you kept repeating the same words only speaking louder?

Lynn: I guess not.

Counselor: And how would you feel about this, Lynn? Frustrated, kind of like you feel in school and at home. So my question is this. Are your actions, which are kind of like a language that you're speaking to them, getting the message across to the people you describe as running your life?

Lynn: I guess not.

Counselor: You "guess"?

Lynn: No. They don't understand at all. They call me "uncooperative" when they're being nice.

Counselor: So, this language, let's call it "uncooperation." Is it getting what you want from mother, school, probation officer, juvenile judge, and others?

Lynn: Nooo, it's not helping me.

Counselor: Now I'm even more firmly convinced that I can help you deal with the people around you. And when you deal with them, I believe you will be able to get rid of the hurt, the fear, and the entire barrel of turmoil and upheaval that you've been drowning in. Would you like to work toward that goal? At least lessen some of the stuff I just mentioned and replace it with something better?

Commentary: The counselor defines actions as similar to a language and then helps Lynn evaluate the effectiveness of her actions as a communication system. This reframing of behavior, more specifically actions, opens a new pathway and provides a wealth of possible interventions for counselors to use with clients who insist on repeating their unevaluated choices. Reframing also aims at helping Lynn, as Daniel Siegel (2012) says, "begin to change the neural proclivities that, without awareness, could remain on automatic pilot" (p. 3–6). This unconventional perception of actions relates to the second purpose of behavior described in choice theory. The first purpose of behavior described by Glasser (1998) is to make an impact on the outside world, to maneuver external circumstances so that the outer world matches the perceptions and wants of the person. As stated earlier, Michelangelo said that the purpose of his behavior (sculpting) was to liberate the statue inside the marble. Using his artistic talents, he shaped or molded the external world, the marble, to match what he wanted. The results were *David*, the *Pieta*, and many other masterpieces that have been admired for centuries. Beyond this basic sculpting purpose, I have added to choice theory the second purpose for behavior, which is illustrated in the dialogue. Our actions, and in fact our total behavior (actions, thinking, feelings, and physiology), are closely analogous to a language designed to communicate with the external world. The most obvious examples of behavior as a method of communication are words, their inflections, and body language. When thinking, feelings, and physiology are linked to actions, they also become part of our language even if they are completely held inside of us and not externally visible. The counselor accepts Lynn's perception that outside forces are controlling her. The counselor is aware of the necessity to help Lynn evaluate this external locus of control. Gradually, the counselor will help her focus on her sense of internal control. In following this process, the counselor does not argue with her, blame her, or imply that she is the source of her own misery or that she is bringing the problems on herself. This attitude represents unconditional positive regard.

Clients can add to the help gained from the counseling session as well as assist in the counselor's own self-evaluation. The following interaction illustrates this brief but crucial technique:

> *Counselor:* Lynn, what was the most useful idea that you will take away from today's session?
>
> *Lynn:* I believe the most beneficial idea is for me to think of my behavior as a way of communicating to others. This is a new idea for me.

Glasser stressed the importance of teaching the concepts of choice theory and reality therapy to clients. Practitioners of reality therapy and cognitive therapy play a directive role in teaching clients specific skills and concepts. Some clients require more instruction on how to self-evaluate than others. Individuals diagnosed with attention deficit disorders, children raised in an addictive family, and especially addicted people themselves have a clear need to learn what is often, for them, a new behavior: self-evaluation (Wubbolding & Brickell, 2005b, 2015). Clients raised in a family characterized by inconsistency have difficulty distinguishing what is effective from what is ineffective. When children are rewarded for a behavior on one occasion and punished for the same behavior on another occasion, they often lack the ability of distinguishing effective from ineffective choices. They grow from one stage of development to the next not knowing what helps them and what hinders them. Counselors sometimes must undertake the responsibility of pointing out and emphasizing effective actions and distinguishing them from ineffective actions. They also help clients discuss their emotions and demonstrate empathy by helping clients label their feelings and express them appropriately.

With young children, counselors often explain the WDEP system and engage in direct teaching. Carleen Glasser (1996, 2017) suggests that the word *self-evaluation* be changed to *help* or *hurt* when teaching young elementary school children; the WDEP system then becomes WDHP.

Self-evaluation can be taught in counseling sessions, in classrooms, in the home, and to the general public. Therefore, counselors can serve as consultants and student advocates to teachers, parents, and administrators. They can facilitate systemic change by assisting other professionals to deal with children of all ages in a more effective and humane manner. Carleen Glasser, senior faculty for the William Glasser Institute, has taught the WDEP system for decades throughout North America (Figure 4).

As you reread the case of Lynn, what two additional questions or exploratory statements would you use to help Lynn self-evaluate? What SAMIC[3] plan would you help her formulate?

1. _____
2. _____
3. _____

**Figure 4. Carleen Glasser Teaching the WDEP System
of Reality Therapy**

Note. Reprinted with permission of Carleen Glasser.

Expanding and Extending Reality Therapy Procedures

The previous discussion of reality therapy procedures is designed to assist you in appreciating and practicing these techniques and skills. These skills are essential for putting into practice and rendering concrete the principles of choice theory. They are the train on the choice theory train track. The procedures summarized by the acronym WDEP deliver the treasures described in the groundbreaking resources given to the world in Glasser's classic books *Stations of the Mind* (1981), *Control Theory* (1984), *Choice Theory* (1998), and *Take Charge of Your Life* (2011). In these books, Glasser presents choice theory as an internal motivational system and as a replacement for the widespread but understandable effort of people to control others. In his lectures, he frequently summarized choice theory by stating that human beings can be happier if they learn to escape from the unreasonable restraints of excessive external control often used in contemporary society.

The procedures of reality therapy constitute specific ways to make practical and useful the principles of choice theory. Techniques used include asking questions, practicing reflective listening, redirecting the client to a discussion of past successes, making exploratory requests, and making nonverbal interventions such as responding to the client's tone of voice and overall demeanor. These signals often indicate nervousness or anxiety as well as positive feelings such as hopefulness and a willingness to take action. It is not practical to provide examples of each of these possibilities. However, as I describe the ever-evolving use of the WDEP formulation of reality therapy, I present several dialogues exemplifying the more advanced use of effective questioning and exploratory requests.

For the sake of both simplicity and effective pedagogy, I have formulated the procedures into four categories summarized by the acronym WDEP. Counselors, students, therapists, educators, supervisors, and managers in business and agencies find this formula useful in both their initial and advanced stages of learning. They apply the system in practicing reality therapy and thereby apply choice theory to real situations. The WDEP expression of reality therapy provides an outline for professional people in their work and represents for them an overall structure and sense of direction. They can keep focused and on track. They know where they are going when they keep this general outline in mind. This outline also serves as a self-help method when effectively taught to clients, students, and the general public.

William Glasser, the founder of reality therapy, has spoken enthusiastically about this formulation of reality therapy procedures and described it in the introduction to *Understanding Reality Therapy* (Wubbolding, 1991) as a "most important contribution in that it provides a system to help in understanding and using reality therapy. . . . I hope that this system will become a household phrase and [be] used by therapists, counselors, teachers and parents" (p. xii). Each letter represents not a single question or concept but rather a cluster of ideas and an array of possible interventions useful when counseling, managing, or using these ideas in any human relationship.

More Than Questioning

Reality therapy is often presented as a series of questions, but to call it only a questioning process is incomplete. Reality therapy includes far more than a series of questions aimed at clients. Rather, the procedures provide a vehicle for establishing a therapeutic alliance and maintaining it. Research has shown that the relationship between counselor and client is the single most important component for accomplishing behavior change. Rogers (1957) believed that the quality of the relationship characterized by empathy, positive regard, and especially congruence are necessary and sufficient conditions for bringing about the desired change. Congruence includes being genuine, authentic, and self-aware. Reality therapy procedures provide a method for achieving and demonstrating these qualities. Along with the principles of choice theory, they provide systematic assistance to the helper for living in the moment and for being mindful of self, client, and the relationship. From my point of view, they are vehicles for implementing the principles of mindfulness. In fact, they might be called the use of "mindful reality therapy." For more information about mindfulness, consult the work of Daniel Siegel (2007, 2012) who describes mindfulness which I believe is compatible with the advanced use of reality therapy. For more information on the compatibility of mindfulness and reality therapy, see my chapter in *Contemporary Theory and Practice of Counseling and Psychotherapy* (Tinsley et al., 2016).

In summary, I can't stress enough the necessity for the counselor to be present physically, emotionally, mentally, and behaviorally (in this instance, behavior equals actions) to the client. If practiced appropriately, the procedures facilitate this process.

• • •

Answers to statements on page 59: 1. S, A; 2. A, M; 3. C; 4. C; 5. I.

Chapter 5

Career Concerns

Human motivation for behavior begins with a system of human needs, as explained earlier, but we are incapable of simply belonging, achieving power, being free, or having fun. We satisfy these nonspecific sources of motivation by fulfilling specific wants or goals, also known as *pictures*. The collection of specific wants unique to each person is analogous to a file cabinet containing important file folders. Glasser frequently refers to this aggregate of wants as the "quality world" or "mental picture album." As we interact with the world around us, we develop pictures of specific people, real or ideal, that satisfy the need for belonging, specific activities that provide a sense of power or achievement, specific choices that connect with freedom or independence, and specific pursuits that result in the inner sense of fun or enjoyment. These intense desires or wants are detailed in Chapter 2. The focus of counseling is often on assisting clients in prioritizing their wants. In the case of substance abuse, clients' pictures or goals are often blurred and therefore unclear to them. The desired fulfillment of some wants is often immediate, but the satisfaction of others can be more long term or delayed. Some wants may conflict with the wants of others, such as family members or an employer.

In this chapter, we meet three clients with out-of-balance scales. In the first case, the counselor acts as a consultant to Morgan, a manager, who is concerned about his employee, Simon. Simon's wants have lost their congruence with those of Morgan, and Simon's priorities are currently very different from Morgan's.

You will also meet Hanako, who is alone and feels shame because of her failure on the job and in her personal life.

Case Example: Self-Evaluation of Quality World Wants—Employer/Employee

Morgan is the manager and owner of a large automobile dealership and is concerned about one of his employees, Simon. He does not wish to terminate Simon's employment because he has been a positive asset for 17 years, but he is convinced that an intervention is necessary. Morgan states that Simon was once a valuable employee who understood the art of supervising his staff, but in the last year Morgan has noticed that Simon loses his temper over small conflicts, seems to "mope around," does not talk as much as formerly, occasionally leaves work early on Fridays, is irresponsible about entering customer information into the computer, and even becomes impatient with customers to the point that several of them have registered serious complaints.

The dealership has enjoyed a reputation of being customer friendly and of providing high-quality service. The employees are well known in the community and for the most part are respected as being honest and competent. The service department has increased its business in the last 5 years because customers have become less inclined to purchase new cars. Consequently, the parts department has become busier than in the past, which has increased Simon's workload and responsibilities.

Morgan is referring Simon to the counselor, and Morgan has stated that he is giving Simon one more chance to be the way he used to be. In the counselor's consultation session with Morgan, the counselor has provided a detailed professional disclosure statement and has discussed confidentiality and its limits. More specifically, the counselor explains "the purposes, goals, techniques, procedures, limitations, potential risks and benefits of services; the counselor's qualifications, credentials, and experience; [and] how services will be continued if the counselor dies or becomes incapacitated" (Herlihy & Corey, 2015, p. 144). (I will not repeat every detail of the required explanation of ethical principles with each dialogue, but I will refer to the most pertinent ethical issues. Such discussions are not peculiar to reality therapy. Rather, they constitute the standard practice).

As you read the dialogue, observe how the counselor helps Morgan evaluate the attainability of his wants.

Case Example: Counselor as Consultant

Counselor: Morgan, we discussed the various ethical issues governing our consultation as well as some general expectations on your part. Let's start by discussing what you want from Simon.

Morgan: He's been a very effective employee for 17 years, and I thought he enjoyed running the parts department. He gave me no indication that he was unhappy, and in our conversations over the years he has made many helpful suggestions for improvements. He always put in more than the minimum number of hours, and his staff indicated that they were quite satisfied working under him.

Counselor: So he's been a loyal worker and manager and saw his role as more than just having a job. He also seemed to view the dealership as a place where he could be personally invested in its success.

Morgan: Right. He *was* the kind of manager that you could have full confidence in. I could go home at night and feel that the dealership, especially the parts department, was in good hands, and I could be free of worry.

Counselor: And you'd like to get back to that, where you could go home at night relaxed and confident. But you're not at that place right now.

Morgan: That's exactly right.

Counselor: And so you want something from him that you're not getting. And if you got it, you would have peace of mind.

Morgan: Umm hmm.

Counselor: This might sound pretty basic, but I think it's important that together we talk about and define exactly what you want from him.

Morgan: Well, for starters I'd like him to work a full week every week. He goes home early on Friday at just the time when people come to his department to purchase parts they want to use over the weekend on their own cars. Also, the people in the service department are rushing around and need his expertise to satisfy their customers who hope to pick up their cars late Friday or early Saturday.

Counselor: OK. So let's write these down on the flip chart. Let me assure you that no one else will see these papers. A major want that you have, and the one you mentioned first, is that he stays to the end of the day on Friday. It's not like this is a new expectation on your part. In fact, it's what he used to do in the past.

Morgan: That's exactly right again.

Counselor: Now, I want to ask you something that might seem obvious but that is crucial to this whole process. Deep inside, do you believe it is realistically attainable for you to fulfill this want? In other words, is it something that you can reasonably ask of Simon?

Morgan: I believe it is because that's the way he was until about a year ago. He just seems unhappy and restless now.

Counselor: OK. So, you believe it is a reasonable expectation in that you believe it is possible. I can see from your expression that not fulfilling this expectation is especially aggravating and worrisome to you.

Morgan: Yes, my evenings and my weekends are not as enjoyable as they once were. I don't want to fire him, but it may come to that. Then replacing him brings its own problems . . . like finding the right person.

Counselor: So we've nailed down your number one expectation. What is your second want regarding Simon?

Morgan: I would like him to be more friendly and courteous, both to the customers and to his workers. It's like he's always preoccupied.

Counselor: Do you suspect any kind of drug or alcohol involvement on his part?

Morgan: I don't think so, but anything is possible.

Counselor: Drug abuse is a widespread problem regardless of social class or race. I often find that it is a common issue. On the other hand, I don't want to create a problem where there is none.

Morgan: I'll keep an eye out for this problem.

Counselor: I'll give you a paper about drugs in the workplace that contains a list of things to look for. No need to panic about it, however. Now, what would be another expectation or want that you have regarding him?

Morgan: I don't think it's unreasonable to ask him to do what he's supposed to do regarding staying on top of the paperwork and computer records as well as ordering parts from the factory in a timely manner. I'd like him to be more efficient and prompt in this regard.

Counselor: So now we've listed on the flip chart three major expectations: working a full week, being courteous to the people around him, and improving his work habits.

Morgan: If he could do those three things, he would be well on the way to being his old self again.

Counselor: Now, Morgan, let's discuss these from another point of view. Which of these, in your mind, is the most important one?

Morgan: Definitely the first one.

Counselor: Tell me whether you think it is realistic for you to get what you want from him regarding a full week's work.

Morgan: I don't think it is asking too much. To me it is obvious that a leader and manager of a major department in our dealership should go beyond the minimum and, in fact, set an example for the other employees.

Counselor: Let's take a closer look at your three wants or expectations, starting with the first one. How realistic is it for you to get 100% of what you want? Or how realistic is it for Simon to make a 180-degree turn right away?

Morgan: I'm not sure.

Counselor: Has his change from being an outstanding, go-the-extra-mile worker to his current level of commitment been a sudden change or a gradual one?

Morgan: It's been a gradual deterioration over the last year.

Counselor: If that's the case, how realistic is it for him to make a 180-degree turn and suddenly become the ideal employee that he once was?

Morgan: When you put it that way, I suppose it is not realistic to expect an immediate total makeover.

Counselor: OK, so what are you willing to settle for as far as seeing an improvement?

Morgan: I'm not sure, but I definitely want to see improvement.

Counselor: So, I will work with him from a counseling point of view to make an improvement. Of course, whether he does improve will depend on whether he *wants* to make the improvement. What about your second expectation, that he demonstrate more courtesy and friendliness? How realistic is this expectation?

Morgan: I think it is very realistic because once again all I'm asking is that he makes an effort and improves.

Counselor: And your expectation regarding administrative details?

Morgan: Same thing. If I'm to keep him around, I better see some improvement in this as well as in the other two.

Counselor: So *improvement* is the key word here. I will help him examine his behaviors and evaluate them. Then, depending on his motivation, help him make realistic plans to improve. Is there anything that you told me that I should not discuss with him?

Morgan: No, feel free to bring up any of these details, and you can even tell him what I said because I have already discussed his situation with him.

Counselor: OK, Morgan. I'll be talking to him tomorrow. You know my approach, and you are open to the fact that he will have to deal with more than on-the-job issues and problems. Morgan, I have one last request of you. Could you tell me what is the most useful idea that we discussed today.

Morgan: I think the most useful idea is that I might not be able to get everything I want quickly. I will probably need to settle on less than an ideal outcome for a while.

Commentary: It is clear that the WDEP system, especially the self-evaluation component, applies to this session, which was a *consulting* session rather than counseling. One of the differences between consulting and counseling is that the former focuses on a third person. The counselor is not primarily focusing on the emotions, self-talk, or actions of the consultee. Rather, the focus is on a third person, in this case an employee. The counselor does not assist Morgan to face his own resentments or anger at Simon, nor is Morgan asked to "name it to tame it." Rather, the counselor stresses Morgan's wants as they pertain to Simon, his employee. The counselor helps Morgan evaluate whether his wants are realistically attainable. He also assists Morgan in listing his wants in priority. One of the key questions is, "What are you willing to settle for in the short term?" Both of these concepts have wide application in the practice of reality therapy, such as when a counselor consults with parents about their children or with teachers about students' behavior.

Answer the following questions about Morgan's session with the counselor:

1. What in Morgan's quality world are his wants as they relate to Simon? _____
   _____

2. Why do you think the counselor limits the discussion of Morgan's wants to three? _____
   _____

3. What is the theme of the counselor's effort to help Morgan evaluate his wants? _____
   _____

4. How else would you help Morgan conduct a searching self-evaluation? _____
   _____

5. How would you deal with the relationship between Morgan and Simon if there was a racial or ethnic difference between them?
   _____
   _____

Case Example:
Employee Evaluating Wants and Actions

Simon is 43 years old. His marriage ended 9 months ago, and he is employed as an auto parts manager in Morgan's large automobile dealership. Simon arrives for counseling willingly but hesitantly. As in the consultation session with Morgan, the counselor reviews the necessary professional disclosure issues common to all counseling methodologies.

The dialogues are not intended to represent a comprehensive discussion of ethical principles. Users of reality therapy are expected to know the standard of practice and to practice the highest level of ethical behavior as described in the code of ethics of the American Counseling Association (2014) and other professional organizations. I describe reality therapy interventions but not every aspect of informed consent, duty to warn, conflict of interest, multiple relationships, and so forth.

The counselor informs Simon that Morgan released him from any obligation pertaining to confidentiality. Consequently, from the point of view of Morgan, all information is on the table and open for discussion.

Counselor: First, I'd like to review what we talked about during our phone conversation. Our discussion is confidential, just between you and me. I will not discuss your situation outside this office unless you give permission by signing a paper that we call a "release." I want you to know that I have discussed confidentiality with Morgan, and he is in agreement with the need for confidentiality. As we progress, you might want me to make some recommendations to Morgan, but I will do that only with your written consent.

Simon, now that we've covered the professional details, summarized Morgan's discussion with me, and clarified my counseling style, I'd like to congratulate you for coming here today.

Simon: To tell you the truth, I'm nervous about being here and not thrilled with having to ask for help.

Counselor: Yet, despite your hesitancy, you came in, and I think that takes guts and indicates that you are willing to take a step in the right direction.

Simon: I haven't thought about it that way. It seems to me asking for outside help means that I can't solve this on my own.

Counselor: Have you tried solving it on your own?

Simon: Yes, I have.

Counselor: And how's that worked out for you? Have you gotten to a place where you want to be?

Simon: No, it hasn't worked, and there's no doubt in my mind that Morgan is very unhappy with me.

Counselor: Yet he wants to keep you as an employee. That's why he sent you here.

Simon: That's true, and I definitely want to keep working for the dealership.

Counselor: So, you've got Morgan's support and your own motivation. Those are two valuable resources for you.

Simon: I guess so, but I didn't think I had much going for me up until now.

Counselor: Let's talk about a few comparisons. How do you see your performance now compared with what it was 2 years ago?

Simon: Morgan has reviewed this with me, and he's right. At the present time, I'm very unhappy with my job, and I would love to get away from it. I'm too young to retire, and I feel locked into the dealership because I have my own personal financial investment in the company. Morgan has been very generous over the years with a profit-sharing plan and other incentives.

Counselor: As you talk about your relationship to the company and to Morgan, I get the idea that even though you're bored you do feel good about how you've been treated and about the company in general. Is there any better opportunity elsewhere that you've looked into?

Simon: I have always enjoyed my work until about a year ago. And I have looked at other possibilities. But none measures up to the advantages that I have here. As I've told my kids, "Bloom where you're planted."

Counselor: Simon, let's talk about your work, your work habits, and how things are going with the people under you. We've talked about Morgan's viewpoint. How do you see things?

Simon: I'm bored and preoccupied at work, and I find the new computer system much more complicated and time consuming. Not to mention the endless reports we are now required to generate for both Detroit [the automobile manufacturer] and the government. To tell you the truth, I procrastinate this kind of stuff and get far behind on it. Then, when I get to it, I make mistakes because I'm in a hurry and haven't mastered the new computer system. It's not actually new; it's been in place for about a year.

Counselor: I'm going to recommend that Morgan set you up for training in the new system. We could either have someone come in and work with you, or you could go to a trainer or consultant who will teach you the details of this system. I'm sure Morgan will agree to this.

Simon: That is a great idea. I welcome that opportunity.

Counselor: Now on another subject, I'd like to ask you about how you get along with your employees. How's that going?

Simon: I find myself taking out my aggravations and frustrations on them. Morgan has talked to me about this, and I indicated I would work on it. But, in fact, I don't care anymore.

Counselor: Would you say you're happy or unhappy with the way things are going for you right now?

Simon: I'm not at all happy. This computer business has got me down. I am so glad to leave on Friday, get in my truck and drive north to the lake, sit there, and shout, "Free at last!"

Counselor: You said bluntly that you don't care about how you deal with the other employees. Are you happy about this kind of apathy?

Simon: No, I'm not. I said I don't care, but I know that kind of attitude is not very helpful.

Counselor: So you've already made a judgment that apathy about your impatience does not satisfy you. Would you like to change from apathy to enthusiasm?

Simon: Well, if it means keeping this well-paying job, the answer is yes.

Counselor: What about the internal payoff of feeling good about your work and your relationships with your employees?

Simon: I'd like to have the kind of job satisfaction I used to have and better relationships with the people under me.

Counselor: In other words, you'd like to turn your feelings of misery into feelings that we might label as feelings of happiness and success.

Simon: For sure.

Counselor: Do you think it is possible to reach at least some degree of satisfaction in your work with the computer system?

Simon: I sure hope so.

Counselor: Let's discuss your individual wants or goals. How firm are these individual wants in your own mind? Let's start with something pretty basic. Do you want to keep your job at least until you find something better?

Simon: Yes, I need the job for a lot of reasons.

Counselor: You say "for a lot of reasons." Let's get back to that in a few minutes. Second, do you want to increase your efficiency in the area of computer skills?

Simon: Yes, I really need to do this.

Counselor: And finally, do you really and truly want better relationships with the employees and coworkers and especially with Morgan?

Simon: Definitely, I must answer yes to all three of these.

Counselor: Now Simon, I'd like you to respond to a very important request. Are you ready?

Simon: OK.

Counselor: Without kidding yourself and in all sincerity, are your current actions you have described in detail helping you or hurting you in satisfying your wants relative to keeping your job, regaining enthusiasm, and getting along with the people around you?

Simon: No, definitely what I'm doing is personally destructive.

Counselor: Wow! So you put it even more strongly than I suggested! You said "personally destructive."

Simon: Yes, this direction in which I'm headed just adds to my crappy life.

Counselor: You mentioned that you were a good worker until about a year ago. My instinct as well as my experience leads me to guess that something happened about that time. In other words, your behavior at work is the tip of an iceberg. There's more upset in your life than what we've discussed. Of course, I could be wrong.

Simon: I've not discussed this with anyone at work. But my wife and I separated about that time, and it turns out she had been working on the divorce a few months before that. She moved out of the house and moved in with a much younger man. I was against the divorce but was willing to go along with it, especially when I found out what her extracurricular activities were all about.

Counselor: And no one at work knows about this. Keep in mind, as we discussed earlier, this information is between you and me only. What do you want to tell me about your personal life since then?

Simon: What do you want to ask me about?

Counselor: What part did alcohol consumption or drug usage play in your life before the separation and since then?

Simon: Not much.

Counselor: How much?

Simon: A little bit.

Counselor: What would your ex-wife say if she were sitting here?

Simon: That was part of the problem. She exaggerates everything. But I still didn't want the divorce.

Counselor: What kind of exaggeration would she describe? For example, when you went up to the lake by yourself, how much did she think you usually drank on the weekend?

Simon: She'd say I drank a couple of cases of beer, but that only happened once or twice.

Counselor: How did she know that you drank a lot by yourself at the lake?

Simon: Well, a couple of times she washed my clothes before I got a chance to wash them myself, and she found evidence. She asked me if my kidneys were giving out on me.

Counselor: In other words, you pissed in your pants and made a mess of yourself occasionally.

Simon: How do you know this sort of thing?

Counselor: I've been in this counseling arena a long time, and this is not my first rodeo. I've been around.

Simon: I've never talked about this before. It's kind of embarrassing. And you don't make it pretty!

Counselor: It's not pretty. But believe me, we can deal with it. There is a solution for every problem you've discussed with me. I can't make guarantees, but it is my firm belief that if you and I make an effort, your life will be much happier.

Simon: Well, that's encouraging.

Counselor: Simon, let's shift gears for a moment. How realistic is it for you to get what you want? Let's start with work.

Simon: Well, so far I'm keeping my job. Based on what you said about solutions, there must be a solution to the computer problem.

Counselor: And in the past you have demonstrated skill in getting along with people, and in fact it's more than a skill for you. From what I gather, you are spontaneously friendly and don't need to work at it very hard.

Note: At this point the counselor talks about solutions in the present tense. This conscious behavior on the counselor's part communicates a subliminal message of hope to the client. Keep in mind that the counselor will relegate problems to the past and emphasize *current* and *future* solutions.

Simon: You've asked me if I think it is realistic to resolve these problems. What do you think?

Counselor: I think it will be easier to resolve the drinking problem than it would be to resolve the work problems.

Simon: I thought for sure you would say the work problems are more realistically addressed.

Counselor: Well, you could be right. Which of those would be the easiest for you to work on?

Simon: Morgan wants me to work a full week. I think I can do that.

Counselor: Do you really want to work a full week? Describe how realistic it is for you to stay until 6 o'clock on Friday evening and even come in on Saturday when formerly you took off early on Friday.

Simon: I used to do that all the time.

Counselor: When you were more enthusiastic about work.

Simon: That's right. I just don't feel like it now.

Counselor: In spite of your feelings, do you *really really really* want to do this now and in the future?

Simon: Yes. I have to.

Counselor: So it is realistically doable. You see it as a want that you can fulfill? Am I right or wrong?

Simon: You are right, and I agree.

Counselor: One last thing. I always ask this of my clients. Based on our conversation, what idea is most useful to you?

Simon: I think it's two ideas. There is an urgency for me to make changes. And second, I need to show improvement quickly.

Commentary: In this session, the counselor helped Simon evaluate the realistic attainability of his wants. In one notable interchange, the counselor deviated from the focus on the evaluation of wants and asked Simon to evaluate his *behavior*. Even though the dialogue is primarily intended to illustrate the self-evaluation of quality world wants, it is clear that the best use of the reality therapy procedures is an integrated one. Evaluation of wants need not be separated from other forms of self-evaluation. This interaction illustrates that there are many other possible directions that a counselor might take in the dialogue, some of which are only foreshadowed in this brief conversation. Also worth noting is the counselor's effort to help Simon examine the internal satisfaction derived from his behavior without diminishing the value of his "external motivation," that is, the possibility of changing his behavior because of the implied threat of job loss given him by Morgan.

Answer the following questions based on Simon's session with the counselor:

1. What is Simon's current quality world picture and what are his wants? _____

   _____

2. Why do you think that up to this point the counselor stressed the discussion of Simon's wants to the job itself, his computer skills, and his interpersonal relationships? _____

   _____

3. What is the theme of the counselor's effort to help Simon evaluate his wants? _____

   _____

4. How would you help Simon evaluate his use of alcohol? How would you evaluate the information Simon provides about his drinking habits? Do you need more information that is attainable only from other individuals? _____

   _____

5. How would you deal with Simon's feelings and self-talk about his separation and divorce? _____

   _____

6. What direction would you take to help Simon conduct more self-evaluations, such as evaluating his level of commitment, his perceptions of other people, and his self-talk? If he were an ethnic minority person, would your interventions be any different? If so, how? _____

   _____

In helping clients self-evaluate, the skilled practitioner assists clients in evaluating the many aspects of their quality world. After helping them define, clarify, and articulate what they want from the world around them, the counselor guides clients to evaluate the attainability of their wants. Key questions include, "In your opinion, do you have a reasonable chance of fulfilling your want?" "Is what you want attainable?" "Are your goals clear enough in your mind that you can determine, at this point, whether you can achieve them in the near or distant future?"

Many people have not learned the art of examining the realistic achievability and fulfillment of their wants. Such judgments are often easy for counselors to make, and they may conclude that clients would find self-evaluating in this manner a simple process. However, counselors are ahead of their clients in seeing the unrealistic attainability of clients' wants, which is the reason that the counselor is the counselor and the other person is the client.

Case Example: Helping a Client Explore Wants

In this hypothetical case, Taro is a male counselor using reality therapy with Hanako, a female client who is 28 years old. Hanako has phoned the counselor and reported that she feels sad because she is alone and unmarried and is ashamed because of her lack of achievement in her job as well as in her personal life. As you read this dialogue, keep in mind that both client and counselor are Japanese.

The counselor begins the session by exploring perceived locus of control.

Counselor Taro: It's good to see you today. I hope you did not have difficulty finding my office.

Hanako: No, it is near the bus stop.

Counselor: Please have a seat in this chair. I believe it is comfortable.

Hanako: Thank you very much. It is quite comfortable.

Counselor: May I offer you a cup of tea or coffee?

Hanako: Thank you very much. I would like a cup of tea. (*The counselor's secretary serves both Hanako and Taro tea.*) It was a very stressful ride on the bus.

Counselor: When you were on the bus, what thoughts went through your mind that you found stressful?

Hanako: I kept thinking how ashamed I am about so many things.

Counselor: I think it takes courage to admit such thoughts so early in the counseling process. Could we come back to that issue in a few minutes?

Hanako: Yes, it's very difficult to talk about such things, but I know it is important for me to talk about my stress with someone who is wiser than I am.

Counselor: Hanako, take a few deep breaths and pay attention to the breath as you inhale and exhale. As you breathe in, breathe through your nose and keep your shoulders level, don't raise them. Inhale deeply and allow the air to travel to your stomach and even throughout your body. Imagine it traveling to your arms and hands, to your legs and feet. As you slowly breathe out through your mouth, try gently to release just a little bit of the stress.

Hanako: (*Breathes five times and focuses her attention on her breathing.*) That's very relaxing. I feel a little better.

Counselor: That's an activity that you can use on your own several times a day or when you feel upset and out of control. The best way to lessen anxiety is to choose to breathe deeply and to pay close attention to the breathing. Later in our time together today, we will return to the thoughts you had on the bus. But for now, I would like to explore with you a few ideas that might help you.

Commentary: Even while Taro seems to be using the reality therapy procedures, he is also setting an environment that is safe and friendly. He avoids any hint of arguing with Hanako, blaming her, or criticizing her. His tone of voice, his gestures, and his posture all indicate a gentle and genuine empathy for Hanako. These behaviors illustrate a central point in the practice of reality therapy. *There is no absolute distinction between environment and procedures. They are inseparably linked to each other* (as shown by the dotted line between the procedures and the environment in Figure 3).

The session continues.

Counselor Taro: Hanako, could you describe some of your hopes, your dreams, what you are striving for?

Hanako: I'm 28 years old, and I've been employed since college. I've been working for 6 years, and I've only received one promotion during that time. Besides, I have almost no social life. I know the role of women has changed a lot in the last 10 or 15 years, but I still don't feel comfortable going to a club without an escort.

Counselor: How do you feel about your desire to go to a club?

Hanako: I feel ashamed about even desiring to go to such places.

Counselor: You feel shame at the desire to go and yet sorry that you don't have the opportunity to go. Would you be interested in relinquishing some of the shame even if you don't choose to go to a club alone?

Hanako: Yes, I would like to get rid of some of the shame.

Counselor: That could be something that we could work on together; getting rid of some of the guilt feelings. Would that be a worthwhile goal?

Hanako: Yes, I would like to feel less guilty, less shame, even if I have no desire to go out alone.

Counselor: In other words, you could make a more firm decision, one not colored by such an intense emotion.

Hanako: Yes, that would be a worthwhile goal.

Commentary: Taro responded to Hanako's comment about her thoughts that she experienced on the bus. His idea was to begin with something that she was very willing to disclose and used language that indicated inner control without pushing Hanako to believe that she has inner control. He asked her what thoughts went through her mind. She can still believe that she has no control over the stress or the thoughts. He does not push her to conclude that she is choosing her thoughts. And because clients generally can control their breathing, he very quickly helps her make a choice that leads to an added sense of inner control. The importance of deep breathing cannot be overemphasized. It is a behavior that a client can *choose.* It is an indirect way to achieve a higher sense of inner control. It is an especially useful tool to use with clients who have an external locus of control, that is, clients who perceive that they are victims of their own feelings or of external circumstances. This activity, furthermore, assists us to live in the present. In his book, *Mindfulness in Plain English,* Venerable Henepola Gunaratana (1992) observes:

> When we truly observe the breath, we are automatically placed in the present. We are pulled out of the morass of mental images and into a bare experience. In this sense breath is a living slice of reality. A mindful observation of such a miniature model of life itself leads to insights that are broadly applicable to the rest of our experience. (p. 79)

Deep breathing helps the human brain make more effective neural connections and illustrates total behavior as presented in choice theory. Finally, it exemplifies a crucial Ericksonian principle that is congruent with the work of William Glasser as he illustrated in his ingenious demonstrations conducted during his training sessions:

Sometimes the solution seems to have nothing to do with the presenting problem or with the client's upsetness.

• • •

Discussion Question
1. How was the activity of deep breathing connected to Hanako's presenting problem? _____
_____

The session continues.

Counselor Taro: I'd like to explore with you how you view your situation. I have found that a good way to discuss it is to explore your thoughts [perceived locus of control] about what you have control over and what you do not have control over. Talk to me about how much control you believe you have over your sadness.

Hanako: Not very much.

Counselor: So, right now you have very little ability to get rid of these sad feelings. That seems like a very accurate and insightful observation on your part. Yet it seems to me that you *do* have the ability to evaluate and make judgments about *how* you feel.

Hanako: I never looked at that sort of thing as a strength!

Counselor: Would you be willing to give some thought to this ability and to see it as something positive, as something that you have going for you?

Hanako: I don't know how to do that. Would you tell me how?

Counselor: I would suggest that each day you spend a few minutes sitting quietly while you reflect. While you're sitting there, think about the fact that you have the ability to evaluate how you feel, and not only the ability but a skill in assessing and evaluating how you feel. I'm asking you to do this because when you begin to see your strengths you will begin to be more joyful and less sad. It's a slow process, but it is a way of taking control of your life and of being convinced that you have more control than you at first thought.

Hanako: I can do that. I don't quite see the value of it, but I'll take your word that this will happen.

Counselor: I would now like to explore your earlier statement regarding your feelings. You believe that you don't have much control over how you feel. My next question is very important, and I ask it without any hint of criticism or blame. Are you ready for the question?

Hanako: Yes, go ahead.

Counselor: In discussing the amount of control you have over your sadness, you said "not very much." It sounds to me like you believe you might have *some* control over it. Would that be accurate?

Hanako: Well, yes, I suppose it is true that I bring some of it on myself. Sometimes I nurse it along.

Counselor: You sound like you're willing to take responsibility for nursing and nurturing the sadness. What amount of the sadness do you feel responsible for? Describe it as a specific percentage.

Hanako: Just taking a guess, I suppose it's about 15%.

Counselor: So you do have some sense of control over your feelings. I believe 15% is quite a lot! I would have been surprised if you would have said 5%. Now, let's try to build on your willingness to be responsible. And instead of blaming yourself, I suggest that we work on replacing the 85%. In this way there is no need to feel the least bit upset about causing the 15%. After all, it's only human in many circumstances to feel bad and to choose to increase the bad feelings. As a counselor, my job is to help you to feel better, to make better choices, to take more charge of your life. In so doing, you can actually change your inner story that you tell yourself and even make changes in the biology of your brain. And so, if you are willing to make choices to alter your actions, you will have an even greater sense of responsibility. This responsibility will not focus on negative feelings but rather on increasing positive feelings.

Hanako: It seems to me that you are talking about helping me realize that I can view the world and I can view myself in a different light than the way I have been recently seeing both my circumstances and myself.

Counselor: We have much more to talk about, but your thinking is right on track.

Commentary: In the conventional instruction of reality therapy, it is not customary to teach techniques for exploring the perceptions of clients. Emphasis has always been placed on exploring wants or goals and behaviors, especially actions, designed to satisfy wants or quality world pictures. Although this part of the process is necessary, I wish to add the importance of helping clients discuss their perception of how much responsibility they have now or could have in the future. The counselor assisted Hanako in examining her thoughts about her perceived locus of control. Although the session is free of psychological language, the counselor helps her examine her perceptions by making inquiries focusing on how much of her sadness is the result of her own lifestyle and choices. If the counselor has been successful in establishing an empathic relationship and can demonstrate genuine compassion, the client does not conclude that she is being blamed or criticized. Hanako is very willing to admit that she is partially responsible (15%) for how she feels. The counselor describes how accepting responsibility is a strength. He subtly shifts the discussion from the 15% of sadness to her intellectual judgment about her degree of responsibility. Not only is taking 15% a strength on her part, but her ability to judge her degree of responsibility and willingness to disclose it is a strength. The counselor, therefore, helps her address her negative feelings in a very indirect way. Previously she felt at the mercy of her circumstances. The counselor helps her to begin to see that she already possesses a foundation of strength and ability. Therefore, she progresses from a sense of external control to a sense of internal control. Her perceived locus of control makes a slight shift.

Exploring Wants or Goals

Central to the effective practice of reality therapy is the discussion of clients' wants related to the five-need system and what specifically they are striving for. Human motivation rests on the satisfaction of survival or self-preservation, love and belonging, power or inner control, freedom or independence, and fun or enjoyment. More specifically, we human beings formulate specific wants or pictures related to the five-need system. Because of the central place of specific human strivings (wants or goals), the reality therapist helps clients develop and clarify their wants or their specific pictures of what satisfies them. This clarification constitutes a prerequisite for self-evaluating the realistic attainability of wants or goals.

Areas for exploration include a discussion of what clients are seeking:

From family
From spouse
From children
From friends
From job/career
From manager
From subordinates
From the organization
From religion or spirituality
From recreational activities
From the client him- or herself
From the counselor, therapist, or counseling process

Examples of possible inquiries and reflections for each of these categories of wants include the following:

- What are you seeking from the world around you that you are getting or not getting?
- Tell me how much effort you will exert to satisfy your desire.
- Describe what you will settle for if you cannot attain everything you desire.
- Explain what you might have to give up or how you would have to change to get what you want.

In the brief dialogue that follows, the counselor helps the client select one topic from the quality world to explore. Space does not permit an exhaustive discussion of every possible category. You are invited to create hypothetical dialogues illustrating the exploration of other topics from the client's quality world.

Counselor Taro shows Hanako the list beginning with "From . . ." and explains the following:

> *Counselor Taro:* Hanako, I'd like you to look at this list and make a decision about something that you would like to work on during our sessions. In other words, what would you like to gain from the counseling that you could apply to one of these topics?
>
> *Hanako:* There are quite a few that pertain to me, but I would like to accomplish something regarding my job, my career.
>
> *Counselor:* Is that a topic you would rate easy to work on or hard to work on? Also, is it *very* important or not so important to you?
>
> *Hanako:* I think it might be somewhat easy to work on, and it is very important to me.
>
> *Counselor:* You did mention that you were disappointed that you did not get a recent promotion. In fact, you mentioned it within the first few minutes of the session. And you are now quite decisive about selecting it. Do you see yourself as a decisive person?
>
> *Hanako:* No, I don't. I think I have a hard time making up my mind.
>
> *Counselor:* So those topics might be connected! As time goes by, maybe we can work on both of them at once.
>
> *Hanako:* I never thought about connecting those two issues.
>
> *Counselor:* That's my job, to help you make connections that you have not previously made. Let's start with what's going on at work. Talk a little bit about what you are unhappy about at work, besides not being promoted.
>
> *Hanako:* I don't know where to start. Could you give me a suggestion?
>
> *Counselor:* Tell me about how you get along with your coworkers.
>
> *Hanako:* I get along with most of them, but I have trouble with my team. Some of the men flirt with me, and I believe that some of my team members are jealous. I hear that they say nasty things about me behind my back. Not all of them, but some of them.
>
> *Counselor:* Are you interested in making peace with them or at least having a truce?
>
> *Hanako:* Yes, I don't like the coldness that two or three of the team show to me.
>
> *Counselor:* Do you want to say anything to them directly?
>
> *Hanako:* Oh, I see on television in American movies that people often confront each other. This is embarrassing for me, even when I see it on television.

Counselor: I thought this would not be your style. But I wanted to ask you to comment about it. Your answer seemed very decisive. So you do make some decisions quickly and soundly at times. But the point is, you would like to be more friendly with them and have them be more friendly with you.

Hanako: Yes, I think that would be a valuable goal for me.

Counselor: You also mentioned the promotion. Is there the possibility of another opportunity for a promotion in the near future?

Hanako: Yes, there is. The rumor is that there will be a supervisory position available in about 6 months.

Counselor: So that would be another goal to achieve.

Hanako: Yes, it would.

Counselor: So in summary, you've established three goals for the counseling: to be more decisive, to get along better with a few of your team members, and to achieve the position of supervisor.

Commentary: In this portion of the dialogue, the counselor assists the client to formulate goals or to clarify wants. These wants are specific and appear to be achievable. In subsequent sessions, the counselor will help Hanako evaluate the attainability of her wants.

Exploring the Client's Level of Commitment

As people develop specific desires in their quality world or specific pictures in their mental picture albums, they choose varying levels of intensity aimed at satisfying their wants or fulfilling their pictures (Wubbolding, 2000b, 2011, 2013). Clinical experience has shown that clients describe their intensity of desire in one or more of five levels. (Refer to Chapter 4 for a description of the five levels of commitment.)

A client does not usually describe a specific level of commitment without direct assistance from a counselor. Rather, it is sometimes implied in the verbal and nonverbal exchange between client and counselor. The effective reality therapist can interpret the total behavior of the client and make explicit the implicit and unspoken level of commitment.

Also, the level of commitment can remain unclear until the client has formulated a plan and either fulfilled it or not. A student can *sound* firmly committed to a study schedule and yet not support the commitment with action. This behavior would indicate a lower level of commitment than the one expressed to the counselor.

At this point, we return to the dialogue between Hanako and counselor Taro. This abbreviated dialogue represents the counselor's attempt to help Hanako connect her feelings of depression with action. If she changes her actions, the pain of depression subsequently diminishes, at least to some degree.

> *Counselor Taro:* Hanako, you said you were sad and felt ashamed for not being promoted and not having the relationships you would like to have. You mentioned that the weekends were especially difficult and other free time that you may have: holidays, evenings, but especially the weekends. How serious would you describe these unwanted feelings?
>
> *Hanako:* All I can tell you is that they weigh heavily in my heart.
>
> *Counselor:* In other words, you are carrying a heavy burden around with you, one that you would like to set down and walk away from.
>
> *Hanako:* That's exactly right. I would like to drop this rock and walk away from it. In fact, I'd like to run away from it.
>
> *Counselor:* Well, walking away from it and running away from it would take some energy and action! Could we lump all these bad feelings together and give them a single label?
>
> *Hanako:* That's fine with me. I've read about depression and that seems to be a good name, kind of like an umbrella covering a lot of turmoil.
>
> *Counselor:* Walking away from it or running away from it demands quite a bit of energy. Are you interested in exerting some energy to deal with it and get rid of some of the depression?
>
> *Hanako:* Yes, I would, and I believe I can.
>
> *Counselor:* And so you have a choice: to remain in the debilitating cloud of depression or to exert some energy to drop at least part of this burden and to see at least a sliver of light breaking through the dark cloud.
>
> *Hanako:* Yes, I see the choice, and I definitely want to take action.

Commentary: The counselor does not run away from the emotional component of the total behavior. In fact, counselor Taro helps Hanako describe the sadness, the shame, and assists her in renaming it. He is assisting her in making a small change in her thinking by giving the debilitating feelings a new name. The next step is encouraging her to connect her feelings of depression to actions. It is notable that at no time does the counselor imply that Hanako is choosing to depress herself. Rather, he implies that she has within her the capacity and the range of choices to move beyond her oppressive feelings.

This conceptualization fits with the adapted definition of the human mind as a relational process attempting to regulate (a) information or input from the external world and (b) behavior or efforts to influence and manipulate the external world (D. Siegel, 2012). In the future, the counselor will assist Hanako in developing relationships and directing her energy toward gaining what she desires and toward more satisfying connections with other people.

You are invited to formulate and continue the dialogue between Hanako and Taro.

Counselor Taro: _____

Hanako: _____

Counselor: _____

Hanako: _____

Counselor: _____

Hanako: _____

Counselor: _____

Hanako: _____

Counselor: _____

The counselor might also assist Hanako in discussing her thinking or her cognition about the depression by presenting inquiries that focus on her inner self-talk. It is likely that together they can identify implicit statements such as, "I can't do anything about my feelings, about the job, about my depression." She might also be telling herself, "Even though what I'm doing in my relationships and in my free time is not helping me, I'm going to continue to do it." As the counselor moves to the self-evaluation component of the WDEP system, he will assist Hanako in conducting a searching self-assessment of her actions and her inner statements, both those that are explicit and those that are implicit.

In these cases and in those in subsequent chapters, you are invited to give serious thought to the counselor's statements, to evaluate them, and to formulate your own responses aimed at client self-evaluation.

Chapter 6

Cross-Cultural Applications

As you read this chapter, notice the similarities as well as differences in the counselor's approach and statements. In this chapter, we meet several clients with a common theme: they are in trouble. LaMar is a troubled youth. Shuichi is also troubled. Jade is a resident of a halfway house who develops a sense of internal control. Norman has many issues to deal with and is referred by school authorities.

Case Example:
Evaluation of Behavioral Choices and Direction

LaMar, age 16, is an African American ninth-grade student in a school that is 11% African American, 15% Hispanic, 4% Asian American, and 1% Middle Eastern and East Indian students. The remaining 69% identify themselves as Caucasian or White, some of whom are of mixed race. The socioeconomic level is mixed, with an average income slightly above that of a midsized city with a reported unemployment rate of 7.3%. The conventional wisdom is that the unemployment rate is much higher. The reported unemployment rate is less than that of some cities but more than that of others. The population of this midwestern city is approximately 310,000 people.

LaMar is repeating the ninth grade and flunking several classes. He believes that the teachers do not understand him, have little appreciation of his situation, and pick on him because of his race. He believes that his White teachers favor White students and that his two African

American teachers are part of an unjust system. He enjoys only one class, social studies, in which the teacher teaches that the system is unjust and biased against minorities who live in a state of perpetual victimhood. LaMar believes he has little control over his life. Two teachers have referred him to the school counselor because of his failing grades and what they refer to as "disrespectful behavior and obscene language directed toward them and other students."

LaMar lives with his mother who is employed part-time and receives public assistance. She has contacted the school several times and remarked that she is unable to control him and that she knows he has used drugs and has been truant. She is doubtful that the White counselor can be of assistance to him, but she is willing to cooperate with the school administration and the counselor. The counselor has spoken on the phone with LaMar's mother regarding confidentiality in working with clients who are minors and discussed in detail standard B.5.b. of the *ACA Code of Ethics* (ACA, 2014).

As with all written dialogues, the nuances of nonverbal behavior are not observable. The skilled practitioner of reality therapy incorporates an appropriate tone of voice, expressing a caring and genuinely empathic attitude. Nonverbal behavior also includes the use of gestures, facial expression, body posture, use of silence, and other therapeutic interventions.

Counselor: Come in LaMar and have a seat. We have met before, and it's good to see you again. I understand that you've been sent to me by a couple of teachers.

LaMar: Yeah. They told me to come here again.

Counselor: What do you think about being sent here?

LaMar: I've talked to counselors before. It's just a bunch of bulls_____.

Counselor: So, not much has changed for you?

LaMar: What do you know about what I go through? You're White. How could you know what it's like for me in this school?

Counselor: To tell you the truth, I've worked here a long time, and I was once a student. But I have no idea what it is like to be you and to be a student in your classes.

LaMar: Then how can you help me?

Counselor: I believe I can. But I have no idea about how much frustration you must feel. Let me ask you this. Do you feel that these people around here are in some way against you?

LaMar: Sure. All they do is pick on me. Other kids do the same things I do, and they don't get in trouble. They're just suck-ups.

Counselor: And you don't want to be a suck-up. Is there any other student or teacher who would accuse you of sucking up?

LaMar: No.

Counselor: So that's one put-down you've managed to avoid. I wonder if there are any other attacks or put-downs that you've avoided.

LaMar: No, they don't like me because I'm Black.

Counselor: What about Mr. Johnson, your math teacher?

LaMar: My guys have names for him.

Counselor: You don't have to tell me. I've heard them before.

LaMar: I'd like to tell you what we call him. The names we use.

Counselor: No. I don't want to hear them. I've heard it all before anyway. I've heard all the put-downs. But anyway whatever you tell me is between us. It's between us unless you talk about hurting yourself or somebody else or if you've been abused.

LaMar: Yeah, I did hear that about you, that what we say to you stays in this office. It has a name.

Counselor: Yes, it's called confidentiality.

LaMar: I don't see how you can help me.

Counselor: Actually, whether I can help or not depends on what you want. I have a very strange question for you, LaMar. Do you think I need to know everything about you, such as what it must be like to be Black in a school and a city where most people are different from you?

LaMar: That is a weird question. How can you help me? You're White.

Counselor: I'm not sure I can. Maybe you're just condemned to be powerless, hopeless, miserable, and live a life of being discriminated against.

LaMar: See, I knew you couldn't help me. You can't understand.

Counselor: I didn't say I *couldn't* help you. I said *maybe* I couldn't help you. I also said I believe I can. In fact, for my part, I am 100% certain I can. I have full confidence because I am a damn good counselor. I'm obviously White and I know how to deal with White people.

LaMar: Yeah. You're good for some people but not for me. You don't understand.

Counselor: LaMar, I just heard something different in what you said. Up 'til now you've been saying I *can't* understand. But now I just heard you say I *don't* understand. It seems to me there's a big difference.

LaMar: What are you talking about, man?

Counselor: What I hear is a kind of, a tiny bit of, just a little bit of desire on your part that I do understand. I can't help thinking that you want me or somebody else around here to appreciate you and accept you as you are. Maybe even like you!

LaMar: (*Hesitates and talks very slowly at this point.*) Yeah, maybe, I guess so.

Counselor: Here's a different idea. Suppose I or someone else on the faculty really and truly understood what you go through every day: being aggravated in class, singled out, living in a rough neighborhood, probation officer on your back, your mother hassling you, getting busted, and so on and on. Do you really think your life would change for the better if these adults understood?

LaMar: You bet. If people understood, my life would be better off.

Counselor: So, what you really and truly want is for your life to be better off, to be free of all these weights that you feel like you're carrying around on your back.

LaMar: That'd be nice, but it's never going to happen.

Counselor: Are you absolutely sure it's never going to happen? How do you know that?

LaMar: I don't know anybody where it has happened.

Counselor: I do. There are people in this building who are doing pretty well.

LaMar: Yeah, bunch of suck-ups.

Counselor: You know, LaMar, what you're going through reminds me of another situation. A couple of years so ago I had a student in here who had moved in from another neighborhood. In fact, he got kicked out of his previous school, had trouble with drugs, probation officers. He had a parent who hated the school and everybody associated with it. He thought everybody was a racial bigot. I got to know him and saw him in a different way. I looked for the good that was in him and listened very carefully to him. I'll never forget the expression on his face. He felt hurt, but of course he couldn't admit it. Well, he could admit it as time went on but not at first.

LaMar: What do you mean?

Counselor: Well, what I saw in him was a 17-year-old young man, about to make a serious decision about what kind of life he would live, what kind of person he would be, what road he wanted to go down: a road of unhappiness, crime, drugs, or a road of success, learning something useful in life, and having relationships with people who were interested in helping him stay out of trouble. After talking to him just a few times, he told me about how he felt rejected and hurt by society. And yet the way he expressed it was by getting p.o.'d at anybody and everybody. Somebody would accidently brush up against him in the hallway, and he'd feel he needed to teach 'em a lesson. After a while he came to the realization that there's just too many people to teach lessons to. One time he said to me, "Why should I let other people decide whether I'm gonna fight and get in trouble? It's a lot easier to just ignore some things." He even began to realize that he had more control than he had first believed.

LaMar: Whatever happened to him?

Counselor: I don't know what finally happened after a year, but I know he started to get along around here a lot better and his grades improved.

LaMar: He became a suck-up.

Counselor: A happy suck-up who didn't get in trouble. Actually, most people didn't call him that, only one or two. When someone makes a turn-around, it's funny how other people don't pay any attention to him. They're just thinking about themselves. A friend of mine once told me, "Don't worry about what other people think about you. They're not thinking about you at all, they're thinking about themselves, just like you are."

LaMar: I just don't like the way things are going for me.

Counselor: Things are definitely not going in a way that's very much fun for you. Your life is pretty miserable.

LaMar: That's for sure.

Counselor: So there is one thing we can agree on. This guy who doesn't understand you or couldn't begin to appreciate you does know that your life is pretty crappy right now and you're unhappy. I have a hunch it's been a while since you agreed with some adult around this school.

LaMar: What do you mean?

Counselor: We agree, you and I, that people are on your back and you're feeling pretty lousy about the way your life is going. So I have a very important idea for you. Tell me whether you want your life and your time here at school to be better or worse for you.

LaMar: Yeah, of course I want it to be better.

Counselor: And you believe that all these people are making your life hell.

LaMar: Yeah, of course they are.

Counselor: So the question is, do you want to go in a different direction or do you want to keep going in the direction you're heading now?

LaMar: It's not my problem. They're the ones doing it to me.

Counselor: I never said you were the problem. However, I do have enough confidence in you that with my help you can find a solution.

LaMar: (*Looks at the counselor and seems to ponder his next comment.*) I'd sure like that.

Counselor: So the way I see it, LaMar, is that as we sit here right now you have two choices: one is to keep going in the same direction you're going and the other is to try a different pathway. (*Makes a dramatic gesture with his two arms stretched in two different directions indicating two different roads.*)

LaMar: What do you mean?

Counselor: You can choose to continue to do things that make your life miserable, or you could choose to at least *try* a few decisions that would improve your situation.

LaMar: I heard about this kind of stuff. "Blaming the victim."

Counselor: Have I used the word blame? When it comes to what's going on in your life, I don't recall blaming you. I did say I believe you have a solution inside of you. Well, maybe not a solution, but the possibility of making a few better choices that *just might* help you feel less frustration and give you some relief.

LaMar: I can tell you this. I'd try anything to get people to leave me alone.

Counselor: So which choice do you think is the better choice for you: to be miserable or to work at feeling better? (*Utilizes his arms once again to emphasize a fork in the road.*)

LaMar: When you put it that way, there's only one choice: to work at feeling better.

Counselor: That's what I can help you with. If you want to feel worse, you could continue doing what you're doing. Don't change anything. And all these people around you will continue to hound you and pick at you. And guess what? They will blame you, and you can blame them. The game will end in a tie. The only problem is they will still be here drawing a salary and you will feel as miserable as you do now. And who knows where that path will lead you.

LaMar: So you think *I* could make things better!

Counselor: I don't have any doubt about it. You see, LaMar, I don't see you as a weak character. I see you as someone who *feels* like you're being targeted. Maybe you believe that someone has put a target on your back. My job is to help you rip off that target. In other words, my job is to help you take a few steps toward feeling better. My question is, "Are you willing to commit to a different pathway, a different road and different choices?"

LaMar: Well, at least you believe I have some positive choices. I don't have to end up in prison.

Counselor: Prison? There's not a doubt in my mind that you can make other choices. The key question here is which pathway is better for you? The choice you have is to keep the target on your back and be miserable and to have other people blame you or to rip it off and work at feeling better. How you answer that question, from my point of view, will determine how you get along the rest of the school year and maybe even after you graduate.

LaMar: Putting the words "graduate" with "LaMar" is not something I've ever heard before.

Counselor: You heard it now. The pathway that I can help you with is not easy. But as I said, you are definitely not a weak character. At least, you don't appear that way to me. So the question is, do you want to make some choices that will help you? Which direction is better for you?

Commentary: In this dialogue, the counselor establishes the relationship with LaMar by admitting and agreeing to the existence of a barrier between them. Paradoxically, the barrier then becomes less of an issue. The counselor helps LaMar examine the realistic attainability of his wants and appeals to his need for power by observing that LaMar does not appear to be a weak person. The session builds to the point where LaMar can make a self-evaluation of his overall behavioral direction and moves gently from a perceived locus of external control to a perceived locus of internal control. Will he choose to proceed in a direction that is more effectively satisfying to him, or will he choose a direction that brings more misery? LaMar feels put upon by society. At no point does the counselor take sides in the sociological macro issue of whether society at large is just or unjust. The practitioner of reality therapy deals with the client's world as seen by the client. In this case, LaMar believes in societal unfairness. Without blaming him or his teachers, the counselor assists LaMar in evaluating which cluster of choices is more beneficial to him. The stress is placed on what LaMar has control over rather than what he perceives as an unjust system. On the other hand, the counselor's work with LaMar does not preclude nor discount the merit of systemic interventions. The counselor can approach the staff members in a consultative manner with the goal of assisting them to maintain a "firm, fair, friendly" environment in the classroom (Richardson, 2015; Wubbolding, 2015b). Blaming the teachers and other school staff is as ineffective as blaming LaMar for his feelings and perceptions. Also, from the perspective of reality therapy with its emphasis on building and retaining relationships, an effective consultant approaches colleagues as allies and not in an antagonistic manner.

Answer these questions about this session:

1. How does the counselor attempt to see LaMar's point of view? _____

2. How does the counselor deal with LaMar's initial belief that because the counselor is of a different race he cannot help LaMar? _____

3. Do you agree or disagree that a counselor needs to understand the past history of clients in order to assist them? Why or why not? _____

4. What other self-evaluation interventions would you use with LaMar? _____

5. From the point of view of reality therapy, what are several internal statements LaMar might be repeating to himself? _____
_____

6. How does the counselor assist LaMar in evaluating his self-talk? _____

7. What is your own degree of comfort or discomfort in dealing with a client who is racially different from you? _____
_____
_____

The following brief comments about each of the previous seven questions are designed to elicit more discussion from you:

1. The counselor emphasizes Lamar's perceptions but does not stress reflecting on his feelings.

2. Do you believe that LaMar's thoughts are mere excuses, or would you agree with them?
3. It is impossible to adequately appreciate or completely understand the experiences of many clients.
4. Interventions focusing on client self-evaluation are many and varied.
5. LaMar's self-talk includes many "shoulds" and "should not's."
6. Helping LaMar evaluate his self-talk is subtle and indirect.
7. Whatever your feelings, keep in mind that they are legitimate and will change.

Case Example: Evaluating Self-Talk More Explicitly

The following dialogue represents an alternative direction in the counseling session with LaMar. Contained within this dialogue is a focus on the explicit self-evaluation of the client's self-talk.

Counselor: LaMar, because these people around you treat you unfairly and because of many things in your world, you've stated that you feel there's no way they will get off your back.

LaMar: You got that right.

Counselor: Tell me what thoughts go through your mind about all this.

LaMar: What do you mean?

Counselor: Let's put it this way. My guess is that you spend quite a bit of time internally going over some thoughts about the people and about everything the social studies teacher tells you.

LaMar: Yes. I think a lot about it.

Counselor: I'm wondering about some of your thoughts, and I'm not talking about how you feel, just your thoughts. I'm wondering what you are saying about yourself in this messy world in which you live.

LaMar: I'm thinking I'd like to get away from it.

Counselor: And yet you can't. Not just yet.

LaMar: No, I can't.

Counselor: So tell me, is one of the thoughts that you tell yourself, maybe not in so many words, but is one of the thoughts summarized by the phrase, "I can't" or "I can't do anything to make my life better"?

LaMar: It sounds like you're saying it's all my fault.

Counselor: If I thought that, I would say it, and there would be no doubt about what I meant.

LaMar: Well, they just seem to be on my back all the time.

Counselor: And the result is you believe that you can't do anything to make your life better.

LaMar: Well, I probably could do something.

Counselor: And yet at times you say, "I can't" even though you don't think it all the time.

LaMar: I suppose I think that. In fact, to be honest, I say that a lot of times to myself.

Counselor: Now LaMar, suppose I understood your situation completely and you believed I understood it, and I said to you, "LaMar, you're right. You're powerless. You're without any choices. At least you're without choices to get along better here. You're probably going to drop out. You're going to get in trouble with the law. And who knows what's going to happen to you."

LaMar: People have already told me all that.

Counselor: Now I have a very important question. When people say that to you, and if I said that to you, and most important, when you repeat the words "I can't" to yourself, does it help you or does it hurt you?

LaMar: It might be true. It's the real world.

Counselor: Well, it might not be true. And I'm not asking you about the real world. I'm asking you about your inner thoughts about the real world. Do you see the difference?

LaMar: Yes, there's the world outside of me and then there's my view of it.

Counselor: Yes. And I'm describing your inner self-talk *about* the world outside of you. Now I have another very important question. Of those two things—the world outside of you and what you tell yourself about the world—which is easier to change?

LaMar: I don't know what you mean.

Counselor: Can you quickly change the people around you, or can you more easily change over time what you tell yourself about the world?

LaMar: I see what you mean. I can more easily change what I tell myself. But what good would that do?

Counselor: Good question. There's no sense changing it if it doesn't make your life better. How do you think it could make your life better?

LaMar: I don't know.

Counselor: OK, let me give you another situation. Suppose the basketball team is in a close game and there's about a minute left and our point guard gets fouled. He approaches the free throw line and he tells himself, "I'm not a very good free throw shooter. I make a very low percentage of my free throws. And this noisy crowd is screaming for me to miss the free throws. I just can't do it." What do you think about this self-talk?

LaMar: Won't help him make the free throw. He better not tell the coach if there's a time out before he shoots it.

Counselor: Wow! You've really said something there. In fact you've said two things. First, you said, "It won't help." So this kind of self-talk stands in the way of his success. And so, the screaming crowd cannot *force* him to miss the free throw? You've also said, "He better not tell the coach during the time out." Why not?

LaMar: Because if he's a bad coach, he'd yell at him. If he's a good coach, he would encourage him and tell him he could do it.

Counselor: So we have two elements here. The player needs to tell himself "I can" and he needs a good coach. Oh, by the way, does the coach have to have been a player at this very school to be a good coach?

LaMar: No. And I see what you're getting at.

Counselor: What I'm getting at is the need to tell yourself something different such as "I can." But it may surprise you that I'm also getting at the idea that maybe a coach would help you. In fact, I believe you could be your own coach. Then you'd have somebody that really understood your situation.

LaMar: (*Very thoughtfully.*) I think I could do that.

Counselor: If you had a good coach, what would he tell you about shooting the free throws that you have to make here at this school?

LaMar: He'd tell me "You can do it but you need to practice and follow my instructions."

Counselor: Now, LaMar, I'd like to trade seats with you right here and now. I'm going to be LaMar and you be the Coach.

(*Counselor and client switch seats.*)

Counselor: Coach, I want you to help me.

LaMar: Look kid, I know you can do it. You're a good player. Focus on the ball going into the basket. The hell with the crowd! And when you step up to the line this time and every other time, I want you to tell yourself, "I'm a good free throw shooter, and I will put the ball through the hoop."

(*Counselor and client switch back to original seats.*)

LaMar: I guess I told him!

Counselor: I notice you have a different expression on your face. I also heard you say something that gives me hope. You said, "I *will* put the ball through the hoop." That's even better than "I can."

LaMar: I see what you mean.

Counselor: Oh, I almost forgot. One last thing, does that coach have to be the same race as the player in order to inspire the player?

LaMar: No, he just needs to be a good coach.

Counselor: Hmmm. And I see what you mean.

(*They both smile and realize they don't need to add anything else.*)

Counselor: One final question. What is the most useful idea we've talked about?

LaMar: That I can be my own coach.

Commentary: At this point, the counselor could help LaMar with positive self-talk. LaMar would make plans to formulate self-affirmations, to tell himself something different when his self-defeating thoughts begin. Simple phrases such as "I can" or "cancel that thought" serve as antidotes to toxic thinking. I would encourage him to post on his mirror one self-affirmation that he could formulate with the help of the counselor for the purpose of repeating it early in the morning and at night.

This session illustrates how a counselor can help a client progress in a gradual way from cognitions that focus on external control to self-talk reflecting a sense of internal control. The counselor is careful not to overwhelm the client with choice theory language. Rather, the analogy of the basketball player and the coach, familiar to teenagers, provides an additional intervention for assisting LaMar in evaluating his self-talk summarized in the phrase "I can't." The counselor is emphatic about *replacing* the self-talk with a more effective alternative statement without implying criticism. It would be tempting to drive home the point that repeating "I can't" is ineffective. But the counselor is aware that LaMar might misunderstand this exchange and interpret it as criticism. LaMar has experienced enough criticism. He does not need to hear even a misunderstood line of criticism from the counselor.

At the very end, the counselor helps LaMar evaluate his relationship with the counselor. This evaluation is extremely indirect. The coach need not be the same race as the players. LeMar recognizes that the coach needs to be competent and to care about the players. There are many applications and extensions of this principle available to the counselor. But the counselor chooses to place an open-ended thought on the table and shows respect for LaMar while believing that this indirect self-evaluation will take hold in LaMar's thought processes.

Here are several additional discussion questions:

1. How would you evaluate the counselor's response to LaMar's statements that the counselor cannot understand or appreciate him? _____

   _____

2. How else could you respond to LaMar's ideas about the counselor's inability to understand him? _____

   _____

   _____

3. What would be your self-talk about LaMar's resistance shown to you as a counselor racially different from him? _____

   _____

   _____

Some people would say that the real problem is not LaMar's behavior but the oppression by his school and by society. Without debating the merits of this presumed racial prejudice, I ask you to consider these suggestions:

1. The counselor should, of course, become an advocate for LaMar by discussing his situation with his teachers, but such advocacy is inadequate. The counselor should be able to conduct training for the *entire* staff regarding the equitable treatment of all students.
2. These systemic interventions should, at no time, communicate that the counselor assumes that the organization is oppressive and that the staff is biased. As in all human interactions, there is more than one viewpoint of events. In this case, there is a wide variety of possible perceptions, and the counselor should not imply that he is taking sides. A motto for the counselor/consultant/trainer is "always approach people as allies" and "assume that other people's motives are at least as laudable as your own."
3. If LaMar's teachers feel criticized or judged by the counselor, they will certainly become alienated from the counselor and possibly more resentful toward LaMar. Strained relationships between staff and counselor help no one. Empathy for the teachers instills confidence and trust in the counselor. When teachers realize that the counselor has their best interest at heart (the education of students) and when they become convinced that they all have common goals, the result is a more need-satisfying school atmosphere.
4. The interventions described in the dialogues are the opposite of "blaming the victim." Rather, they empower a person who *feels* like a victim. When clients realize they have choices, they

become uplifted, ennobled, and in charge of their lives. Skilled practitioners of reality therapy do not wait for the external world to become imbued and saturated with the principles of social justice. Historically, the world has been characterized by racial injustice and intergroup strife more than by societies free of conflict. Such an ideal world has never existed, and there is no evidence it will exist in the future (Sowell, 2013). The counselor's responsibility is to facilitate and assist in maintaining and enhancing a school atmosphere that is just, fair, firm, and friendly (Glasser, 1990; Wubbolding, 2007, 2015b) and thereby contribute to the improvement of human relationships.

Case Example:
Exploring Need Satisfaction by Discussing "What Do You Really Want?" or "What Are You Longing For?"

A logical place to begin the counseling process is by asking clients to be as specific as possible when identifying and clarifying their hopes, goals, dreams, and what they are seeking. A skillful reality therapist guides clients in a compassionate and empathic way as they disclose their specific desires. Part of the process summarized with the letter W (*wants*) includes identification of deeper wants related to the five fundamental motivators or needs. The brief dialogue that follows illustrates this process.

Shuichi, a 15-year-old male, is brought to a counselor because he is flunking several subjects in school and is uncooperative with his parents. This dialogue with the counselor takes place after one or two counseling sessions.

> *Counselor Mayu:* We've discussed a few things that you hope could happen that would make your life better. You said you would like your parents to leave you alone.
> *Shuichi:* Yes, I would like them to get off my back and stop bothering me.
> *Counselor:* And if they got off your back, what would you have?
> *Shuichi:* I could do what I want.
> *Counselor:* Talk a little about what you would have if you could do what you want.
> *Shuichi:* Nobody would be bothering me all the time.
> *Counselor:* Tell me what you would feel and think if you could do what you wanted.

Shuichi: I'd be free from their constant lecturing.

Counselor: Your most basic desire is freedom.

Shuichi: Right!

Counselor: And you don't have nearly as much freedom as you want?

Shuichi: Right again!

Counselor: What about school. What do you want from the school?

Shuichi: I want to be out of school.

Counselor: And if you were not in school, you'd be even more free: no parents bothering you and no school checking up on you.

Commentary: In this dialogue, the counselor helps the client identify specific wants or desires and then assists him in bringing his fundamental source of motivation to the surface: freedom or independence. Very soon after this dialogue, the counselor will help the client evaluate (E) the realistic attainability of having complete and total freedom or independence. At this point, however, the counseling focuses on the quality world of the client as preliminary to self-evaluation. The components of the reality therapy delivery system (WDEP) are not steps to be followed one after another in a rigid manner and with only four questions; nevertheless, when clients make self-evaluations, they do evaluate specifics such as the realistic attainability of their strivings. In the process of counseling Shuichi, the self-evaluation component will follow later.

Exploring the Client's Perception of What Other People Want From Him

The interventions made by the counselor in the following dialogue illustrate how to help a client explore another aspect of his perceptions. In this interchange, the counselor does not help Shuichi examine his perceived locus of control. Rather, Shuichi presents his opinion or perception of what other people expect of him.

Counselor Mayu: Shuichi, we've discussed some of *your* desires, what you are seeking from the people around you, especially your parents and the people at school. I'd like you to describe what you think they want from you.

Shuichi: I don't know what they want, and I don't care.

Counselor: I know you don't really care what they want, but I'd like you to use your imagination and try to figure out what they would like to see happen regarding your choices.

Shuichi: My parents want me to be like my older brother.

Counselor: Describe what you think they mean by that.

Shuichi: They say they want me to act more mature.

Counselor: What do you see your brother doing that they think is more mature?

Shuichi: Coming home right after school, doing 3 hours of school work, passing all his courses with high marks.

Counselor: What about friends? What do you think they want you to do about your current group of friends?

Shuichi: They want me to give them up and find what they call "nicer friends," and they want me to behave better.

Counselor: So, from your point of view, they want a lot that you can't give up or change.

Shuichi: I could if I wanted to. I don't want to make those changes. But I do want them to leave me alone.

Counselor: Do they leave your brother alone, or are they always on his back?

Shuichi: They don't bother him. They think he's perfect.

Counselor: Tell me what your life would be like if you did all these things that you described before.

Shuichi: I don't know. I've never tried it.

Counselor: Would you feel better or be happier if they left you alone?

Shuichi: I sure would.

Counselor: And they do leave your brother alone, the brother that does the schoolwork. But let's come back and talk about that later. I'd like you to describe your school situation. Is there any teacher you regard as helpful?

Shuichi: How do you mean?

Counselor: Is there anyone you like, even a little bit?

Shuichi: Well, there is my science teacher. He's a pretty good guy.

Counselor: When you skip school, do you miss seeing your science teacher?

Shuichi: Yes, he's the one bright spot in the school day. He doesn't punish me.

Counselor: I suppose he doesn't have reason to punish you.

Shuichi: No, I like science, and I'm pretty good at it. I am passing his course.

Counselor: And you seem to give him what he wants: accurate answers on tests. You probably ask questions every once in a while too. Maybe even pay attention in class.

Shuichi: Yes, I think that's true.

Counselor: One final request. What have you found most useful in our conversations?

Shuichi: You showed me a better way to do things without putting me down.

Commentary: The counselor helps Shuichi look at his situation from a different point of view. The goal of this discussion is to help the client become aware of and mindful of his surroundings and to reflect on what others think about him and want from him. Shuichi also becomes more aware of his own perceptions, and in describing them implicitly and indirectly, he evaluates his viewpoint. The counselor does not rush to the self-evaluation component of reality therapy. Encouraging the client to be mindful of his own wants and perceptions, especially his perceptions of what he believes other people want from him, is a necessary prerequisite for genuine behavioral change.

In the previous dialogue, the counselor made the following comment:

Counselor: And they do leave your brother alone, the brother that does the schoolwork. *Let's come back and talk about that later.* I'd like you to describe your school situation. Is there any teacher you regard as helpful?

It is notable that the reality therapist resists the urge to insert or to lead the client to self-evaluate at this point. It would be perfectly legitimate for the counselor to intervene in the following manner:

Counselor: And they do leave your brother alone, the brother that does the schoolwork. He does his work and feels happy or at least feels some degree of freedom. Is what he's doing working for him? On the other hand, is not doing your schoolwork helping you?

Clearly, there are many ways to utilize the principles of reality therapy. The dialogues illustrate one or two possible interventions. I encourage you to use your creativity to generate other procedural interventions that feel natural to you and that express your personality, your comfort, and your cultural instinct.

Case Example:
Evaluation of Perceived Locus of Control

Jade, a Caucasian female probationer who is 28 years old and has no children, is referred to a counselor by the court after being arrested for dealing drugs. She is a resident of a halfway house for women.

In several counseling sessions, Jade has described that she feels powerless, oppressed by the court system, singled out by the police, and discriminated against in five previous entry-level jobs that she held in the last 6 years. Consequently, she feels that her locus of control is external in that she is "put upon" by society. She is also unhappy with the treatment she has received in the halfway house. Her response to this sense of oppression has been a pervasive fear. She has discussed her fear of the future, where she will end up, how society will treat her, especially now that she has a record, or as she says, "a number on my back," and whether she will be able to obtain a job as the unemployment rate climbs higher. She also fears that she will be alone and that no man would be interested in her because of her obesity and unattractiveness.

In efforts to understand her plight, the counselor, a female, has demonstrated appropriate empathy and support for her. She has helped Jade identify her emotions and taught her how to discuss them. At this stage of the counseling process, the counselor believes that to continue to further reflect upon her feelings might only serve to relegate her to a condition characterized by an increased sense of powerlessness and could facilitate her continued self-pity. The counselor believes that the counseling relationship needs to move beyond this initial stage of involvement.

> *Counselor:* Jade, we certainly established that you believe you have experienced a high level of rejection and that up to now you have felt clobbered by society. At the same time, the court, the halfway house staff, and possible future employers will have expectations of you. I know you feel an intense fear and a sense of being alone and beyond help. So I want to ask you this question: Will future employers and the court as well as the staff at the halfway house believe that you are helpless and that there can be no hope for a better future?
>
> *Jade:* No. They think I can do what they want me to do. But they don't really understand.
>
> *Counselor:* We've talked about your outlook and have used the word "control." You have stated that you believe you have very little control in your life. I want to ask you to stop and think very carefully for a moment about what I'm about to say. I want to bring to your attention this point, and it is the most important point I could bring up to you at this stage of our work together.

Commentary: In this dialogue, the counselor helps Jade look at the expectations of others because these expectations focus on her sense of control. Implied in the counselor's statement is a gentle challenge to Jade's belief that she has no control over her life. After all, other people believe she has control. The counselor will take the lead in the conversation and assist her in evaluating her perceived locus of control. Moreover, the last line of the counselor's comment is crucial in helping Jade begin to examine her sense of control. Three elements are encapsulated in the simple phrase "at this stage of our work together": (a) the counseling relationship is developing, and it will not remain the same in the future; (b) Jade will need to exert effort and "work" as the counseling relationship progresses; and (c) the counselor is clearly more than just a reflecting mirror, she is a partner in the counseling process. The implication is that "we are in this process as a team." Jade may not completely understand this subtle message at this point, but the counselor will return to these principles and re-emphasize them as Jade grows out of her sense of powerlessness and begins to see that she has more control than she previously thought. Jade has choices available to her. The counselor's job is to help her perceive her inner strength, her inner control, and realize that she need not remain a helpless victim.

Counselor: Is it really true, Jade, that you have no control at all in your life? This is a very important question, and I'd like you to think about it for a moment before you answer.

Jade: Are you saying that I'm to blame for everything?

Counselor: No, I've never said that or even hinted at that. I think other people have pointed the finger of blame, and you've seen that finger many times. My job is to help you look forward and move on from here.

Jade: What was the question again?

Counselor: Deep down inside of you, do you really believe you have no control over your life?

Jade: But look what they've done to me. Look what's been happening.

Counselor: I understand what you've told me. But I want you to answer that question.

Jade: (*States reluctantly with a shrug of her shoulders.*) I suppose I have some control over a few things.

Counselor: In other words, you're not completely at the mercy of other people and systems. You do have some choices. That's what I mean by having control.

Jade: But not many choices.

Counselor: I'm not saying you have an unlimited number of choices. Can I tell you a story about someone who seemed to have almost no choices?

Jade: Sure, I'll listen.

Counselor: There was a man who was a prisoner in Nazi concentration camps for 3 years during the Second World War. One of these horrible camps was Auschwitz in Poland. The Nazis put many people to death and also tortured many. People starved and died horrible deaths by the thousands. But quite a number survived, including a man named Viktor Frankl. He wrote about his experience, and he said that the people who survived realized and deeply believed that they had a choice. They had very few choices as far as what they could do, but he saw a choice he could make. He decided to think of this horrible experience and this diabolical world in which he was forced to live as having some usefulness for him later in life. He thought it must serve a purpose, possibly to give him strength for his future. So even in this highly regulated and torturous camp where everyone was coerced and life was almost unbearable, he believed that he did not need to yield to the temptation to give up or to feel internally like there was no hope for him. In other words, he had the choice about how he would think and view his circumstances in the prison.

Jade: That's a frightening story. But what's it got to do with me?

Counselor: Frankl saw himself and other people around him as being the objects of a major persecution. The authorities were definitely against him and against many people in those days. From what you've told me, up to now you have felt that some of the authorities were after you. Do you see any similarity to the way Viktor Frankl thought and how you might think about your situation in the future?

Jade: Oh, I think I see what you mean. You're saying that I have more choices than he had.

Counselor: I agree 100%. Are you saying that you have some control and are willing to make some choices that might indicate *to yourself* that you are the one driving your car down the highway?

Jade: Yes, I believe that I have *some* choices available to me. But I'm still scared of the future and what will happen if I make changes.

Counselor: I think it's very interesting that you said "if I make changes." I noticed you said "changes" not a "change." You said something very hopeful by making it plural not singular. You seem to believe that your source of control is inside you and that you have realistic choices available to you.

Jade: I believe that I could do a few things better than in the past, but I still fear what that would be like.

Counselor: I believe I could help you leave aside some of your fears if you are willing to replace them with action-centered choices and plans. For instance, let's talk about some realistic choices available to you today.

Jade: Today!! Are you saying I could do something immediately?

Counselor: Let's put it this way. If you do nothing different this afternoon, will your life be any different?

Jade: Well, no, I guess not.

Counselor: If you do nothing today, will your life be any better than it was yesterday?

Jade: Hmmm, when you put it that way, my life would not be any different or any better.

Counselor: So in spite of your fear, in spite of the urge to wait, in spite of not *feeling* like doing something different, are you willing to take one step today?

Jade: But I don't see how one step is going to make a difference.

Counselor: If you choose *not* to take that one step today, if you choose to remain in one place standing still, would you be acting in your own best interests? Would you be choosing to remain stalled? Or would doing nothing get that car moving down the road?

Commentary: Critique the last statement made by the counselor. She asked three questions. Put yourself in the place of the client. Did the counselor ask too many questions all at once, resulting in the client feeling confused, or do you believe it is generally effective to ask more than one question at a time? (I just asked you two questions at one time.)

Jade: Well, it's obvious that I need to put the key in, start the car, and get it moving.

Counselor: That's what we call taking charge of your life. Even a small choice can make a difference. I used the word "realistic" because the choice need not solve your problems all at once. The choice might be to get started. I wonder if your fears and other reasons might present a roadblock in your mind. I've heard that expression occasionally in the work that I do. Some people say it's like climbing a mountain.

Jade: Yeah, that's exactly what it's like. All I can see right now is a mountain.

Counselor: Well, I guess that's progress. You were stuck in the valley. What is the first thing to do when you climb a mountain? In other words, before you start climbing, what are some preparations?

Jade: I need a backpack and a map.

Counselor: I can help you select the backpack. I can help you read the map. And I can be your guide as you start the climb. In other words, I can't do it for you, but I can be there with you, especially in the beginning.

Jade: I'll count on that.

Counselor: As you talk about this now, Jade, how do you feel: hopeful or hopeless?

Jade: I feel a little better, not so afraid.

Counselor: So merely talking about solutions and discussing a better road to take can help you feel more courage and more self-confidence.

Jade: With your support and with the help of the staff at the halfway house, maybe I can get a break when I see the judge again.

Counselor: What would be something you could do today that would impress the judge if he knew about it?

Jade: He wants me to be free of drugs and to have a job.

Counselor: Do *you* want a job?

Jade: Yes, I'd like to have an honest job where I don't have to keep looking over my shoulder.

Counselor: It is hard to find a job these days, but I can promise you one thing. No one is going to drop a job off at the doorstep of the halfway house with your name on it. Are you prepared to make an effort this afternoon to look for a job? I can give you some help in how to go about searching. Keep in mind, if you get turned down once, twice, or 10 times, that means you're 1, 2, or 10 steps closer to finding a job.

Jade: I could do that.

Counselor: I know you *could,* but *will* you?

Jade: All right, all right. You're kind of pushy, aren't you?

Counselor: That's my job. What time will you start today? Does setting a time sound like a good idea?

Jade: That is not what I expected, but it is a really good idea.

Commentary: In general, the counselor took the lead in assisting the client to move from a sense of external control to a perception of internal control. Or perhaps it is more accurate to say that she moved from a sense of external control to a sense of less external control and a perception of having more control than she previously thought she had. The concept of locus of control, formulated by Rotter (1954), did not originate with reality therapy; nevertheless, it is at the heart of its effective use. If a person perceives that she is a total victim and is completely powerless, she will remain in the perceived state of victimhood and will remain powerless and perhaps sink deeper into the pit of hopelessness. Please note that at no time did the counselor blame Jade. In fact, the counselor made it clear that she is not blaming Jade. However, she doesn't facilitate Jade's denial of culpability. The counselor simply bypasses this issue at this time. When Jade progresses along the pathway of more effective choices, it is very likely that Jade will be able to accept responsibility for her previous choices.

> *We are all products of our past.*
> *But we need not be victims of our past.*
> —William Glasser

• • •

In the beginning of the session, the counselor accepts Jade's sense of external control and yet challenges it. Jade resists and insists that people outside of her have control of her life. The counselor focuses on internal control and uses the story of Viktor Frankl as a metaphorical tool to help Jade evaluate her locus of control. The counselor resists driving the point home; instead, the counselor lets Jade think about the implications of the story. Jade begins to see that she has choices that were at first unrecognized. Throughout the discussion, the counselor also avoids criticism of Jade's sense of external control.

The counselor further utilizes the metaphor of the car, illustrating that people can drive their behavior in either helpful or harmful directions. She pays close attention to the language of the client. When Jade alludes to change, she uses its plural, "changes." Effective reality therapists listen carefully and respond to even the slightest movement by the client toward a sense of internal control. The response to such movement need not be immediate. The counselor may, for instance, wait for several slight changes in the client's manner of expression and summarize them. "Listening for themes" is a useful skill for building and maintaining the counseling relationship (Wubbolding, 2017).

To deal with the client's fears, the counselor tempers the idea of making choices by qualifying the concept with the phrase "realistic choices." Jade need not revolutionize her life by making a 180-degree turn. She can experience success and inner control by making a 1-degree turn. The counselor stresses the notion that actions replace fears. This is based on the principle that making action-centered choices replaces fear with courage.

Until this point in the counseling, helping Jade self-evaluate her behavior has been indirect. Then the counselor asked the more conventional self-evaluation question, "Is what you're doing helping you?" In this case, the question is adapted and becomes, "If you do nothing different this afternoon, will your life be any different?" To help Jade make realistically doable alternative choices, the counselor introduces the metaphor of climbing the mountain, a valuable simile for clients who feel overwhelmed. They need not conquer the mountain; they merely need to take the first step. This first step and subsequent steps are more manageable with a counselor serving as a coach or a partner.

The reality therapy practitioner knows the significance of immediate success or immediate need satisfaction, so she asks Jade to reflect on how she feels after talking about the possibility of moving from misery to a more joyful place in her life. She then encourages realistic action as she links the action to her goal, which is to be free of the judge's oversight and by implication being regulated by other authorities. At the end of the dialogue, Jade challenges the counselor by calling her "pushy." To avoid a defensive response and to infuse a little humor as well as to shun the urge to control Jade by correcting her statement, the counselor simply agrees. Thus, throughout the session the counselor attempts to accept the client and yet refrains from colluding with her perceived sense of external control. Even labeling the counselor as "pushy" is acceptable.

Now that you have read the dialogue and the commentary, please reread the dialogue with the commentary in mind. Also, reflect on what you would do differently within the bounds of the reality therapy procedures. Resist the urge to merely reflect on the client's feelings.

Two Ericksonian Principles

The next case illustrates the application of two Ericksonian principles and how they intersect with the practice of reality therapy. Choice theory provides justification for integrating them into the artful application of the WDEP system of reality therapy. *The counselor uses the material presented by the client.* A counselor learning that a client obsesses about thoughts and feelings of guilt concerning past "sins" and other shameful deeds might assist the client in sharpening his or her memory about past successful and enjoyable experiences. I suggest that you note the manner in which the counselor assists the client to identify an ineffective behavior and transform it into a productive and altruistic choice. Another Ericksonian principle is that *the problem can be the solution.* A counselor utilizing this intervention might assist a client in redirecting and transforming anger. The client thus converts anger into energy and focuses it on something unselfish and humanitarian. The next case dialogue illustrates how the counselor combines these two principles to help an adolescent client.

Case Example:
Incorporating Two Ericksonian Principles

Norman, a 15-year-old male, is referred for counseling by school authorities with the cooperation of his mother. He is under the supervision of a juvenile probation officer because of his arrest for drug abuse. Moreover, his truancy, disrespect shown to teachers and school administrators, his consistent fighting at school and in his neighborhood, and his unwillingness to help his mother at home have presented the adults in his life with ample reason for mandating that he attend individual counseling sessions. I have not identified the client with any racial or ethnic group because the application described here could be used with virtually any client. I firmly believe in the universal applicability of reality therapy, but this does not negate the necessity for modifying its use in a multicultural context, which I have illustrated in other dialogues. Prior to this session, the counselor had explained in detail various ethical issues specifically related to counseling minors. Practitioners of reality therapy follow the standard practice regarding confidentiality, its limits, and the many issues described in various codes of ethics.

> *Counselor:* Hello Norman. I see you made it here on time and that your mother drove you here. I have received some information about you, and I will be asking you to describe your situation. But first, I'd like to ask you what thoughts went through your mind as you came to the office and as you walked in the door.
>
> *Norman:* I don't want to be here. I have other things more important to do.
>
> *Counselor:* But you came anyway. I'm wondering about the reason you agreed to come and chose to be here.
>
> *Norman:* I didn't choose nothin'. They made me come.
>
> *Counselor:* Tell me who "they" are.

Norman: The judge and my P.O., the school people, and even my mother ganged up on me.

Counselor: So you have a lot of people jumping on you, ordering you around, telling you what to do.

Norman: Yeah. They wanna run my life.

Counselor: You think they're working against you, and yet you chose to come here.

Norman: I didn't choose anything. They forced me.

Counselor: They forced you? How could they force you? It seems to me you're freely sitting here of your own accord.

Norman: They said if I don't come I go to juvenile detention.

Counselor: Oh, I see. So, they put a lot of pressure on you, and the pain of juvenile detention would be worse than coming to a counselor.

Norman: I guess so.

Counselor: How do you feel right now as you sit here?

Norman: This is s_____.

Counselor: Well, we've hardly begun, and yet you're sure of that?

Norman: Yeah, all you shrinks are just like everybody else. You just want me to do what I'm told.

Counselor: So you think this is a waste of time. But my question is, how do you feel right now? Angry? Annoyed? Afraid? Frustrated?

Norman: How about all of those?

Counselor: So your thoughts are that this is baloney and a waste of time. And your feeling is that you're upset about being here.

Norman: That's about right.

Counselor: We'll come back to all of that as time goes by. I would like to hear what you would like to gain from our time together.

Norman: Gain? Are you kidding! I don't want anything from this nonsense.

Counselor: OK, so you've defined pretty clearly what you want out of what we call the counseling process. You want nothing. You know sometimes it takes quite a while for my clients to reach a point where they can describe what they want as clearly as you just did. But because you don't want anything and you're nevertheless here in the office, I'd like to hear you describe what other people think should happen as a result of our conversations.

Norman: They want me to be a "nice boy." They want me to act different from the way I act now.

Counselor: So they want to see some change in your actions.

Norman: They want me to do a lot of things that I don't want to do.

Counselor: So there's a gap between what you want to do and what your teachers, the principal, your P.O., the judge, and your mother want you to do.

Norman: That's what I'm telling you.

Counselor: So the gap is as big as the Grand Canyon.

Norman: It might even be bigger.

Counselor: And it might even be smaller!

Norman: Whatever it is, it ain't gonna change.

Counselor: Wouldn't it change if they decided to let you alone?

Norman: Yeah. Can you make that happen?

Counselor: It's possible. But I can't do it alone. Tell me what exactly do they want from you that they are not getting. Try to be specific.

Norman: They want me to stay away from drugs. They want me to go to school every day and be respectful to the teachers. They even want me to do some volunteer work in my neighborhood.

Counselor: Tell me what your mother wants from you.

Norman: She wants me to respect her and help around the house.

Counselor: And all these people tell you that you are not doing these things and so they have sent you here to me.

Norman: Yeah. They're always on my back about something.

Counselor: Norman, you described your feelings earlier. Which of those is most on your mind: angry, annoyed, afraid, or frustrated?

Norman: I'd say frustrated.

Counselor: Norman, tell me where exactly, in what part of your body, you feel this frustration.

Norman: In my hands.

Counselor: In your hands!! Talk a little more about that. Why do you suppose this frustration is in your hands?

Norman: I don't know.

Counselor: Let's put it this way. What do you do with your hands that might be your way of expressing your frustration?

Norman: I fight with other people at school and on the street.

Counselor: Would you say that you usually win the fights, or do you lose?

Norman: Most times I win, but sometimes I lose.

Counselor: It must be hard to lose a fight, especially on the street. At least at school, there are people who try to break up a fight. When you win a fight, what kind of gut feeling do you have?

Norman: I feel like I can take on the world.

Counselor: How long did that feeling remain after your last fight?

Norman: Not very long. My hands started to hurt.

Counselor: Hurt because the frustration returned.

Norman: I never thought of it that way.

Counselor: As you think of it that way here and now in this moment, what is your next thought?

Norman: I don't have any next thought.

Counselor: OK. I can understand that. Let's think about that together, and maybe something could happen as a result of both of us thinking about it. Would that be OK with you?

Norman: Yeah, that would be OK. Ya know, you're really strange.

Counselor: You're right. People tell me that. But what do you mean by that comment?

Norman: Nobody talks to me this way. When I say "I get into fights," they look at me with fire in their eyes. They sometimes get afraid, but they always preach at me about fighting.

Counselor: If I added my voice to the preaching, would it help?

Norman: No.

Counselor: That's why I don't preach to people. They've usually heard the sermons before, and I don't try to do things that don't help or that aggravate people or that add to their frustrations. Besides, I don't have a preacher's license!

Norman: (*Smiles broadly.*) Like I said, you're strange.

Counselor: Thank you, I'll take that as a compliment. You're a very good listener.

Norman: That is really, really strange. Nobody has ever said I listen. In fact, they say I don't listen.

Counselor: Well, you're listening now. And I'm doing my best to listen to what you say. And I heard you talk about your hands where your frustration seems to settle, and I think we both agree that you express your frustration with your hands. I'd like to help you with this frustration. I believe I can help you get rid of some of the pain, frustration, and your general feeling of being upset at the way people treat you. I want to ask you a question or two on a different topic. Is that OK?

Norman: Yeah, that's fine.

Counselor: When was the last time you did even a small favor for your mother?

Norman: That's a tough question. I don't remember doing anything for her.

Counselor: Does she cook for you?

Norman: Yeah, she cooks.

Counselor: How's the food?

Norman: It's pretty good.

Counselor: So she does things for you: cooking, providing a roof over your head, and maybe she does other things for you. But we'll come back to that later. The thought has just occurred to me: *If* you were to do her a favor, what would it be?

Norman: I would do the dishes.

Counselor: Wow! You didn't even hesitate with that response. You didn't have to think about it. How hard would it be for you to help her with the dishes tonight?

Norman: I could do that.

Counselor: I know you could. What do you think about actually doing it?

Norman: Will that get her off my back?

Counselor: I doubt it, but you might get a smile out of her. When was the last time you smiled at her?

Norman: You're asking me very hard questions. I never smile at her.

Counselor: I'm willing to bet that you could smile, because I saw you do it before. And you don't strike me as a weak person.

Norman: I could do that.

Counselor: Would you be willing to help her with the dishes tonight and smile at her? What do you think about saying, "Mom, that was a good meal"?

Norman: You're loading me up with a lot of stuff that I normally don't do.

Counselor: Can you handle it?

Norman: Of course I can.

Counselor: I think you can do it. For one reason, it doesn't take much time. And your friends won't even see you doing it.

Norman: Yeah.

Counselor: Will you do these things?

Norman: All right, all right. I'll do them.

Counselor: Oh yes, one more thing. When you wash the dishes, could you pay close attention to your hands? I suggest you wash the dishes without wearing rubber gloves. Pay attention to how your hands feel. And after you do the dishes and dry off your hands, pay more attention to how they feel.

Norman: Why should I not wear rubber gloves?

Counselor: I don't know. It just seems like a good idea. Are you willing to do this project?

Norman: Yes.

Counselor: Could we write this down on a piece of paper now?

Norman: This is really weird.

Counselor: Yes, it is weird, but like you say, no one talks to you like this. I bet it's been a while since you've had an enjoyable yet serious conversation with an adult without preaching and accusing. Don't get me wrong; I'm not against preaching. But as you said, it would not help the situation.

Norman: (Writes down his plan.)

Counselor: Oh yes, one more thing. I almost forgot. Could you call my office number on your cell phone after you do this tonight? I probably won't be here, but would you leave about a 15 second message describing how it went. Be sure to mention something about your hands.

Norman: Another strange thing, but I could do that.

Counselor: I know you could, but will you?

Norman: (Smiles again.) Yeah, yeah.

Counselor: You're smiling again. I think you're on to me. We'll talk again next time.

Commentary: In this dialogue, the counselor asks Norman what he wants from the counseling experience. As expected, Norman sees no value in counseling, wants nothing from the counselor, and sees no possible satisfying outcome. On the other hand, the counselor sees Norman's lack of desire as a positive even though there is little to build on with this quality world deficit. The counselor deals with Norman's avoidance by acknowledging that he has clearly stated his want. He wants nothing. Thus the counselor responds to Norman in a genuine but unexpected manner. Consequently, the counselor shifts the discussion from the scarcity of Norman's counseling goals to his perception of the wants of others. Norman readily enumerates what other people want from him and how unreasonable they are in that he believes he should be left alone and free of the repressiveness of the adult attempts to curb his behavior.

Even though the counselor would have previously discussed informed consent issues, the client's initial understanding of them gradually evolves into a fuller grasp of them. Users of reality therapy contrast the role of the counselor with the role of other adults in the child's life. Fulfilling this delicate responsibility is the result of training, supervision, experience, and the recognition that the healthy development of adolescents embraces a wide variety of relationships with adults. In short, the counselor avoids all criticism of the authority figures encountered by Norman.

The counselor combines utilization with the problem as solution. Using Norman's description of stress in his hands, the counselor sees that this problem can become a solution. With the help of the counselor, Norman formulates a plan to use his hands in a generous, kind, and altruistic manner, helping his mother wash the dishes. Part of this plan is to attend to his total behavior: not only washing the dishes but also thinking and reflecting on how his hands feel during what is actually a self-cleansing process.

In this counseling relationship, self-evaluation occurs in a very indirect manner. Norman will discover that using his hands to assist his mother is more effective and personally satisfying than using them to hurt other people or to keep his mother away from him. In the dialogue that follows, the counselor helps Norman reflect on this experience.

There are several additional subtleties in the dialogue. Norman implies that he will wash the dishes *for* his mother. The counselor translates this willingness from doing the dishes *for* his mother to washing the dishes *with* his mother. Clearly, the focus is on the effort of Norman to choose behaviors that represent a positive achievement. But more important, the counselor hopes that Norman will satisfy his own need for belonging with his mother. And if the experience is successful, the mother *might* feel good about Norman's behavior if only for a few moments. Thus they both share time together during which they make a connection with each other by achieving a simple household task.

Please note, even if successful, this plan might seem trivial when compared with Norman's overall plight. I present this dialogue for the following reasons:

1. It represents the beginning of a new direction for the client. If Norman can take one step along this positive path, he can take many steps. The British writer G. K. Chesterton remarked that trifles make perfection, and perfection is no trifle.
2. It illustrates how to listen carefully to the subtle expressions of clients and utilize their problems by reframing them as solutions.
3. The plan also illustrates yet another Ericksonian principle congruent with reality therapy: *sometimes the solution appears to have no connection with the problem.* Washing dishes might seem to be completely disconnected from Norman's antisocial behavior. But a plan that satisfies the client in a healthy and productive manner is a way to replace destructively self-serving choices.

Future sessions with Norman might include a discussion of the experience of washing dishes with his mother: how he felt about it; how his hands felt when he used them to serve his mother; how she felt; and what she thought about his willingness to assist her. Finally, helping Norman implicitly evaluate his behavior and facilitating his plan of action is a metaphor for the much broader and yet more detailed practice of reality therapy in which skilled counselors help clients replace ineffective behaviors. This viewpoint of replacement is slightly different from the viewpoint of overcoming problems. Another example is helping a depressed person develop an exercise program. It is a well-known fact that exercise is a very useful tactic for banishing feelings of depression or, more accurately, replacing them (Arden, 2014).

The next session, which takes place a few days later, could take many directions. I selected the following direction as one example.

Counselor: Thanks for calling and leaving the message about washing the dishes with your mother. I'll bet you never expected that washing dishes would satisfy the judge, the school, the probation officer, and most other people! But I wonder what happened between you and your mother as you were washing the dishes.

Norman: You're right, I never expected that from visiting a shrink. This was really weird.

Counselor: Well, you might be right. But I prefer to think of it as just different. Sometimes when I talk to people in my office, I don't know what will happen as a result. I just try to listen and help clients get what they want and make better choices that will help them get rid of some of their problems. Would you like to get rid of some of your problems?

Norman: I'd like to get rid of all of them.

Counselor: That's a big order. How about at the end of this session today you give me just a couple of your problems?

Norman: I can think of a few.

Counselor: That sounds good. I can only take a few at a time.

Norman: You really talk weird.

Counselor: As I said, I prefer to think of it as different. If I talk to you the way everyone else talks to you, would it make any difference?

Norman: No, I've heard it all before.

Counselor: So, if there are five people hammering on you, one more hammer won't do much. I'm more concerned with helping you deal with the world without hammering back at them. But let's get back to the experience with your mother. How did she act when you helped her with the dishes?

Norman: She didn't say much. But she did say thank you at the end. She looked at me with a very strange expression.

Counselor: Kind'a different! So when you reach out with helping hands instead of angry hands or stressed hands, you get a different kind of response from people. I guess there's something to be learned from this single effort on your part. By the way, how did your hands feel when you were doing the dishes? What did the soap feel like?

Norman: It sure felt different. But my hands were really clean when I was finished.

Counselor: You learned that you can use those hands to help your mother. And when you use them in that way, they feel clean. I think they felt clean not only because of the soap but because of what you did for her and with her. How do you evaluate or judge this experience with your mother? Do you think it helped or hurt her?

Norman: I think it helped her.

Counselor: What did it do for you, help or hurt?

Norman: It helped for a few minutes.

Counselor: Would you be interested in at least thinking about and talking about how you could take those few minutes and extend them into even more minutes?

Norman: Are you trying to turn me into a suck-up? I don't want people to think of me as a suck-up.

Counselor: Don't worry Norman. For people to see you as a suck-up is waaaaay down the road. That will take a long time. And if that happens, we'll deal with it. I wasn't thinking of you in that way. I was thinking of you getting to the point where people are off your back and you feel better about the way things are going. It seems to me that something has to change in your life if you're going to feel better about everything.

Norman: They need to just leave me alone.

Counselor: In other words, they need to change.

Norman: You got that right.

Counselor: Now I have a very important question. One that I would not ask in the beginning of our talks together. But I think the time is right to ask you this question.

Norman: All right, all right. I'm ready.

Counselor: (*Using a softer tone of voice and speaking more slowly to indicate the added seriousness of what is to follow.*) Deep inside of yourself, without kidding yourself, without avoiding facing yourself, do you believe the people around you such as school people, the probation officer, the teacher, the police, and everybody else are going to change? Don't answer it right away. Just think for a few seconds.

Norman: (*Pauses for about 7 seconds.*) I wish *they* would change.

Counselor: That's what you wish. But the real issue is, do you think they will change?

Norman: I guess not.

Counselor: So who's left that can make a few changes or at least one change? I'll give you a hint. The person is in this room. And it's not me.

Norman: I guess I'll need to make some changes.

Counselor: Norman, it seems to me that today you are standing at a fork in the road. You can go down the road of trouble and people on your back (*Gestures using arms outstretched to indicate two roads.*) or you can go down the road of happiness and being free of people ordering you around. It's your choice. Which will it be?

Norman: I don't like people ordering me around all the time.

Counselor: Getting orders from people around you is the road of misery.

Norman: So the only road open, the best road, is what you call happiness highway?

Counselor: That's the way it looks to me. But keep in mind, if you make that choice, it's not always a smooth highway. There are bumps and detours. There are people who still will tell you what to do. There's just not as many. But there are teachers, and if you get a legal job, you'll have a boss. But overall, what do you think? Is this road better or worse than the road of breaking the law, skipping school, flunking, drugs, telling people off, and on and on and on?

Norman: I guess you want me to say it's better.

Counselor: Well, as a matter of fact, I do want you to say that. I'd be lying if I said I didn't care. But the real answer has to be yours. I can help you with the positive path. But you already know the negative path, and I am not willing to help you get in more trouble.

Norman: I could give it a try.

Counselor: Actually, you already gave it a try when you helped your mother with the dishes. You said you felt better. And she even felt better about you. Isn't that what you said?

Norman: Yeah. That's what happened.

Counselor: So you showed to your mother, to yourself, and even to me that you can take action steps down that road. You've already done it. So let me ask you this. Of all the choices you've made, which one would be the easiest to work on in the sense of making a better choice starting today or tomorrow?

Norman: I don't know about the easiest, but going to school would be the most important.

Counselor: Would you like to give that a try? Going to school every day for a week? How hard would that be?

Norman: I could do it if I wanted to.

Counselor: Do you want to?

Norman: If I don't go, I'm going to get in more trouble.

Counselor: Yes, and you're already in trouble because that's why you were sent here. Now let's see if we can lessen the trouble. Are you willing to go to school every day for a week?

Norman: I can do that.

Counselor: I know you can. But will you?

Norman: You just don't let up.

Counselor: No I won't let up because that would be giving up on you. And you said you wanted to go down the happiness road. And your car has started down that road. I'm behind the car pushing it to go faster. I'm not pushing you to do something you don't want to do. I'm just encouraging you to do what you said you *do* want to do. I firmly believe that if you go to school you will be subject to less hassle, less criticism, and less blame. Now, do you believe that showing up is enough?

Norman: Well, no.

Counselor: What will you do when you are at school?

Norman: I know what you're going to say. I'll have to be on time and not cause trouble.

Counselor: You know what to do, and you are strong enough to do it. It's necessary to take a few more steps down that road. Are you willing to follow through on those three plans?

Norman: You mean go to school, be on time, and don't get in trouble?

Counselor: That's exactly what I mean.

Norman: I'll do it for a week.

Counselor: So it's a realistic plan? It's doable?

Norman: Yes, it is.

Counselor: Are you firmly committed to it even to the point of writing it down and carrying the plan with you in your pocket?

Norman: Yes. I'll write it down.

Counselor: I'd like to have a copy of it. After you write it down, I'll photocopy it. Is that OK with you?

Norman: Yes, that's OK.

Counselor: What's the best thing we talked about in our conversations?

Norman: We talked about a solution instead of everything I do wrong.

Commentary: In this admittedly simplified session, the counselor helps Norman reflect on various aspects of his successful interaction with his mother. The purpose is to help Norman move from a sense of being controlled by people around him to a sense of internal control. He comes to realize that he is in charge of his life more than he previously believed. He can even use his body to contribute to his own welfare and to that of people around him. He experiences for a few minutes the journey from the perceived external locus of control to the perceived internal locus of control (Rotter, 1954). The significance of this change cannot be overemphasized. If and when Norman retreats to a sense of external control, the counselor can remind him of his brief rewarding experience with his mother (internal control).

The counselor then helps Norman focus on the broader environment in which he lives without overburdening him with the responsibility of radically changing all his behaviors. Altering his behavior at school seems to require an enormous change in his pattern of making choices. His progress will be slow, with occasional failures. Consequently, the counselor utilized the philosophy summarized as SAMIC planning: keep the plan simple, attainable, measurable, immediate, and controlled by the planner. The adults in Norman's life were attempting to coerce him into making an immediate 180-degree turn in all of his behaviors. The counselor not only shuns coercion but helps Norman see that a slight alteration in his behavior will result in more need satisfaction.

In subsequent sessions, the counselor will help Norman describe positive experiences with other students (the need for belonging). Norman will also reflect on how following through on the plan helped him feel a sense of accomplishment (the need for power or achievement). The counselor will point out that attending school was a choice (the need for freedom). He might have enjoyed conversations with other students or experienced fun in some other way (the need for fun). The counselor operates from a philosophy of choice theory, an internal control system. It is the job of the counselor to assist clients in defining what they want and judging whether their behavior is helping or hurting them and the people around them. Then the counselor helps clients make plans. Reality therapy is a system based on internal controls that satisfy one's needs and wants. It is the opposite of coercion, which often results in resistance and blatant nonconformity to reasonable rules.

This session was simplified and meant to illustrate interventions that a counselor can implement. It is not my intent to create or to encourage the false perception that reality therapy can proceed as rapidly as it appears to in sample dialogues. Though reality therapy is sometimes a brief or short-term system, it is not a quick fix. As Glasser frequently stated in his lectures, "We have no magic." The successful use of reality therapy often requires many counseling sessions, patience, unswerving hope, and a never-give-up attitude on the part of the counselor. At the basis of successful reality therapy is the counseling relationship and the therapeutic alliance. Establishing these mutually satisfying processes is sometimes very rapid, and at other times it requires much more time.

Discussion Questions

1. Identify three self-evaluation statements from these cases that you can use in your work. Think about how you would use them even if you are not currently practicing as a counselor. __

   _____

   _____

2. List two interventions made by the counselor that you disagree with. _____

   _____

   _____

3. Describe two alternative possibilities for the interventions you disagree with. If they are not congruent with reality therapy, describe how they differ from the WDEP system of reality therapy.

   _____

   _____

   _____

Chapter 7

Dealing With Loss, Posttraumatic Stress, Self-Injury, Conflict, and Anger

The recent history of the counseling profession indicates that counselors increasingly deal with a wider variety of presenting issues and more serious client disturbances. Among these client problems are wide-ranging symptoms of loss, posttraumatic stress due to abuse, sudden death of loved ones, and near death experiences and injuries during wartime. Additionally counselors face varying levels of conflict in families, between partners, and in the community that are often accompanied by anger, resentment and many other feelings, harmful self-talk, and tension-inducing actions. These client concerns are often exacerbated by varying world views and cultural differences. The cases in this chapter illustrate several effective ways to help suffering clients find relief.

Evaluating Perceptions: Couples Counseling

Maria and Hans, ages 36 and 38, respectively, have been married for 16 years and have two children. Maria and Hans are experiencing tension in their marital relationship. Prior to the first session, Maria phoned the counselor and explained her perception of the problem. Her husband travels frequently, and she believes excessively, for his company. When he is home, he watches television and seems to increasingly withdraw from family life. Maria says she has gradually assumed more and more responsibility for raising the children, keeping the house, paying the bills, grocery shopping, and so

135

forth. She relates that she is exhausted and feels alone and taken for granted in what was once an enjoyable marriage. She adds that her older child, Elyse (age 15), is her pride and joy because she is a well-behaved high-achieving student with many "nice" friends. Her son, Bruno (age 13), on the other hand, is totally apathetic, cares little about school, plays video games for hours every day, and is flunking most of his classes. She feels a glimmer of hope because her husband has agreed to attend the counseling sessions.

For counseling to be effective, the counselor believes she needs to connect with Hans via telephone as she did with Maria. If she speaks only with Maria before the first counseling session, Hans could think that the counselor and Maria have established a partnership and an alliance against him. In fact, Maria might hold a similar belief. Through a phone conversation with Hans, the counselor hears Hans's story. Hans says he is required to travel so that he can provide the necessities as well as many luxuries for the family. Maria has her own late model car, dresses exquisitely, and can spend money as she sees fit. He says that he takes the family on trips during the summer and over the school's winter vacation. He feels rejected by Maria who he says is child-focused and is uninterested in him. He states that he even prepares his own meals when he arrives home late and would appreciate meals prepared by Maria.

After satisfying the requirements of informed consent, the counselor asked each of them to summarize how they see their relationship. Then the session continues.

Counselor: You've both summarized what you told me on the telephone. What else do you have to say about this marriage?

Maria: As I said, I feel like all the responsibility for the family is on my shoulders, and he absolutely refuses to help in any way. He thinks I'm nothing more than a nanny and a housekeeper. At the same time, I can't help thinking that he will meet someone in his travels and that will be the end of our marriage.

Counselor: You say that with quite a bit of concern in your voice. Do you want to keep the marriage together?

Maria: Yes, I do. I wish we could bring back the old days when we paid attention to each other and spent more time together.

Counselor: I noticed you said, "*we* paid attention to each other." We'll come back to that point after while. But for now I want to clarify whether or not you want to keep the marriage together. In other words, do you want me to be a divorce counselor or a marriage counselor?

Maria: Divorce? No. I want the marriage to stay together.

Counselor: So, from your point of view, there is enough value present in the relationship for you to stay together. Now Hans, I want to ask you something similar. What role do you believe you have in this relationship?

Hans: I believe I do a good job of supporting the family and trying to help Maria raise the kids. She just doesn't appreciate me or what I do for the family. When I travel, I have to deal with union representatives, plant managers, and even some of the disgruntled employees in the organizations that I visit. When I return home, I'm tired of talking and listening. It's getting more and more difficult to fly, and the flights are a lot less convenient than they used to be. They seem to be late most of the time, and security is a royal pain. When I come home, I really don't want any more hassles, and I have to get up early the next day and go to the office.

Counselor: So, from your perspective, is the marriage worth saving or not? For your part, do you want me to be a divorce counselor or a marriage counselor?

Hans: I knew you would ask me that question. I want to remain married to Maria.

Counselor: Just out of curiosity, when was the last time you told each other that the marriage is worth saving?

Maria: It's been a long time.

Counselor: Hans?

Hans: She's right. It's been quite a while.

Counselor: I often ask a husband and wife to say to each other, "I want to keep our marriage together." But I don't think you're quite ready to look each other in the eye and say that just yet. So let's move on.

Hans: Wait a minute. Why do we need to delay saying this? I think we can say it. Maria, do you want to say this out loud to me?

Maria: Of course I do.

Counselor: No, you're not ready.

Hans and Maria: Yes, we are!

Counselor: OK, give it a try.

Hans: Maria, you go first.

Maria: Hans, I definitely want to keep this marriage together, but we do have to make some changes.

Hans: Maria, I too want to keep this marriage together, but I want you to make some changes too.

Counselor: Wow!! You went further than I thought. Maria, you said "definitely" and Hans you sounded very definite in your tone of voice. And you even see the necessity for change.

Commentary: The counselor made a concerted effort to extend the content of the phone conversations to initiate a face-to-face relationship with both Hans and Maria. She asked them whether they wanted her to be a divorce counselor or a marriage counselor. This question constitutes an attention getting and quick start intervention for couples counseling. It elicits a description of each person's perception regarding the possibility of maintaining the relationship. It can also trigger each individual's current and future contribution to the marriage. In my experience, most couples express the desire for the counselor to serve as a marriage counselor. This signals that they are at least willing to try to improve the marriage or the relationship. They often add a description of their perception that the other person is the one who needs to change. An unskilled reality therapist often intervenes by demonstrating a lack of appreciation for the artful use of choice theory by making such precipitous statements as these: "You cannot control the other person and coerce him or her to change. I can help each of you make changes in your own behaviors and work on the marriage, but I cannot help you change the other person." This is an accurate statement, but a counselor can be too hasty and impulsive in providing this information. These statements could be interpreted by the clients as criticism, and they may feel that the counselor is correcting them. I suggest listening carefully for clients' cues indicating that they, at least marginally, believe they cannot change the other person and currently perceive that expecting others to perfectly conform to their respective quality worlds is unrealistic. It is not reasonable to expect clients who have relationship problems to express them in choice theory language.

The counselor also utilizes a paradoxical statement when she says that she doesn't think they were ready to look each other in the eye and express their desire to maintain the marriage. The purpose of this statement is to ensure an immediate success and need satisfaction for a couple perceiving tension in their relationship. If they challenge the counselor, as Hans and Maria did, they gain a sense of achievement and bonding, that is, belonging. If they agree that it is too soon, they experience success in agreeing with each other and in agreeing with the counselor.

The counselor further pointed out that they agree on the fact they perceive the necessity for changes in their behaviors. They might believe that the other person is the partner who should change, but the counselor focuses on the possibility of change rather than on the futility of causing the other person to change.

The session continues.

Counselor: I noticed that you seemed very definite, very convinced that change would need to happen. Before we talk about specific changes, I have an important question. If you maintain this perception that changes need to be made, will this perception help or hurt the relationship in the future?

Maria: I believe that we need to maintain this viewpoint. It will help.

Hans: I agree. This fits with the management philosophy that I employ at work: a positive outlook helps the company.

Counselor: And so this attitude will improve and make more satisfying the company that you keep with each other. How useful is that idea to you?

Hans and Maria: We both agree that our relationship will work out for the better.

Commentary: This last segment of dialogue is the culmination of previous interactions. Earlier comments by the counselor are an attempt to facilitate a process whereby Hans and Maria evaluate their respective perceptions and make a judgment about the value of how they see their marriage improving. The dialogue presented in this case could be expanded to include the totality of reality therapy. The detailed use of reality therapy with Hans and Maria could include helping them define what they want from each other, assisting them in the examination of their behaviors, and conducting a searching and clear-eyed evaluation of the attainability of their wants and the effectiveness of their choices.

This dialogue illustrates specific interventions aimed at client self-evaluation. In this case, even though many more diverse interventions would be appropriate, the purpose of this dialogue is to illustrate one aspect of self-evaluation: helping clients evaluate their perceptions.

Case Example: Cross-Cultural Application

Arif, a Malaysian woman living in the United States, is a self-referred client. She is 33 years old, has no children, and was married to a Malaysian, Ziyad, for 4 years. Ziyad died of cancer 5 years ago, and Arif is still deeply grieving his death. These few details constitute the totality of information known to the counselor. This is often the real situation: The counselor knows very little about the client before the first appointment.

Counselor: Arif, we've been through the information on informed consent and other ethical issues as well as the type of counseling that I practice, called reality therapy. You told me a few details over the telephone, and I'm wondering what is on your mind today as we begin our conversation.

Arif: I'm feeling sad about the death of my husband, Ziyad. He died 5 years ago, and I'm wondering how you can help me. I have my doubts about any help that I can receive after all this time.

Counselor: I believe I can be of some help, but it might take a while before you come to believe that it is possible.

Arif: I'm not sure if you can really understand.

Counselor: What do you see as barriers to the counseling process and to my understanding?

Arif: I don't want to upset you, but I don't know if a man can understand what I've been through.

Counselor: And what else?

Arif: (*Hesitates, looks away, and is clearly reluctant to say anything more.*)

Counselor: I'm wondering if the fact that I'm not only a man but ethnically different from you creates a barrier.

Arif: Like I said, I don't want to insult you, but I do have some doubts about whether you can understand me.

Counselor: Yet you came anyway! It seems to me that you made a courageous choice to come here in spite of your doubts. (*Tries to identify a theme for counseling and provisionally hypothesizes that "courage" might be a theme.*)

Arif: I have a number of friends, and they encouraged me to seek help from a counselor. They said talking it over might help.

Counselor: I'm curious as to your reasons for selecting me.

Arif: (*Appearing somewhat embarrassed*). Well, to tell you the truth, your office is not far from where I work, and you were willing to schedule me today after work. In fact, my friend called before I did, talked to you, and got the impression that you would be able to help me.

Counselor: That's a good reason. In fact, over the years, I have referred people living in other cities, and I always encourage them to go to someone nearby who is easily accessible. Many people will not continue to seek help if they have to travel a great distance. But I am glad you came because I believe help is available and that I can help you. You have already taken a step that is admirable.

Arif: You are near by, and I can walk here from work.

Counselor: What about the racial difference between us?

Arif: Well, I thought that could be a problem too.

Counselor: You brought up some legitimate concerns. Gender difference, ethnic differences. Maybe there are others. I guess we'll find out. I admit these could be obstacles, but you came here anyway, so let's just talk about how things are going for you. Your husband, Ziyad, died 5 years ago, and a friend sent you here. What reasons did she give for suggesting that you come here?

Arif: I have a number of friends, some White and some Malaysian, and all of them say that it's time for me to move on.

Counselor: And I'm willing to bet you're getting tired of hearing that.

Arif: I am. I'm tired of hearing it, but they keep it up. And I don't feel comfortable telling them to stop.

Counselor: I'm just curious. Are you expecting me to encourage you or show you how to move on?

Arif: I think my friends want you to help me to put all of this behind me.

Counselor: I'd like to rephrase what they're saying. Is that OK with you?

Arif: (*Shows a hint of frustration.*) Go ahead.

Counselor: They want you to put your husband behind you, to make his death part of history, and to give all of your energy to the present and the future because you cannot change the past. Is that what you hear when they tell you "it's time to move on"?

Arif: (*With tears in her eyes she nods.*) Yes.

Counselor: I will make you a promise. I will never say to you that it's time to move on.

Arif: (*With surprise in her voice.*) Everyone else tells me to move on. I thought you would show me how to do this.

Counselor: That is why I'm a counselor. I don't try to help people do what other people think is best for them, at least most of the time, and especially in your situation.

Arif: That's a surprise.

Counselor: How would it help if I said that it's time to move on?

Arif: It would not help.

Counselor: I believe it would make things worse. And so my question to you, Arif, is this: Why do you have an obligation to move on?

Arif: I don't know.

Counselor: It may be the opinion of many people that after 5 years it's time to move on, but for the life of me I can't find any proof that you should move on. It was a very important part of your life, and in fact I think it would help if you continue to carry it with you. But I do believe counseling can make the burden a little lighter.

Arif: That sure is different from what I've been hearing.

Counselor: Would you be willing to work on that? Making your burden a little lighter?

Arif: Yes.

Counselor: One of the ways we can begin to accomplish that goal is if you just tell me about your husband. What was he like? How did you meet, and so on?

Arif: We were both studying in Missouri. There were not many Malaysians in school, and we met at a social gathering for foreign students.

Counselor: What attracted you to him?

Arif: First of all we were both from Malaysia, about the same age, and spoke both Malaysian and English fluently. He was studying engineering, and I was studying computer science. We started to date, and just after graduation we were married. Then about 4 years after we were married, he was diagnosed with stomach cancer. The doctors said that because of his youthful age the cancer would spread rapidly. It did spread very quickly, and he died 8 months and 12 days after receiving the diagnosis.

Counselor: And you were heartbroken at his death. I can see that in your face.

Arif: Yes.

Counselor: And I can see that you are still heartbroken. And when people say move on, they don't seem to appreciate the depth of your sadness.

Arif: That's exactly right.

Counselor: I'd like to hear more about him and about your relationship.

Arif: He was very generous, and we agreed to support students who were at the university and in the early stages of their adjustment to the United States. We also worked together in the program called Habitat for Humanity. And we had many laughs about various incidents.

Counselor: What would be one of the incidents that you enjoyed?

Arif: One time, one of the American volunteers wanted to please Ziyad and me. She tried to fix a Malaysian lunch for us to eat while we were working. It tasted awful, but we smiled and ate it anyway. The most we could say to her was that "we also enjoy American food."

Counselor: Were you satisfied with your comment to her?

Arif: Yes, we didn't want to say anything more than that, and we really appreciated her kind consideration and her intention to do us a favor.

Counselor: Tell me more about Ziyad.

Arif: He was very ambitious and worked long hours, and we would argue about that.

Counselor: How serious were these arguments?

Arif: They weren't a major source of disagreement. We learned to live with different viewpoints about this. Overall, we got along beautifully.

Counselor: What were some things you liked to do together?

Arif: We learned to do many things Americans do. We learned to play golf and tennis, and we would have friends over for dinner and to watch sports on TV.

Counselor: (*Smiling.*) In Malaysia, they don't do those things?

Arif: Oh, of course, we did, but we didn't do it quite the way you Americans do it. At home Ziyad's family and mine were a bit more formal.

Counselor: One thing about Americans, we can be very casual. Of course, there are social and even geographic differences when it comes to entertaining people in our homes.

Arif: Yes, I noticed quite a difference between the times we would have people over to watch professional football games on Sunday and more formal cocktail parties with business associates.

Counselor: I have a question I'd like to ask you, Arif, as an aside. I have a friend who is Japanese and who is fluent in English, a young man. We'll call him Koji. He's about 25 years old, and he has told me and my wife that he likes to speak English because it is so informal. He said Japanese tends to be a much more formal language. Is that true of the Malaysian language? Or at least true of people that your families would associate with?

Arif: It is more formal in some circles, and I certainly noticed the difference. Americans, regardless of position or job, use more slang words, and they love to laugh. They seem to have some very strange games, like Bingo! (*laughs*), and American football is very different from any sport I grew up with. It seems the goal is to knock the other person to the ground. And baseball: I keep wondering when will something happen in this game! Americans love it. I hope I'm not being insulting to you, but it bores me.

Counselor: No, I am not insulted. In fact, we have a friend who visits us from England, and when we take him to an American baseball game he says, "Do they have to play nine innings, can't they just play five innings?" Also, it does seem that Americans can make a sport and a game out of just about anything. Arif, I'd like you to tell me something. When you told me about your husband, how did you feel?

Arif: I felt sad as I remembered him, but at the same time I felt good that you seemed genuinely interested.

Counselor: So there were a bit of good feelings or maybe even joy in talking about him. He certainly seemed like someone I would like to know.

Arif: I did feel good that you wanted to hear about him.

Counselor: And how did you feel when we were talking about sports?

Arif: I enjoyed telling you my response to American sports, and you seemed to enjoy hearing about it.

Counselor: Could you bring some pictures of you and him next time.

Arif: Sure, I'll do that.

Counselor: So you can have moments of enjoyment, and yes, I enjoyed hearing your point of view about American football and baseball. What about your friends? Do they enjoy hearing you discuss your memories of Ziyad?

Arif: At first they did, but after a while they didn't really want to hear about Ziyad anymore.

Counselor: When they turned you off in your efforts to talk about him, how did that affect you?

Arif: I felt rejected by them, and in fact I felt mad at them.

Counselor: I have a hunch you didn't tell them how you felt.

Arif: You're right. I guess I'm just not a very good assertive American!

Counselor: Do you say that as a matter of fact or as a self-criticism?

Arif: I suppose I *should* become an assertive American.

Counselor: Sort'a like you *should* move on?

Arif: I guess so.

Counselor: The more people say this sort of thing to you, the worse you feel.

Arif: Yes.

Counselor: I'd like to make an agreement with you for you to say two things to yourself: first, "It is perfectly OK for me to be emotionally where I am"; and second, "I don't have to be an assertive American." One statement is positive and one is negative. Maybe we will figure out a way to make both of them positive.

Arif: I might sound like an assertive American, but I would like to say this counseling is sure different than I thought it would be. (*Smiles broadly.*)

Counselor: Arif, sometimes it works out very different from what I expected also.

(*Both Arif and the counselor laugh!*)

Counselor: When you talked about your husband, I noticed that you said you felt glad that I asked about him, and now you actually laughed. So I have a very strange question: How do you feel about how you feel? In other words, how do you feel about being glad that someone wants to hear about your husband, and how do you feel about laughing as you just did?

Arif: I feel more at peace. And I feel hopeful.

Counselor: I feel hopeful for you also. If you can feel better just from a brief conversation like the one we've had, I believe you can feel better for longer periods of time. And by all means, do not try to *move on.* In fact, can we make an agreement to leave that phrase out of our conversation?

Arif: I think that's a wonderful idea.

Counselor: I'd also like to make an agreement. And this, of course, depends on whether you think it's a good idea. Each time we meet, could you share a little bit more about your husband and about your relationship? Such things as what you did that brought you joy. What do you miss most about him?

Arif: That sounds like a good idea, but why do you want to hear about it?

Counselor: Because it is important to you, and it also helps me understand you.

Arif: I believe this counseling can help me.

Counselor: There's not a doubt in my mind about this. The next time we meet, I would like to ask you not only about Ziyad and your relationship but also about whether you are currently able to take even a short amount of time now and then that serves as a vacation from the pain that you feel.

Arif: What do you mean?

Counselor: I'd like to help you extend the moments of joy that you have felt here today and probably feel at other times. I hope the counseling will enable you to keep your memories but make them less painful. In closing, Arif, I'd like to tell you a little story. I have a lot of stories that I tell to illustrate various aspects of the reality therapy that I use in counseling. Would you like to hear it?

Arif: Of course, go ahead.

Counselor: I read an article in the paper titled "There's No Such Thing as Closure." A man had a female acquaintance who had a very successful career. She was married to a man whom she idolized and with whom she had a beautiful relationship. One day the author of the article was conversing with her. She told him about her first marriage to a man who had died many years before. Keep in mind, her current marriage was successful with minimum pain and tension between her and her husband. She described her first marriage as a very happy one and that her husband had died 20 years earlier. As they ended their conversation, she began to walk away and with eyes full of tears she spoke of her first husband. She said, "I think of him almost every day." Arif, I think this story illustrates that the past is always with us, and if we fight it as many people urge us to do, we are fighting an impossible battle. It is only human to experience pain about our history, but it need not close off our present or our future. I hope you will be able to feel less pain while retaining your memories.

Arif: I have a lot to think about.

Counselor: How do you feel right now at this moment?

Arif: Better.

Counselor: Give me a percentage of how much better you feel.

Arif: About 20% better.

Counselor: Wow! That much! By the way, what's the best thing you thought of as a result of our conversations?

Arif: That I have hope and that if I take small steps they make a big difference.

Commentary: In this session, the counselor helped Arif conduct evaluations of both her own behavior and the impact of other people's behavior on her. In future sessions, the counselor will help her formulate strategies for discouraging her friends from lecturing her or even encouraging her to "move on." This will be a challenging effort because of her reluctance to adopt what she calls "assertive American behaviors."

The counselor also helped her to indirectly evaluate her current behaviors of talking about her deceased husband by asking her how she feels after discussing him. The counselor then indirectly helped her evaluate her current grieving by telling her a story illustrating that it is OK to retain some grief long after the death of someone close to her.

In the next session, the counselor will inquire, "What else do you want to tell me about yourself so that I can help you?" or "What do I need to know about you to be of assistance to you?" "Is there anything we should *not* discuss?" In the future, when the timing is right, the counselor will ask her, "What is the major challenge you face here and now?" Also, at some point he will ask her to formulate plans for dealing with her friends and associates who continue to push her to move on. The counselor might even offer specific suggestions about what to say and suggestions about lessening the pain of her grief.

You are invited to formulate three interventions (questions or statements) that you would use to assist Arif in evaluating her actions, her thinking, her feelings, and the realistic attainability of satisfying her wants.

1. _____
2. _____
3. _____

Also, how would you help the counselor evaluate his behavior? What questions would you like to ask him? What observations would you give him?

1. _____
2. _____
3. _____

Case Example: Posttraumatic Stress

Vivian, age 43, enlisted in the military at age 26 and is a 12-year veteran, a former sergeant who served in Iraq and Afghanistan. She was the only female in her unit. She has never been married, and for the past 5 years she has lived with her widowed aunt. Vivian rarely ventures out of the house except to go grocery shopping. She is startled by loud noises and suspicious of people she encounters in the neighborhood and at the grocery store. She states that she had sought psychological therapy from a very large agency, but she says they were only interested in her as an example of sickness. She decided to seek counseling from a reality therapist and was encouraged to do so by her aunt, whom she trusts more than anyone else. Her overall feelings are that of a dejected, lonely, and isolated person. She has been diagnosed with posttraumatic stress disorder (PTSD).

Counselor: Vivian, we've been through the preliminary and necessary ethical discussion about confidentiality, professional disclosure, and all the other issues involved in the counseling relationship. So now I would like to ask you a few questions. Feel free to answer them or to tell me that you don't want to discuss a topic. How do you feel about coming to this office and discussing your personal life?

Vivian: I'm feeling very tense and fearful. I was very hesitant about keeping this appointment.

Counselor: I'm glad you kept the appointment. It took courage on your part to come here today even though you felt fearful. What did you think might happen today?

Vivian: I don't really know. I don't go out very much. But my aunt said everything would be OK.

Counselor: I'd like to help you relax, and I think the best way I can do this is to assure you that absolutely no harm will come to you in any way in this office and during our counseling sessions. You are perfectly safe in this office.

Vivian: Well, that's good to hear. It helps me feel a little less tense.

Counselor: I often ask my clients to do something very simple and relaxing in the beginning of our sessions. They seem to benefit from it. Please sit with both feet flat on the floor with your eyes open and breathe in through your nose and out through your mouth, gently, as if you're blowing out the candles on a birthday cake. I'll join you in this, and we'll do it about five times. OK, let's start.

(*Counselor and client briefly practice deep breathing.*)

Counselor: How do you feel right now?

Vivian: A little less tense.

Counselor: Good. This kind of activity can be helpful. You might want to practice it at home.

Vivian: Sounds good.

Counselor: I have a question I'd like to ask you. Is there anything that you do *not* want to discuss? Or put another way, is there anything I should not ask you about?

Vivian: (*Long pause, a very serious and somber expression on her face.*) No, you can ask me about anything.

Counselor: You seemed a little reluctant to answer. So if there is anything that you do *not* want to discuss, please let me know if the topic is out of bounds. I realize you're a veteran. Would you be willing to tell me about your time in the military?

Vivian: I was in a unit that patrolled the highways, and I saw what happens when the trucks explode because of the IEDs [improvised explosive devices] used by the enemy. What I saw on a regular basis no human being should have to see. In fact, my truck was bombed. Two of my buddies were killed, and I was one who survived with minor injuries. I witnessed many dead bodies on the roadsides.

Counselor: Do these memories haunt you even to this present day?

Vivian: Yes. They're with me constantly. I think about these horrible experiences during the day, and they keep me awake at night.

Counselor: What about the people around you when you go grocery shopping?

Vivian: I'm very much aware of them and can't help thinking that they wish to harm me.

Counselor: Have any of them ever tried to do anything to you in the last 5 years?

Vivian: No.

Counselor: But the fear still lingers. Vivian, this must be very painful. But considering everything you've been through, it is very understandable.

Vivian: But I don't like this at all.

Counselor: Are you interested in getting rid of some of the fear?

Vivian: But I have no idea how to do it, or even if it's possible.

Counselor: I believe it is possible, and I believe that together we can develop some ways to lessen your fears. But at this point I'm only wondering if you are interested in achieving that kind of outcome.

Vivian: It would be nice.

Counselor: It sure would. I believe that working together we can develop some ways, some things you can do differently, that will help you relax and feel less tense when you do things such as go to the grocery store. Are you interested in finding a pathway that would be more enjoyable for you?

Vivian: I wish I could find such a pathway.

Counselor: This search for a pathway sounds like a pretty good goal. I don't think it will take long to formulate a few plans or to take a few steps on that pathway. You seem highly motivated to make some changes. As I said, you have already taken major and courageous steps by deciding to come here, and then by actually keeping the appointment.

Vivian: Nobody's ever said that sort of thing to me before.

Counselor: Well, to me it is evident, and I really believe it. Tell me some more about your military experience.

Vivian: I enlisted with the idea of serving my country, being patriotic. But it didn't turn out that way. I was the only woman in the unit, and it was not a pleasant time for me.

Counselor: With all these young soldiers around, I suspect they were frightened also.

Vivian: They were, but there's no excuse for how they acted.

Counselor: I think I know what happened. They not only attacked the enemy, but they attacked you.

Vivian: That's exactly right.

Counselor: At some point, if you want to discuss this event or events, I'll be willing to listen with the idea that I firmly believe even without knowing the details that you were not to blame in any way.

Vivian: But what if you're wrong?

Counselor: I'll be glad to admit it. But right now, I want to assure you that an attack on a woman is not her fault. Besides, if anyone blames you, does it help?

Vivian: No, it doesn't help, and I've never discussed it with anyone.

Counselor: So, if you *do* want to discuss it at any time, feel free to do so.

Vivian: Maybe, at a later time.

Counselor: OK. Now I would like to discuss with you a few less intense topics. Tell me about the last time you enjoyed yourself, had a really good belly laugh.

Vivian: (*Long pause and tears in her eyes.*) It's been a very long time. Maybe when I was in high school.

Counselor: I thought you would say it's been a long time. I think you're due for a little enjoyment.

Vivian: I can't find anything to be very happy about.

Counselor: But I didn't say "very happy." I said, I think you're due for a *little enjoyment.* I'd like to tell you a joke or two! Is that OK with you?

Vivian: (*Eyes wide open with a curious look on her face.*) I don't see what this has to do with counseling.

Counselor: It will become obvious in a few minutes. Do you know what the greatest achievement of the early Romans was?

Vivian: No, I haven't a clue.

Counselor: Learning to speak Latin!

Vivian: (*Smiles.*)

Counselor: Do you know what their motto was?

Vivian: I don't have a clue about that either.

Counselor: Volvo, Video, Velcro! It means "I arrived by car, I watched a film, I stuck around."

Vivian: (*Smiles broadly.*) That's funny.

Counselor: I'd like to know how you felt for an instant after you heard these corny jokes.

Vivian: I felt a little lighter.

Counselor: So, the change in your feelings even for an instant proves to me and, more important, I hope it proves to you that you *can* feel better.

Vivian: So there is a reason for telling me a joke.

Counselor: I have a lot more jokes, but I don't want to overdo it just now. And you are right that there is a purpose. My belief is that you will be able to replace the tension and fear with something better, such as enjoyment and maybe even fun.

Vivian: I would like that very much.

Counselor: And as I said, you are highly motivated. I see you as a courageous person for coming here today, highly motivated, and able to change your feelings. These are three qualities, strong qualities, that will work to your advantage. What do you think about that?

Vivian: I haven't thought of myself as having strong qualities.

Counselor: And that's why you came here. My job is to help you look at things differently, to look at yourself differently, to think differently, and to do some things differently. Now I would like to ask you, when was the last time you took a brisk, enjoyable walk that did not involve going to the grocery store?

Vivian: I don't remember. Certainly not since I've been out of the military, and definitely not while I was in the military.

Counselor: One of the things that I do in my counseling is help clients make plans, specific plans, that lead to better feelings. Would you be willing to make a plan, one that would be helpful?

Vivian: It depends what it is.

Counselor: OK. Before we get to the plan, I have a very important question. Perhaps this is the most important question I will ask you today. Are you ready?

Vivian: I'm ready.

Counselor: The question is this. If you don't do anything differently, will anything change?

Vivian: (*Long thoughtful pause and distant facial expression.*) I guess not.

Counselor: And the second question might be a little painful to answer. Is the way you're living now, your current lifestyle, helping you as much as you would like it to help you?

Vivian: It's not helping me at all.

Counselor: So are you willing to make a few changes? Not terribly dramatic changes. But are you willing to alter a few choices that you're making?

Vivian: That is the scariest question that you've asked me.

Counselor: I realize that. And I would not think it would be helpful for you to do anything to increase your fears.

Vivian: So what did you have in mind?

Counselor: What do you think about the value of taking a walk?

Vivian: I don't know. I haven't done any walking except to go to the grocery store.

Counselor: I am aware of that fact. Is your neighborhood safe?

Vivian: For me, no neighborhood is safe.

Counselor: What I mean is, is it a high crime area?

Vivian: No, there are no crimes and also there is a park nearby.

Counselor: Could we work out a plan, a helpful plan, for walking in the park?

Vivian: I could do that.

Counselor: It would be very different, wouldn't it? And it would be a big step toward replacing some of the sadness and unhappiness that you feel. I would like to suggest that when you walk you relax your mind and just be aware of your feet on the ground, your legs moving, your arms swinging.

Vivian: What's the value in that?

Counselor: It helps you live in the present moment rather than ruminating about the past and the pain. Also, could you be aware of the trees, the plants, and what you see around you?

Vivian: But what if there's somebody behind the trees?

Counselor: OK, I understand. Being aware of the trees is not a good idea. What about just noticing the grass, the small plants?

Vivian: I can do that.

Counselor: Oh, another thought about walking. When you notice someone walking toward you, could you just glance at their face and nod to them?

Vivian: That would be different because I often think that they might attack me.

Counselor: I understand you might have those thoughts. But would you be willing to nod to them anyway? In fact, maybe not nod to everybody. How about two or three people?

Vivian: That would be very difficult.

Counselor: What was the question I asked you before? I said it was a very important thought.

Vivian: You asked whether anything would change if I don't change something in my life.

Counselor: That's the question. You are not a weak person. You've shown that to me and to many other people. Are you willing to take this step today? A walk of about 10 minutes?

Vivian: That's more doable.

Counselor: I'd like you to think about one more thing before we stop. I have here a blank piece of notepaper. Would you like to leave a little bit of your tension here today?

Vivian: I would like to do that, but how?

Counselor: Would you tear off the amount of tension that you'd like to leave here. Please be realistic.

Vivian: How about 10%?

Counselor: That sounds good to me.

Vivian: (*Tears off one tenth of the paper and gives it to the counselor.*)

Counselor: Vivian, I'm going to keep this 10% in your folder, and next time you can either take it back or else I'll throw it away.

Vivian: I won't want it back. But how does it help?

Counselor: It has an important purpose. It symbolizes something. What do you think it represents?

Vivian: From what we've said, and from what you've said, and even from what you've assumed, it seems to imply that I am able to lessen my pain.

Counselor: There's not a shadow of a doubt in my mind that over time your life can improve immensely. Oh, by the way, I almost forgot something. After your walk, could you call my office and leave a message on my voice mail telling me how the walk went. You don't even need to leave your name. If I'm here, I'll answer the call, but if I'm not here, just leave a 10 second message. In fact, right before you call, do your breathing exercise.

Vivian: You're very persistent.

Counselor: You're absolutely right. And you know who else is determined? You are. Today is Monday. I'd like to see you again on Thursday.

Vivian: That sounds good. I'll be here. What do you think about me taking a walk every day?

Counselor: That sounds good, but don't overdo it.

Commentary: The counselor began by teaching Vivian a behavior that she can control, one that she is in charge of completely. The mindful breathing activity contains several lessons. She has more control over her life than she believes. This exercise might seem insignificant. Nevertheless, the implicit lesson that Vivian learns is that there are more effective behaviors available to her. She learns in an indirect way that there is hope for her, that she can have a better life. Learning that even seemingly insignificant choices are available to her can be a source of confidence and optimism. Sometimes, a counselor will state that this seems insignificant. And indeed it might be insignificant in the life of a counselor or another self-actualizing person. But a client feeling powerless and hopeless learns from this "triviality" that this small step can be a beginning. Wehrenberg (2008) describes the technique of diaphragmatic (deep) breathing as one of the 10 best-ever anxiety management techniques. She states, "Breathing changes physiology immediately. When the body is tense breathing is affected even before panic starts" (p. 51). She adds that such breathing "slows sympathetic arousal and stimulates activity of your parasympathetic nervous system—the part of your nervous system that calms down physical arousal. If you keep it up your panic symptoms will subside" (p. 51).

Vivian does not seem to be experiencing panic at the present moment, but she clearly feels some degree of anxiety. She can transfer the breathing exercise to times when she experiences panic attacks. The counselor could also teach her to combine deep breathing with progressive deep muscle relaxation.

Next, the counselor attempts to empower her by asking if there is any topic that is out of bounds for discussion. Clients often respond in one of three ways: nothing is out of bounds; they will identify a topic when it arises; they state a particular topic that is undesirable for discussion. Sometimes an adolescent will suggest drugs, parents, or some other specific topics to be avoided. The reason for asking is that clients can feel safe and less defensive and even recognize that they have the right and the ability to make choices.

The inquiry about Vivian not making any changes is the key self-evaluation intervention in the session. The counselor implies that Vivian's behaviors, her actions, are within her control. The significance of these counselor inquiries cannot be overestimated. They take on special efficacy with clients who feel they are victimized by their experience, their environment, or their past history. This brief segment of what would be a much longer counseling session demonstrates to Vivian that she will have a positive and uplifting counseling experience. She stated that she believed she was simply an example of a sick person in her other relationships with professional people. The counselor does not reinforce this belief because of the inappropriateness of criticizing other professional therapists or counselors.

The counselor attempts to demonstrate genuine empathy and to be seen by the client as meriting her trust by understanding and appreciating the military culture. The American Counseling Association's Veterans Interests Network (VIN) emphasizes that effective counseling with members of the U.S. military requires cultural competence or appreciation and knowledge of life in the military (Bray, 2014; Myers, 2016). Similarly, the American Psychological Association calls for an appreciation of not only the problems of military personnel but also their strengths such as never quitting, decisive leadership, and many others ("Understanding Military Culture," 2016).

In the following segment, the counselor explains the rationale for what appears to Vivian to be an incomprehensible approach to counseling.

In the follow-up session, the following dialogue occurs.

Counselor: Vivian, how are you today?

Vivian: A little better. I did take a walk and nodded to a few people. However, I felt very anxious when I walked near the woods.

Counselor: How high was your anxiety level on a scale of 1 to 10, with 10 being the highest?

Vivian: It was about a 7.

Counselor: And how does that compare with your anxiety level when you were in the armed vehicle in Iraq?

Vivian: Most of the time it was about a 9 or a 10.

Counselor: So it was at a slightly less intense level but enough to be intensely painful?

Vivian: That's right.

Counselor: But you were able to muster up enough courage and determination to do what you feared. That was an admirable decision. And I must say I'm proud of you.

Vivian: Doing what I did doesn't really seem like a big deal!

Counselor: When you say that, I think you're talking from your head, not your gut. Your gut tells you it really was a big deal. Am I right or wrong?

Vivian: Never thought of it that way, but you're right. I have a question for you. As I said last time, this experience is very different. Could you explain to me what we're trying to do here?

Counselor: You're definitely a fast learner! Many times clients don't ask this kind of question as quickly as you have. But let me explain.

Reality therapy is a mental *health* system, not a mental disorder system. By disorder system I mean any system or any way of thinking or feeling that is upsetting to a person. As a reality therapist, I approach people in a way that helps them get around their problems rather than conquer them. For example, in counseling people who are depressed, I help them leave their depression behind or find a pathway around it rather than approaching it head on and conquering it. This is a different concept for many people. In your case, I will be glad to listen and try to understand the frustration and pain that you have been feeling. I hope I have shown that willingness already. At the same time, it is important to bring to the surface choices that help you feel in control of your life. In reality therapy, we observe what healthy people do who are able to deal with obstacles to a satisfying life. And then, when someone says their life is not satisfying to them, we help them do what the people in the first group do. In your case, you are unhappy about what might happen when you walk near the woods. Consequently, I will attempt to help you improve and get around those unhappy feelings while acknowledging the healthy courage that you demonstrated in fulfilling a plan that involved walking around your fear rather than "conquering" it. Put another way, we look at how people who are doing well spend their time, and we help our clients make similar choices. People who feel pretty good often take walks. It is my belief that after you take a few walks your feelings will follow along and catch up with you.

This is similar to someone learning to play a sport or drive a car. We look at skillful athletes and what we call good drivers. We then imitate what they do. It doesn't make sense to imitate a failed athlete or a reckless driver. By analogy, the same can be argued about mental health. I call myself a mental health counselor not a mental disturbance counselor.

Vivian: I think I see what you mean. But I would like to have more explanation of this.

Counselor: I will be glad to go into more detail as we go forward. In the meantime, what's the best idea that you've gotten so far?

Vivian: That I can improve even though at times I will look back to the war.

Commentary: Direct teaching and explanation of reality therapy enhance the effectiveness of mental health counseling. In this vignette, the counselor presented a partial explanation of reality therapy in a seamless manner in answer to Vivian's inquiry. My suggestion to practitioners is keep it simple (KIS) and keep it brief (KIB).

Describe three questions or reflections you would provide for Vivian that you can derive from the WDEP system of reality therapy.

1. _____
2. _____
3. _____

In addition, what parts of reality therapy would you wish to explain to Vivian? Perhaps one would be the significance of her developing the skill of self-evaluation.

1. _____
2. _____
3. _____

For a person with PTSD, the distinction between past and present behavior can become blurred. There is calendar time and mental or psychological time.

Case Example: Integrated Use of Self-Evaluation

This case contains examples of several types of self-evaluation. Try to identify them and list them as you read the case. They are explained more fully in the commentary following the dialogue.

Bella is a 34-year-old women who lives in a one-room apartment in a poverty stricken neighborhood. She uses food stamps and is on public assistance. She has four children ages 12, 8, 6, and 5. Child Protective Services has removed the children from the home. Her history includes abuse and neglect of her children, self-injury (cutting herself), and mental health diagnoses such as bipolar, schizophrenic, and sociopathic. Other agencies have terminated her and as a last resort have sent her to a counselor who is described as "practicing reality therapy." The most recent agency stated that they doubted she would even keep the first appointment. The race and ethnic group of Bella is not indicated. She could be of any ethnic group and a member of any religious group.

Counselor: Bella, I'm glad you came today. I've read the summary of your situation, and I see you've been to quite a number of agencies.

Bella: Yeah, and they didn't do s_____ for me.

Counselor: Yet you kept this appointment, and I think that shows determination on your part to get the help you need. You know a lot of people would have given up long before this.

Bella: Yeah, well, what can you do for me?

Counselor: Let's put it this way. What did the other agencies say they could do for you?

Bella: They couldn't do nothing for me.

Counselor: But what did they *say* they could do for you?

Bella: They said I have every diagnosis they know of and my "rehabilitation" was up to me.

Counselor: And you are unhappy about that sort of thing?

Bella: Wouldn't you be?

Counselor: Yes, I'd be very upset by that attitude. But you have not given up. I have a question, Bella. How realistic is it for you to make improvements in your life?

Bella: I'd be fine if they just gave me my kids back and more money.

Counselor: I would like to help you to work toward that goal. But I would need something from you first. Would you be willing to come here and talk two times a week for 6 months?

Bella: You mean you want me to come here?

Counselor: Absolutely. My job is to work with people who have a rough way to go in their lives. And you certainly fit that category. You'll notice that I do not blame you for anything.

Bella: Well, the judge did. The police did. The hospital did. My neighbors did. The social worker did. Even my mother preaches at me.

Counselor: Has any of that kind of conversation helped you travel the road any better?

Bella: Hell no.

Counselor: Because of your answer, I will not blame you. I don't think blaming you would help much. In fact, you just told me that when other people put you down it didn't work for you. So, suppose I make statements that put you down for what we all know you've done or at least what you've been accused of: hitting your kids too hard, drinking, cutting yourself. I don't see how more of this is going to get us anywhere. I don't intend to soft-pedal anything. But I don't see any point in talking about what you have already talked about a thousand times. I suggest we move on from that. Would that be satisfactory to you?

Bella: That sure would be different.

Counselor: I believe it would be different. You didn't come here because you wanted me to sing the same old songs to you. I'd like to help you learn to sing some different songs for yourself.

Bella: That sounds great. But what can you do for me?

Counselor: I can help you take charge of the way you're living and make some other choices. But I would need to see you two times a week for 6 months. You must know that I can't solve all your problems. But I can help you improve and lessen the pain that you've felt. What if you could feel 50% better than you feel now? Would that make our conversations valuable to you, or would it be a waste of time?

Bella: If you can't help me 100%, this would be bull just like the other people who said they could help me.

Counselor: I am 100% sure that I can help you if you will come two times a week for 6 months. And I believe that if your pain becomes half what it is now, that will be a big step.

Bella: I guess you're right.

Counselor: Two times a week. Six months. Your choice. If you say no, I'm not the one giving up. Just the opposite. I believe that in 6 months, and even before that time, your life will change for the better.

Bella: All right, all right. I'll try to be here.

Counselor: I know you'll try. But do you believe that anything less than a firm commitment is going to help you?

Bella: OK, OK. I'll come. You better solve my problems, or I'm going to be really mad.

Counselor: At this time, all you have to do is show up. And you said you would do that.

Commentary: In this dialogue, the counselor and the client agreed to structure the relationship as illustrated in Figure 3 under "Environment, Build Relationships, A." The counselor does not overburden the client by putting responsibility on her. She feels victimized, and informing her about the need to make more effective choices might be interpreted as blaming her with the result of increased feelings of victimization and powerlessness. The immediate result would be a strain in the relationship or even a severed relationship with the further result that she would not return. However, the counselor does help her conduct several evaluations. Two evaluations are not focused on her wants or behaviors but on her external world. The counselor helps her evaluate whether the diagnoses are helpful and whether the conversations and preaching have been helpful. Asking her to evaluate the world around her at first appears to be outside the acceptable application of reality therapy. Because choice theory/reality therapy (CT/RT) is an internal control system, asking her to evaluate what appears to be the behavior of other people might seem inappropriate. Yet the counselor is accepting her as she is, not as the counselor thinks she should be. She sees herself as being controlled by the people and systems around her. So the counselor helps her make explicit evaluations. These evaluations precede her more detailed self-evaluations of her own behaviors. The counselor will say to her, "You've evaluated the helpfulness of what other people have said to you. Now I'd like to ask you to decide whether your own choices are helping or hurting you." Consequently, what begins as a process of her external evaluations will gradually evolve into a process of her internal self-evaluations.

The counselor assists Bella in bridging the gap between her external evaluations and her subsequent self-evaluations of her choices by asking her to conduct two rather mild self-evaluations: whether it is realistic to make improvements and whether 50% will help her or is a waste of time. Finally, the counselor takes a risk by asking her to make a judgment on her level of commitment. However, this last discussion of her level of commitment might be better placed in a subsequent counseling session.

Subsequent Sessions

The treatment plan formulated by Bella and the counselor aims at helping Bella satisfy her need for belonging by learning to communicate differently than she has in the past. She will talk to people in a more courteous manner and be conscious of speaking in a lower tone of voice rather than an elevated, angry tone. She will also adopt a more civil conversation style and keep an open mind when the social worker visits her every 2 weeks. For instance, she will ask the social worker questions about how to perform her housekeeping chores. She will call the proper authorities and explain to them that she now has a relationship with a counselor and sees the person two times per week and that she wishes to earn the right to regain custody of her children. This behavior aims at helping her satisfy her need for inner control or power. To satisfy her need for freedom more effectively, Bella will also write down three choices each day, such as, "I chose to go grocery shopping today." "I chose to become irritable with the cashier." "I chose to resist the urge to shoplift." When feeling the urge to cut herself, she will search the television programs until she finds a program or even a commercial that is humorous and thereby satisfies her need for fun. The purpose of this choice is to help her replace the urge to cut herself by substituting a positive behavior.

With the details changed, the description of this case is based on one that a counselor related to me. At the end of the 6-month period, the client was able to spend weekends with her children although she still needed time away from them. Her self-mutilation did not totally disappear, but it became significantly less frequent and less dangerous. The client missed only a very few counseling appointments. Toward the end of the 6-month period, the counselor asked her about her faithfulness in attending the sessions. She simply related that she liked talking to the counselor and felt better about herself and the direction of her life.

Case Example:
Self-Evaluation of Stated Values Versus Behavior

A type of self-evaluation used with clients who demonstrate at least a moderate level of commitment to change emerges when their behaviors demonstrate incongruence with their stated values. When clients assert that they hold certain values, the counselor should believe them. At the same time, the counselor needs to be vigilant enough to observe discrepancies between stated values and chosen behaviors. The following case illustrates the self-evaluation of this delicate issue.

Sean is 56 years old, and his spouse is deceased. He referred himself for counseling and has described in detail that his two grown children are afflicted with many problems. His son, Patrick, age 31, has lost his business because of his gambling problem. In describing

Patrick's problem, Sean makes this significant statement: "I want to help him." An astute reality therapist listens carefully for statements that indicate the client's sense of internal control and a desire to do something different, and in this case the counselor makes special note of Sean's statement. (Please note how he utilizes this statement in subsequent counseling.) Sean further describes how Patrick's three daughters are performing poorly in school and are behavioral problems. Sean believes that because of their youthfulness (ages 11, 9, and 7) they can be, as he says, "turned around." Sean's daughter, Kathleen, age 29, has never married but has a daughter (11 years old) fathered by one of her many live-in boyfriends. Kathleen struggles successfully to maintain both a full-time and a part-time job; with the help of her father, she is able to send her daughter to a private school that stresses discipline and achievement. Her daughter appears to be a conscientious overachiever but is showing a consistent rebellious attitude toward her mother. Kathleen calls her father every day and complains about her daughter's behavior. She says that her daughter talks back, won't listen to good advice, has given up on her "good" friends, and is now starting to associate with troublemakers. The daughter storms out of the house and meets up with her new friends at the nearby mall and has harassed several merchants.

The session with Sean follows.

Counselor: Sean, you've described in detail your family situation. Let's talk about how you would like your adult children to be different.

Sean: The way I was raised, and I believe it's important, is for parents to be responsible. I think Patrick should stop his gambling because it is getting out of control. He plays poker with his buddies on the weekends and hangs out way too much at the casino. I don't know how he picked up that disgusting habit, but it's getting him in trouble. His wife is about ready to take over his paycheck and hide the money from him. It's no wonder his kids can't stand him. I came here because I want to help him.

Counselor: Let me stop you for just a second Sean. How do you know he hangs out at the casino?

Sean: I've seen him there.

Counselor: OK, I understand. Please continue.

Sean: I want to tell you more about my daughter too. As you can tell, these kids are a disappointment to me. She's a good worker and holds two jobs, but her apartment has had a revolving door on it, one guy after another. They come and live for a while, and then they're gone. They pop in on weekends and stay for a few days.

161

Counselor: Do you suspect any abuse between them and your granddaughter?

Sean: No, she introduces me to her current boyfriends. She usually keeps one for a few months, and then they drop each other and she moves on. But I've never thought any of them had such tendencies. If I believed that, I'd call the police immediately.

Counselor: That sounds like a wise and necessary choice. I'd like to talk to her sometime, but we can review that possibility later. Meanwhile, I'd like to help you explore some of your thoughts about how to handle these situations and other ideas. When you called, I got the idea you wanted to get rid of some frustration about all of these things. You even mentioned that you felt you weren't a good father to your children.

Sean: Yes, that's the reason I wanted to talk to you, but I need to explain the situation.

Counselor: Yes, I agree with that. So we have two major topics here with a lot of overlap between them. On one hand we need to talk about your own internal attitudes, feelings, thoughts, and actions. On the other hand, we can also talk about how to handle your son and daughter.

Sean: That makes a lot of sense to me. If I could figure out a better way to deal with this situation, I would feel some relief from the stress that has overtaken me.

Counselor: Which of these general topics would be easier to work on?

Sean: It's certainly easier to talk about the kids than it is to talk about myself.

Counselor: I thought you might say that. But I would like to begin by asking you a few questions about your own approach to these troubles. Is that OK?

Sean: Of course, that's why I came—to solve these problems and to give me peace of mind.

Counselor: OK, you said a lot there. I think these two subsets are connected: solving problems and achieving peace of mind. Let's talk about achieving peace of mind first, and I have an initial question for you, a very important one. Is there anything I should *not* ask you about?

Sean: No, you can ask me anything.

Counselor: My first question is about trying to *get* the kids to change. You certainly worked hard to bring them around. As a matter of fact, you've taught your kids to work hard. Your son had his own business in his 20s, and your daughter works two jobs. Many people say this kind of ambition is in short supply, especially when they're out of work. Your children might be doing things that you don't like and that are not going to help them very much, but they seem to have energy and determination.

Sean: I never thought of it quite like that, but that is true. Some of my friends complain about their kids who are in their 20s and even beyond. They say they're lazy. They live at home, don't help with bills, and some don't even look for a job.

Counselor: I've not heard you even hint that your kids are lazy. In fact, they seem to have incorporated your work ethic. I think you can be proud of that fact.

Sean: Now that you mention it, I think you're right. Sometimes I only look at their faults and don't give them credit.

Counselor: That may be part of addressing the problems and giving you peace of mind. Let's talk about making plans to look for their strengths and about telling them how you see their positive qualities.

Sean: You know, I do value hard work and conscientious parenting. But I've not mentioned it to them in so many words.

Counselor: So there is quite a discrepancy here between what you think is important, the value you put on work and parenting, and what you say to your children.

Sean: Yes, there is. I value one thing and say another.

Counselor: What do you mean another? I think I know what you mean, but I'd like to hear you say it out loud.

Sean: I value work and parenting, but then when I talk to them, I limit the conversation to lectures and criticizing.

Counselor: Now I have another very important question. Is this gap between what you treasure most in your life and how you deal with your kids helping or hindering your relationship with them? Keep in mind I'm not asking about what you do but rather about the gap between what you value and how you talk and deal with them. And if I can be blunt, it sounds like more than a gap. It sounds like a chasm.

Sean: You're right, it is more than a little crevice. It is a chasm.

Counselor: I believe the key question for now is whether this discrepancy that you've discovered is helping or hurting you as well as helping or hurting your kids?

Sean: It's definitely not helping.

Counselor: And most important, what impact does this gap have on your relationship with them?

Sean: It's really screwed things up.

Counselor: So let's talk about how to bridge this chasm or close it. Also, I suggest that we think of it as a gap, not as a huge chasm or gulf. And I suggest thinking of it as temporary. One thing is certain. You have judged that there is a discrepancy between your values and your actions.

Sean: You got that right.

Counselor: So let's talk about plans. Let's talk about actions, choices that you can make in the very near future so that your external behaviors and your internal values are more congruent.

Commentary: Early in this session, the counselor observed in a tentative fashion a possible discrepancy between Sean's values and actions. Sean mentioned that he disapproves of his son's gambling, but Sean is aware of the gambling because he himself has visited the casino. The counselor has not yet explored whether Sean's visits are occasional or whether he gambles as consistently as his son.

The next segment contains a description of additional interventions. The counselor feels that another serious element would require consideration if Sean is a habitual gambler. However, the counselor also realizes that Sean might not be ready to face the gravity of the inconsistency between his values and his external behavior. As the session develops, Sean discloses a less intense and more manageable breach between his value of parenting with hard work on one hand and his manner of communication on the other. Such counseling represents a very useful attitude and skill on the part of the counselor that can be stated as follows:

> *Help clients first achieve small successes before*
> *leading them to confront more difficult or*
> *more self-threatening issues.*
>
> • • •

This principle is not an absolute rule. Sometimes it is quite appropriate to discuss harmful, self-destructive, and exploitive behaviors early in the counseling process. Knowing when to apply a principle and when to proceed more abruptly cannot be taught with absolute certainty. Rather, counselors and therapists learn this with experience, and more specifically with experience that is self-evaluated. You might ask, "Is there any principle that can serve to help my self-evaluation?" My answer is yes. The principle is: Will the direction the counseling takes and the order in which I deal with the presenting issues help or hurt the counseling relationship and will it help or impede the client's progress?

The session continues.

Counselor: Sean, you mentioned that I could ask you about any issue. Is that still true?

Sean: Yes it is.

Counselor: You said that you believe in living a reasonably frugal lifestyle and that you didn't appreciate the fact that your son spent so much time in the casino and that you've seen him there. If you say he spends too much time there, how do you know that the time spent is too much?

Sean: I thought you might bring this up. I know it because I pass by the casino on the way home from work and often stop there to play the slots for a few minutes.

Counselor: How often do you stop by the casino?

Sean: I'd say about three days a week.

Counselor: Sean, I have a very serious question, and I'd like you to think about it for a moment. Does that action of stopping at the casino *fit* or *not fit* with your value about spending too much time gambling.

Sean: (*Pauses.*) I do talk about the dangers of gambling and the need to be temperate regarding the use of money. But to tell you the truth, I don't always live according to that principle.

Counselor: And, in your judgment, is three days a week in line with that principle or is it outside that principle?

Sean: It's definitely not in line with what I think is important.

Counselor: You have a real strength here Sean. You are willing to admit not only to yourself but you are willing to say out loud that your actions don't coincide with your values. Do you want to make any changes?

Sean: If I'm to live according to the value that I preach to my son, I suppose I need to make a change in what I do.

Counselor: You said "I suppose." Is that commitment firm enough to get the job done?

Sean: No, I really need to be stronger in my willingness to make a change. I read your book and you talked about levels of commitment. I know what you're going to say. You're going to ask me if I'm willing to raise my level of commitment from the equivalent of "I'll try" to a more determined "I will."

Counselor: It's evident that you're learning the process of reality therapy. I believe that will also help you.

Sean: You're right about that. And so I need to repeat my commitment out loud. I even need to write down that I have an unbending commitment to align what I say and do with my value about gambling.

Counselor: When your son realizes that you have made a change, what impact will that have on him? I know we can't say for sure, but what do you think? Harmful or helpful impact on him?

Sean: Well, it can't hurt.

Commentary: When counselors judge that it is appropriate to utilize the mirror technique, they hold a metaphorical mirror before clients and ask them to make a judgment, a self-evaluation. Keep in mind that self-evaluation does not imply a judgment made on one's self. It is not a judgment made on the essential good or evil of a human being. Rather, it is the facilitation of clients' judgments about aspects of their control system or choice system that they have control over in the sense that they can change them.

In this dialogue, the counselor assisted Sean in evaluating whether his behavior matched his values. Fortunately, Sean had the courage to make the judgment that they are incongruent and he is willing to examine the appropriateness of this incongruence. Moreover, he is willing to make a change in his actions. Because of the trusting relationship between Sean and his counselor, Sean is also willing to evaluate the strength of his commitment.

At this point you might say that's all well and good, but what if the client is unwilling to admit to the incongruence and unwilling to make a firm commitment? Even more, what if a client is resistant to all efforts of the counselor to bring about any honest and effective self-evaluation? In other words, what if the client is totally, completely, entirely, unreservedly, and unrestrictedly adverse and resistant to any form of self-evaluation?

I'll answer this question with a multiple-choice question: How should you handle a client described in the previous paragraph?

a. Deepen the therapeutic alliance and trusting environment
b. Continue to see the client while making small talk
c. Refer the client to a counselor you don't like and can't get along with
d. Engage in the psychoanalytic technique of dream analysis and free association
e. Administer the Minnesota Multiphasic Personality Inventory (MMPI)
f. Use your creativity
g. Consult with a colleague or supervisor
h. Set the problem aside and discuss a more neutral topic for a while
i. Utilize another form of self-evaluation
j. Help the client evaluate other people's behavior

k. Look for exceptions to the problem
l. Give up
m. Resort to arguing with the client
n. Return to a discussion of the W of the WDEP system of reality therapy

The correct answers are a, b, f, g, h, i, j, k, and n. At various times, one or another intervention can be helpful in addressing the global resistance of a client.

The dialogues that follow illustrate several methods for utilizing reality therapy with Sean if he is an overall resistant client. In the next counselor–client interaction, we replay the dialogue with Sean, but this time he is less engaging and less willing to conduct his own evaluation. As you read the dialogue, see if you can identify the correct answers the counselor implemented.

Counselor: Sean, you mentioned that I could ask you about any issue. Is that still true?

Sean: Yes it is.

Counselor: You said that you believe in living a reasonably frugal lifestyle and that you didn't appreciate the fact that your son spent so much time in the casino and that you've seen him there. If you say he spends too much time there, how do you know that the time spent is too much?

Sean: He spends hours in the casino every day. I see him there.

Counselor: And so you must be spending a lot of time there too. How much time did you spend there last week?

Sean: That's not the point. That's my business.

Counselor: I know. I understand that, but tell me how many hours on average you spend there every day.

Sean: Not that it makes any difference but about 2 hours.

Counselor: Two hours. That much!

Sean: So what. I'm 30 years older than my son, and besides I don't lose very much money.

Counselor: Do you ever beat the house?

Sean: Not very often.

Counselor: Tell me more.

Sean: I didn't come here to talk about me. I came to figure out a way to help my son.

Counselor: That's what I thought. You wanted to help him. In fact, on the phone before you came to the office you said, "I want to help him." Now if we omit the word "to," there are four words left:

167

"I," "want," "help," "him." Only one of the four words indicates someone other than you. Do you still stand by that statement?

Sean: Of course I do. That's why I'm here. (*Appears slightly agitated; perhaps he sees the possible direction the counseling might take.*)

Counselor: Sean, you seem to be a little uncomfortable with what I said about the four words and about whether you still stand by them.

Sean: No, I'm not uncomfortable, but I think you want to focus on me instead of my son.

Counselor: I don't really think we should focus on you except as a means, a way, a method, for helping your son. This situation is similar to one I heard about a while back. A man had a rather narrow driveway. Next to the driveway was a telephone pole. Every couple of months he would scrape the fender of his car on the pole. He would curse, kick the car, slam the car door, and complain to his wife about the telephone pole. He even called the telephone company and blamed them for putting the pole too close to his driveway. It seems to me he had several choices. He could chop down the pole, continue to scrape it, widen the driveway opposite the pole, or examine his driving when he pulled in and out of the driveway. Let's say that his relationship to the telephone pole was not what it could be. What do you think was the easiest and probably the most effective choice for him?

Sean: I see what you're getting at. The simplest thing for him to do is to examine his driving skill.

Counselor: You're exactly right. And so I would like to help you look at yourself and examine whether there is something you could do more effectively. At no point am I blaming you or putting you down. I'm sure at your work there are people who have made suggestions about how to make improvements to increase the efficiency of the system. Also, I have another question for you. If we spent 90% of our time talking about Patrick and his unacceptable and harmful choices, would all of our talk accomplish anything? Would our discussions make any difference to your son? After all, he's not here?

Sean: I guess not.

Counselor: So let's figure out a way for you to look at how you can influence him more effectively. First, I'd like to ask you to take a look at yourself, your values, and your actions with a view to how they influence your son. I see a direct connection, and I firmly believe that even though you're not at fault there still are some choices that would improve the situation.

Sean: I see your point. But I'm not thrilled with the necessity for *me* to make changes.

Counselor: I understand that. But you came here for help in coping with your son's behavior. I can only ask you to let me do my job. And the way I see my job is to help you look at what you're doing with the idea of helping you figure out a better way to deal with your son. I believe that if you make a change in your own actions you will help him. Now, I want to ask you if you did make a change or two what would you lose?

Sean: I guess if I come here I ought to trust that you know what you're doing. What I would lose if I made a change? Well, I could make things worse.

Counselor: Change does involve some risk. But if the status quo remains, what are you risking?

Sean: I see what you mean. The risk is probably less if I do make a few changes.

Commentary: In this dialogue, the counselor utilized several interventions. Discuss how the counselor used these interventions:

a. Deepen the therapeutic alliance and trusting environment
f. Use your creativity
i. Utilize another form of self-evaluation
n. Return to a discussion of the W of the WDEP system, the client's wants

When a client expresses a generalized or total resistance to self-evaluate or to implement plans, the reality therapist familiar with the WDEP system can return to a discussion of the clients' goals, desires, or wants. When Sean stated that he did not come to discuss his life or his behavior, the counselor reminded him that prior to the first session and repeated in this session Sean stated, "I want to help him" (that is, his son Patrick). The counselor asked Sean if there is anything they should not discuss. The client stated that he was open to any discussion.

Resistance sometimes occurs in sessions similar to the one described here when the counselor does not clarify in his or her own mind the answer to the question, "Who is my client?" If the session evolves from a consultation about a third person to a counseling session for the consultee, the counselor should clarify the relationship. In this case, the counselor did not discuss this informed consent issue thoroughly enough. This error on the part of the counselor illustrates that informed consent is an ongoing issue, not one dealt with at the beginning of the relationship and then set aside. The effective user of reality therapy embraces professional ethics as does any counselor. The mistake made by this counselor is perfectly understandable and can be readily and graciously repaired.

The session continues.

> *Counselor:* Sean, you said you want to help your son, Patrick, and in fact you have tried. Tell me, in your opinion, if what you've done so far has helped the situation improve at least as much as you want it to improve.
>
> *Sean:* No, I don't see any change in Patrick's choices.
>
> *Counselor:* If you continue to do what you're doing, is anything going to change?

Commentary: Asking the question "If you continue to do what you're doing, is anything going to change?" is a very effective intervention for most relationship problems, especially those in which one person blames the other person for the deteriorating relationship. Think of ways you can use this intervention with students who complain about their classes, their teachers, their parents, their families, their friends, and anyone else in their environment. Write three ways to paraphrase this question, such as "What are the realistic odds that you can force that other person to change?"

1. _____
2. _____
3. _____

Once again, I want to remind you that the full impact of reality therapy interventions cannot be fully appreciated by reading the dialogues because they lack the full force of the visual and the auditory communication. The question "If you continue to do what you're doing, is anything going to change?" represents a major intervention. Keep in mind the timing, the tone of voice used, and the clear communication of empathy in an environment that facilitates honest and authentic responses from clients. The reality therapy counselor frequently provides feedback about clients' heartfelt answers and helps clients identify their feeling level about the issue. Clients not only name it to tame it, they can also name it to claim it, especially when it is a helpful, positive feeling.

The session continues.

Sean: I guess nothing is going to change with Patrick if I keep doing what I'm doing. But I don't see why I have to change when he has the problem.

Counselor: You don't have to change. Changing what you do is only one possibility, only one choice. You could continue to do what you're doing, or you could do nothing. You could completely withdraw from the situation.

Sean: I don't want to withdraw.

Counselor: I didn't think so. You said that you want to help him. And you've already said that what you are doing is not working to your satisfaction. So that leaves one possibility, and that is to make a few changes in what you're doing.

Sean: (*Shrugs his shoulders with eyes cast down*). Yeah, I guess so.

Counselor: Judging from your reaction, I don't think you feel deeply committed to changing what you do. You seem doubtful as to whether it would really make any difference.

Sean: That's true, and I'm still less than 100% convinced that I'm the one who should change anything.

Counselor: I too have some doubts about the firmness of your desire to change what you're doing.

Sean: Yes, I'm kind'a wavering about all this. It seems unfair that I should do anything different when it's his problem.

Counselor: At the same time, Sean, you have certainly shown that you have deep feelings of affection for your son. There's no doubt that you want the best for him. These are admirable qualities. It must be very painful for you to witness his downward spiral. You haven't used the word but you've heard the phrase "addicted to gambling." I can't help wondering whether such a thought goes through your mind and accompanies your hurt and your agony. I'm also wondering if you're feeling fear for his future.

Sean: (*Begins to sob uncontrollably.*) He is my only son, and I had such great hopes for him. It breaks my heart and depresses me to see him wasting his life by falling deeper and deeper into a dark pit.

Counselor: It's like a burden too heavy to carry. I wish I could remove the burden. I can't. But I can help you lighten it. And you've taken a major step forward by seeking help, and once again I believe you deserve to be proud of taking this step.

Sean: The situation feels so hopeless.

Counselor: It sounds to me like *you* are feeling hopeless.

Sean: Hopeless, exhausted, and alone.

Counselor: Dealing with your son and with your daughter without your wife makes you feel overwhelmed. Would you like to feel less powerless? Would you be interested in figuring out a way to climb out of this pit, out of this dark hole, and climb up into the light where you can feel hopeful again? Would you like to reenergize your life?

Commentary: Reality therapy is often critiqued as a method in which empathy is lacking. By now I hope you realize that this critique is without foundation, as this brief dialogue illustrates. The demonstration of an affective response to Sean is brief but illustrative of the appropriateness of empathizing with the client. You are invited to think about how you would expand on this demonstration of empathy.

Crucial to the practice of reality therapy is the principle that expressing accurate empathy is a means to an end, not an end in itself. Emotion is not the cause of behavior; rather, it is a behavior that accompanies actions, cognition, and physiology. The cause of total behavior rests in the need system and springs from the world of wants, the specific desires clients focus on at a given moment. Hence the counselor asks Sean a W question, "Would you like to feel less powerless?", and then adds a question about Sean's desire to climb out of the pit. This question contains a threefold implication: (a) Sean's feelings are connected to actions; (b) if Sean changes his actions, he will change how he feels; and, most important, (c) Sean possesses within himself, in his suitcase of behavior, the potential to live a more fulfilling and happier life by taking charge of it through more satisfying and effective choices.

This dialogue also indicated the significance of connecting with the client's total behavior. The counselor responded to the client's physiology by reflecting on it and interpreting it as indicating Sean's deep feelings for his son. He also responded to Sean's current expression of disappointment, sadness, and hopelessness. The counselor's comments presented in the dialogue are not intended to exhaust the wide range of possible interventions, and I invite you to expand this list.

In the next dialogue, the counselor asks Sean to describe his self-talk—what he tells himself about his son and the deplorable situation—and it illustrates the counselor's effort to help Sean examine his inner self-talk about one aspect of his presentation. This sequence paints a summary picture of how a counselor utilizes and operationalizes the principle of total behavior. Prior to this dialogue, the counselor has provided a brief explanation of ineffective self-talk based on choice theory and stressed three basic statements many clients tell themselves either explicitly or implicitly:

"I can't. I have no control over what I do. I have no choices."

"No one's going to tell me what to do."

"Even though what I'm doing is not working, I will continue to do it."

The session continues.

Counselor: Sean, I've explained what is often called self-talk, especially three internal statements that many people tell themselves when they are not feeling happy. Do any of these statements strike you as something you've told yourself?

Sean: Yes, I have often believed that I'm at my wit's end and don't know how to handle this. I haven't seen any workable choice.

Counselor: Up until now. It seems to me that you are beginning to see that maybe you do have some choices.

Sean: Yes, I've thought about this. I don't know if he will make any changes, but it seems to me that I can at least make a more effective effort to have a better relationship with him.

Counselor: So you've come to the conclusion that you can't force him to change but that you can take some satisfaction in what *you* do.

Sean: Well, that's not exactly what I thought, but I believe you hit the nail on the head.

Counselor: I think you have also been having another thought that's not helping you.

Sean: Probably a lot of such thoughts.

Counselor: Let's just focus on one. It seems to me that you've been telling yourself something not explicitly but it kind of goes along with your other thoughts and certainly with your actions. "Even though what I have been doing is not getting me anywhere and not helping Patrick, I'm going to continue to do it."

Sean: It sounds kind of stupid. But I think you're right.

Counselor: I didn't say it's stupid, and I don't think it is stupid. The way I look at it is that it is human nature to tell ourselves such statements and to act on them. It's similar to looking for misplaced car keys in the same place over and over. Many of us do this kind of thing and implicitly tell ourselves, "Maybe the car keys will miraculously appear in the place where I've looked five times already."

Sean: So where do I go from here with these newfound mistakes?

Counselor: Let's put it this way. When you feel like thinking that you have no choices, you could explicitly tell yourself, "I do have a choice in this matter. I just need to search for it."

Sean: What about the other self-talk statement, the one about doing what's not working?

Counselor: I have an observation about that one too. The new statement is, "If something is not working, I'll stop doing it and look for a better plan."

Sean: So what I get out of this are several ideas. Look for a better choice and look for a better plan.

Counselor: I think you've got it. And I have one more question. Of all the things we've talked about, what single idea do you find most useful?

Sean: That I don't live according to my values and that I can make changes that will elevate my behavior.

Commentary: The counselor assisted Sean in focusing on one aspect of total behavior: the thinking component. This brief dialogue illustrates that reality therapy embraces a major cognitive component. Thus a counselor can focus and help the client discuss four aspects of behavior: the component over which we have least control (our physiology), the component over which we have some slight direct control (our feelings), the component over which we have more direct control than feelings and physiology (our thinking or self-talk), and the component over which we have the most direct control (our actions). The conventional use of reality therapy has, in my opinion, underplayed the value and the role of direct discussion of feelings and thinking. This book fills that lacuna by extracting from choice theory a richer and more comprehensive system of reality therapy.

Case Example: Evaluation of Plans

This case illustrates a treatment plan derived from choice theory that enables the client to fulfill needs and wants.

Emi, a 38-year-old flight attendant, approaches a counselor because of an increasing feeling of anxiety about flying and provides the following information before the first session. Emi believes her discomfort is increasing, and she is fearful of informing her supervisors about this condition. She has a well-paying job with 15 years of seniority, yet she believes her coworkers and even the passengers might become aware of her fears and also become fearful or at least perceive her as a less than competent airline employee. She reports that now she "feels anxious about the anxiety." Thus she has two levels of anxiety. She was once married, but her husband, also an airline employee, was killed 2 years ago in an automobile accident while entering a highway from the airport parking lot. She has scheduled an appointment with Kenzo, a reality therapist in Tokyo, Japan. The counselor will help Emi provide details about both her current behavior and her history that is connected with her current lifestyle.

Counselor Kenzo: Good afternoon, Emi. Please take a seat and make yourself comfortable. I'd like to offer you a cup of tea. I will have one myself. A friend of mine in the United States just sent me a box of tea that he says is typically American. It's called Lipton Tea. He also sent me a box of Girl Scout Cookies, much enjoyed by Americans. He says that young girls go door to door and take orders for these cookies. Then several weeks or a month later, the girls deliver the cookies to their customers. The money they earn supports their projects. Girl Scouts is an organization that teaches young girls to help others and serve their communities. You might already know that they volunteer in hospitals, nursing homes, and so forth. They learn self-discipline, self-confidence, arts and crafts, and a willingness to reach out to others. Feel free to help yourself to the cookies. My friend doesn't realize how popular the Girl Scout organization is in this country. It was introduced here in 1919 and goes by the name of Nihon Joshi Hododan (Girl Guides of Japan).

Emi: Thank you very much. I will have a cup of tea and some cookies. In fact, I was a girl guide myself when I was younger. I was very nervous on the way here and when I came in. A cup of tea will help me relax. I'm sure the cookies make a nice snack in the middle of the afternoon. I've also discussed this organization with passengers on flights to and from the United States. As I observe your office, I see that it is very well decorated. It feels very comfortable and inviting.

Counselor: I would like to take credit for all of the decorations, but my wife is responsible for most of it. She's much better than I am at selecting appropriate furnishings. She told me she wanted to be sure the office would be a place where clients would feel at home and would feel safe and relaxed.

Emi: She accomplished her goal. She succeeded in creating a welcoming and pleasant atmosphere.

Commentary: At first glance, this initial interaction might appear to be idle chatter. In fact, during an actual counseling session, this interaction could even be much longer and more detailed. Reality therapy can be structured and used in an overly rigid way, which sometimes lends itself to minimizing and missing the importance of such seemingly trivial conversations. Practitioners who believe the following two statements have an unfeeling way of thinking and may lack empathy with their clients:

1. Because most presenting problems are rooted in relationships, the counselor should immediately begin a discussion about "Who is important in your life and how can you enhance that relationship?"
2. The unspoken motto of a counselor who unthinkingly applies a theoretical principle might be "Let's get moving with this process. I know what the problem is and I know what the solution is. There's no need to waste time talking about trivialities."

Such a scientifically accurate approach might reflect knowledge of choice theory principles, but the rigid application of them is often both unhelpful and off-putting to clients. The skillful reality therapist is aware of the necessity for establishing a friendly and safe atmosphere or environment (Wubbolding, 2015b). This kind of atmosphere, characterized by empathy and positive regard, serves as the basis and foundation for the effective use of reality therapy procedures. According to Glasser (2005a), reconnection with people "always starts with the counselor first *connecting* with the individual and then using this *connection* as a model for how the disconnected person can begin to connect with the people he or she needs." Therefore, Kenzo is very purposeful in his comments and in his actions. In the first meeting with Emi, Kenzo attempted to help her relax and to implicitly learn that she need not feel the highly intense anxiety that she has been experiencing at work.

The session continues.

Counselor Kenzo: Emi, how do you feel right now compared with how you felt before you opened the door and as you entered the office?

Emi: I feel a little better. Not as tense and fearful as I did 10 or 15 minutes ago.

Counselor: So, it is possible for you to relax and feel better after you have felt some fear and anxiety? I am hoping that by working together you will be able to relax. Also, I believe that you will be able to leave at least some of your fears behind you. Would you be interested in establishing and working toward that kind of goal?

Emi: That is exactly why I came here. I want to be like I once was: able to fly without anxiety. And, in fact, to be able to live on the ground without being victimized by my fears.

Counselor: I think your ability to establish and describe these goals will work to your advantage.

Commentary: The counselor *connects* with the client not only with an empathic understanding of her fears and anxieties but also with the change in her emotional state. Emi very quickly changed her feelings of anxiety as she entered the building and the office and became more relaxed and confident. The counselor points this out to her with the purpose not only of understanding her but also of presenting her with immediate and specific evidence that, in fact, she can change for the better. There is hope for the future. If the reality therapist does nothing else for the client at the initial encounter but help her become hopeful about the future, the counselor has done her an enormous service.

The counseling session continues.

Counselor Kenzo: It appears to me that we have already been able to establish a goal for the work that we do together. We could summarize the goal by saying that you would like to feel less anxiety and fear and be more comfortable and confident.

Emi: I agree. But my main concern is that I relax on the airplane so I can serve the passengers better and set an example for the other flight attendants. I am often the senior flight attendant on flights, and everyone expects me to show that all is well during the takeoff and landing as well as when the plane is in the air.

Counselor: So what you're saying is that you have both general goals and specific goals. Let's focus our conversation on some other goals and specific desires that you might have. For instance, can you point to a certain time in the past when you noticed your anxiety and fear increasing?

Emi: It seems like it has been a gradual evolution, or more accurately a decline in my comfort level.

Counselor: Can you remember any specific incident that might have ignited or triggered these negative feelings?

Emi: If I were to point to a specific event, I would say the sudden automobile death of my husband. We had only been married 4 years, and we were older when we married. I have never tried to find a specific cause for the anxiety. It seems pretty obvious now that I talk about it.

Counselor: It's not unusual, in fact it is perfectly normal, to fail to see the connection between an external event and the internal turmoil that a person feels. After all, it doesn't appear obvious that the anxiety you experience about flying is connected to something like the sudden automobile death of a loved one.

Emi: I've also noticed that my fears have increased recently after viewing a 2-hour television documentary on the Concorde, the supersonic jet plane. They showed how it took many years to refine the science necessary for building the airplane. They also interviewed both French and British scientists, engineers, pilots, and others who were qualified to discuss the plane. Then they analyzed in great detail the theories behind the crash of the Concorde as it took off from Charles de Gaulle Airport in Paris. They repeatedly showed in great detail the fire and the aftermath of the crash. For some reason this bothered me more than any other documentary on plane crashes. The increasing anxiety that I have been feeling became almost overwhelming after viewing that documentary. In fact, now that you mention it, I believe that all these past events and more recent ones are connected. I also think that if these fears continue to spiral upward, my job and my career will spiral downward. I hope I have come to the right place for help.

Counselor: I believe you have. It is unethical for me to make guarantees, but I truly believe that you need not fear that this anxiety will spiral out of control and damage your career. Let's talk more specifically about gaining control of these feelings. You mentioned that you are worried about being worried. So not only are you fearful and anxious but you are concerned that the fear and anxiety will have negative and far-reaching consequences.

Emi: Yes, that's exactly right. It's one thing to be worried. But I really don't like another layer of worry on top of the first one.

Counselor: We can deal with all of these issues. But first I'd like to explore with you how your husband's death triggered your subsequent emotional state.

Emi: Well, as I said, he was leaving the airport parking lot and was hit by a speeding truck.

Counselor: Let me interject something here. Each time you mentioned his death you have made quite a point that he died while leaving the *airport* parking lot. I can't help wondering if at some level in your mind the location of this tragedy still influences you today.

Emi: I believe you are completely accurate in your assessment. Whenever I remember him, I always think of how and where he died. Fortunately, I have been able to avoid that employee gate leading from the parking lot to the street. Also, after the accident, the airline changed the exit by removing a blind spot that employees had often complained about.

Counselor: Where were you when he died?

Emi: I was en route from California to Japan and did not hear about it until after we landed.

Counselor: It must have been a horrible moment and a terrible shock. Here was the man you loved, in good health, with a great future, and suddenly he's gone. What a loss this must be for you. I wish I could understand the pain you must feel. And I wish I could take away the suffering that you're feeling.

Emi: People tell me it's 2 years now, and I should move on with my life.

Counselor: You notice that I didn't say that, and I won't say that.

Emi: Thank you very much. I appreciate you saying that you do not understand my feeling of loss. It's so deeply personal. No one can really grasp it.

Counselor: So it could be that the anxiety you're feeling now is still connected with your husband's sudden death. I believe you might be feeling out of control because of his death, and this lack of control surfaces when you fly. My hope is that through our work together you will gain an inner sense of control in your life and added peace of mind.

Emi: No one has made these connections to me prior to this time.

Counselor: It's just a way of looking at your situation. I am not saying it is absolutely true. If you are willing to take some steps to gain a greater sense of inner control, however, I believe that both the feeling of loss and the feelings of fear and anxiety will become less. I'm not saying they will vanish completely or immediately. However, I believe that you will feel better and be able to leave *some* of these hurtful ideas behind you. This does not mean that you will not miss your deceased husband, but the pain about the loss can be lessened.

Emi: Well, that sounds very hopeful.

Counselor: I'd like to ask you a question that might seem to be a diversion, but it really is not. Tell me about your husband. I don't know his name at this point. In fact, I know almost nothing about him.

Emi: He was an executive for another airline. He was originally from the Netherlands. His name is Nick. He had never been married and had given himself to his career. We met in an airport lounge when the airport was closed because of weather. A year later we married. He was very handsome, personable, and kind. He had a wonderful sense of humor, and we "clicked" immediately. We got along with each other very well. We both traveled, loved to spend our free time in Japan, and arranged to meet in other countries. I never met anyone quite like him. He was considerate and very generous. Our times together were like honeymoons. Some people said we were like two teenagers. (*Emi goes into many details about their closeness, their dreams, their joys, and what they hoped to achieve together, including starting and raising a family.*)

Counselor: Clearly, the loss seems unbearable.

Emi: Yes, it feels like that.

Counselor: And yet, somehow you are managing. You have kept your career intact, and you have managed to work and have a life in spite of the pain. When I make this observation, what goes through your mind?

Emi: I think you're right.

Counselor: Has anybody encouraged you to talk about Nick?

Emi: At first some people were willing to listen. But after all this time, they believe I should get past the grief and longing for him. They think they are looking out for my best interest by not discussing him.

Counselor: When you come here, Emi, I want you to feel free to talk about him. I think it is very healthy for you to talk to someone like me who has not been your friend over the years.

Emi: That's very helpful.

Counselor: How do you feel right at this moment?

Emi: I feel relieved. I thought you might say that I should be getting over this.

Counselor: I have not said that, nor will I say that. But I do want to ask you once again a question you've already answered. Are you interested in lessening the pain, the anxiety, the fears, and this cauldron of emotions that stir within you?

Emi: Definitely. It's like carrying one of those backpacks that I see young people carrying as they board the planes.

Counselor: I like that metaphor. It seems to fit your situation right now. We will come back to it. In establishing more specific goals for what you are seeking, I want to present an idea for you to think about. It is central to the counseling that I practice, and I believe it is crucial for you to think about it:

*Sometimes the SOLUTION
has NOTHING to do with the PROBLEM.*

• • •

Emi: I know you will explain that to me in more detail.

Counselor: It simply means that if you develop choices that are inwardly satisfying to you, you will feel less fear and anxiety. These choices might not *seem* to be connected with fear. Nonetheless, they are closely connected. When you are afraid and anxious, you feel out of control. When you make choices that you feel you can control, you tend to feel better and can relinquish some of the distressing symptoms. Also, the fear and anxiety are symptoms of something else. If you have a fever, you demonstrate a physical symptom. But the fever is not the root problem. It is often a sign that you are developing an infection, and the fever is an attempt to fight off the infection.

Emi: So working together I can inoculate myself against these psychological infections.

Counselor: Yes, if you are willing to make some more satisfying choices. This will take effort and often you will not see the connection between the plans and the symptoms. But after a while, you will see and feel the results.

Emi: So where do we go from here?

Counselor: Between now and the next time we talk, I would like to ask you to think about what we've discussed today. There is no need at this point to make any specific action plans. But I think it is important to reflect on the principle that sometimes the solution *seems* to have little to do with the problem.

Emi: Should I write anything down?

Counselor: I'm glad you mentioned that possibility. If you want to write something down, I suggest you reconstruct four or five points from our conversation today. Do you use a smartphone or a computer?

Emi: Yes, I use both of them.

Counselor: OK, but be sure to write down your points in longhand because you use a different part of your brain when you write than when you type. It's closely connected with what is called your "working memory."

Emi: OK, that sounds good to me.

Counselor: Emi, what is the most valuable take-away idea for you from our time together today?

Emi: I think it is that even small steps make a big difference.

Commentary: With the help of Kenzo, Emi has been able to formulate a general goal or hope. As the counseling relationship develops, together they will identify specific elements of a treatment plan. The counselor refrains from pushing Emi to formulate a SAMIC plan. Rather, he attempts to help her *think* about the necessity for action planning, and he resists the urge to rush to a plan of action that would directly address the problem. The counselor wishes to proceed at a gentle and slow pace. In the words of Jeff Zeig (2006), the counselor *seeds* the plan. He gradually sows the idea that something more will happen during the counseling process.

But almost as an afterthought and following the lead of the client, the counselor asked her to "write down" a few recollected points gleaned from the session. This constitutes a plan but not what reality therapists generally describe as a direct plan related to the problem.

At this point, I suggest you reflect on how this session with Emi illustrates a more advanced usage of reality therapy principles than those in earlier chapters and even in dialogues in the first part of this chapter.

Summary of Subsequent Sessions

The next several sessions consist in identifying current behaviors as they relate to four psychological needs: belonging, power or inner control, freedom, and fun. The counselor began a discussion by asking Emi about how she recently has been satisfying her fun need. She described how she and her husband, Nick, had enjoyed sightseeing, especially train trips, which for them was an experience quite different from their jobs. They exercised together. When Nick was away, she often went to movies with girlfriends, some were flight attendants and some were high school and college friends. The counselor noted that much of her fun was associating with other people. She also visited her parents who lived approximately a half-day train ride away. Moreover, she found it useful to keep a journal of her travels, noting humorous experiences and favorite restaurants. She felt a sense of accomplishment when she volunteered in various charitable organizations while she was at home between her trips oversees. She especially enjoyed being a "big sister" for delinquent girls.

After Nick's death, she gradually relinquished these satisfying activities. She became more isolated and dropped out of the organizations that had previously satisfied her needs. She stated that she sat at home and lacked the energy to "get involved" with other people. She gradually came to visit her parents less and less, and they expressed concern about her and joined the chorus of those telling her, "It's time to move on."

As the counseling process developed over the next 6 months, Kenzo helped Emi formulate specific plans related to her needs:

1. *Survival or self-preservation:* Emi formulated an exercise plan and a dietary regimen and returned to what she described as her "vitamin supplements."
2. *Belonging:* Emi decided to call her girlfriends and inform them that she would like to resume some of the activities she had previously found satisfying such as going out to movies and eating a few meals in restaurants each month. She also committed to visiting her parents on a more regular basis twice a month. She asked that her parents not discuss that she should move on and get over the death of her husband. This conversation proved to be very difficult for her because of her respect for her parents. She also asked them to be willing to listen to her as she talked about the experiences she had with Nick when he was alive.
3. *Inner control, power, and achievement:* She made a plan to discuss possible promotions with the airline management. She followed through on this plan and was told in a general way what she would need to do to move toward a higher salary and more responsibility. She began to take steps to achieve this goal. She connected this plan with her belief that "Nick would be proud of me."
4. *Freedom:* Each day she would repeat her deep breathing exercises and techniques, which she reported had begun to help her feel free of her debilitating feelings, loneliness, and anxieties.
5. *Fun and enjoyment:* She embarked on a program that included listening to CDs as well as online courses related to her job. She found these exceptionally enjoyable and related that she could have fun as well as satisfy her need for achievement.

Termination of Counseling Process

After approximately 6 months of counseling with a reality therapist, Emi had learned the significance of human needs and wants as motivators of behavior. She also learned how to implement the WDEP system of reality therapy. She often spoke of the procedures and described how she achieved inner satisfaction from both implementing them and teaching them to her friends and to the other flight attendants who showed interest in them.

The final sessions in the counseling relationship with Kenzo consisted in formulating plans to continue her program of recovery and reflecting on principles such as, "Solutions are not always seen as being obviously connected with the presenting problems." As the sessions progressed, both Kenzo and Emi continued to rephrase and reformulate this principle. But she learned that effective behaviors often replace ineffective behaviors. Satisfying the need for belonging, for instance, helps to relieve her feelings of stress, anxiety, fear, and loneliness. Emi and Kenzo agreed that practicing reality therapy procedures did not "cure" her, but it helped her gain a sense of inner control as well as satisfaction of her other needs. She would continue to improve even though she continued to miss and grieve for her beloved. This sense of loss would remain but would become less painful and debilitating.

Case Example: Lynn Returns

Lynn, 17, first appeared in Chapter 4 as a reluctant client referred by her mother. She had used drugs and was flunking in school. The counselor helped her evaluate her actions as a language designed to communicate a message to the world around her. The counselor also helped Lynn name her feelings of worthlessness, anger, and fear. This brief dialogue illustrates the counselor's assistance in evaluating the plan of action.

> *Counselor:* Lynn, you've made it quite clear that you're not getting what you want at home or at school. You've said that the language you have used, in other words your actions, are not getting across to the people around you. They're not getting the message that you're trying to send them. Now I have a very important question. Do you want to make a plan to do something different?
>
> *Lynn:* Yeah, I know. From now on I'll do better. I'll do everything they want me to do if they're willing to change.

Commentary: Answer the following questions about Lynn's plan:

1. What are your thoughts about the effectiveness of Lynn's plans? _____

   _____

2. Is the plan simple? ❑ Yes ❑ No
   Why or why not? _____

   _____

3. Is the plan attainable? ❑ Yes ❑ No
   Why or why not? _____

   _____

4. Is the plan measurable? ❑ Yes ❑ No
   Why or why not? _____

   _____

5. Is the plan immediate? ❑ Yes ❑ No
   Why or why not? _____

   _____

6. Is the plan controlled by the planner? ❑ Yes ❑ No
   Why or why not? _____

   _____

7. Does the plan include a commitment? ❑ Yes ❑ No
   Why or why not? _____

   _____

8. Is the plan consistent, that is, repetitive? ❑ Yes ❑ No
   Why or why not? _____

   _____

Commentary: The plan formulated by Lynn, "From now on I'll do better. I'll do everything they want me to do if they're willing to change,"
fails to fulfill every quality of an effective plan. Perhaps the plan is
simple and easy to understand, but it is doubtful that it is realistically
attainable. "From now on" is a long, long time, and it is unrealistic to
expect clients to make an immediate, permanent, and drastic 180-degree
turn around. "Doing better" is not measurable. Similarly there is no
indication of when Lynn will begin to implement the plan. It is anything *but* immediate. It is only partially controlled by the planner in
that it is dependent on a change in the behavior of others. Also, there
is no hint of firmness or commitment to the plan. Finally, it is impossible to consistently choose a vague and nebulous plan. But most important, Lynn's statement seems aimed at pleasing the counselor and
lacks an internal behavioral commitment to change.

After reading several of these dialogues, you may be tempted to
subscribe to the observation (less common now than in the past) that
reality therapy is simplistic and is merely a problem-solving technique.
However, the most important level of interaction is the implicit unspoken message, a metacommunication sent by the counselor. In the
space provided, indicate two possible messages received by Lynn.

1. _____

   _____

2. _____

   _____

From my point of view, she received these messages: (a) "I have
more effective control in my life than I previously believed." (b) "If I
am to make progress, I will need to work hard at making more effective

choices." Keep in mind that the overall goal of reality therapy is to help clients take charge of their life, gain more inner control, and satisfy their need system appropriately.

The session continues.

Counselor: Lynn, you said you would do better. If you did better and these other people were to get off your back, I have a hunch you would feel better about the way things are going for you. Am I right or wrong about that?

Lynn: Oh, you're definitely right about that. I'd be a lot better off if they would get off my back.

Counselor: And you've said that you would like to work on making your life better and feeling good about the way things are going. So, if you make a small change tomorrow in what you do in school, what would you be doing?

Lynn: I'd be doing better.

Counselor: If someone were to observe you, follow you with a television camera focused on you, let's say from 8 a.m. until 9 a.m., what would they see you doing that would be different from what they would have seen other days?

Lynn: I guess they would see me coming to school on time and paying attention in class.

Counselor: How would they see you walking into the class?

Lynn: They'd see me walking in with my books and iPad.

Counselor: (*Stands up and walks across the room with a scowl on his face in a slouched posture and pretends to mumble to a fellow student, "I hate this class."*) How does that strike you as far as communicating a new message?

Lynn: That's pretty much how I walk into that first class when I show up for school.

Counselor: If you plan to do that tomorrow, what would be different?

Lynn: Nothing, that's what I've done.

Counselor: And that's a small part of what you said is not working for you.

Lynn: Yeah.

Counselor: So, what is a better way to start the day with your first class?

Lynn: I need to walk in the classroom on time and pretend that I like the class.

Counselor: Show me what that would look like.

(*Lynn walks across the room showing a few opposite behaviors to what the counselor did.*)

Counselor: How did that feel for you?

Lynn: Strange.

Counselor: You're not used to it, huh?

Lynn: It feels phony.

Counselor: How did you feel lately at the end of your school day when you walked into your classes like I walked in?

Lynn: It's how I feel, but I feel crappy.

Counselor: So, what do you have to lose from changing your actions at least for an hour a day?

Lynn: Not much.

Counselor: Would you be willing to practice this for the next five school days even though you *felt* phony in the beginning?

Lynn: Yeah, I guess I could do that.

Counselor: Keep in mind it's only practice. You don't have to feel natural at it. Have you ever played a sport?

Lynn: Yes, I played volleyball.

Counselor: And has a coach ever corrected the way you hit the ball by telling you to hit it in a different way, a way that doesn't feel natural?

Lynn: Yes, the coach corrected me all the time.

Counselor: And I'll bet the coach wanted you to practice this new way even though it didn't feel natural. It might have even felt phony.

Lynn: So if I do this, will they change?

Counselor: We have no guarantee about what other people will do. Are you willing to give it some time?

Lynn: I guess so. I'll try to do this.

Counselor: I know you'll *try*, but will you *do* it?

Lynn: You're getting pushy again.

Counselor: I'm like the coach who is working with you to improve you skill. If I backed off and didn't let you know that you can do this, what message would you get from my wishy-washiness?

Lynn: I'd get the idea you don't think I could do it.

Counselor: And that's just the opposite of what I really believe. Also, it might communicate that I don't care about you, and that message is just the opposite of what I think.

Lynn: Well, I do believe you are on my side.

Counselor: And my goal is to help you get what you want. To help you get other people on your side. But first this means showing them a side of you that they've not seen lately. There is not a doubt in my mind that your life can be better. I don't expect you to believe that at this point, but it's what I believe.

Lynn: I believe it. But it's going to be hard.

Counselor: Well, let's put it this way. What will help you more: a weak commitment to make better choices or a strong commitment?

Lynn: You want me to say a strong commitment.

Counselor: That's exactly what I want you to say even if you don't believe it.

Lynn: Even if I don't believe it?

Counselor: Yes, because you will believe it, you will believe a lot of things after you take action. Did you feel more natural when you practiced volleyball the way the coach suggested?

Lynn: Yes, her way became my way, and I'm pretty good at volleyball.

Counselor: You said her way *became* your way. So her way was not your way immediately. It took time. What else did it take?

Lynn: It took practice, doing it over and over and over again.

Counselor: Well, you've got the idea. Are you willing to follow through on this plan for five days?

Lynn: I can do more than that.

Counselor: Yes, but let's start with five days. Don't overdo it.

Commentary: In this segment, the counselor assists Lynn in being specific about her plans. He does not say that her plans are ineffective. Rather, he helps *her* describe where they fall short and how she can easily make them doable. At the end of the session, the counselor utilizes a paradoxical technique known as restraining (Wubbolding, 2000b, 2011). This technique is designed to ensure the success of the plan as much as is possible. The counselor holds the client back from actions that are likely to fail. Consequently, if Lynn follows through on her plan, she wins; if she chooses more success than was planned, she also wins. Many clients "rebel" against the restraint and fulfill more than what the original plan required. At this point, you might ask, "What if Lynn does not follow her plan at all?" The skillful reality therapist would point out to her the following: "Lynn, you succeeded in three out of four aspects of your plan. You thought about it, you talked about it, and you formulated a plan of action. The next question is, do you want to try again with the same plan, or should we formulate a new plan?" Clearly, the skilled counselor sees the client in a different way than the client sees herself. The counselor refuses to accept the inevitability of failure and misery. The indirect and subterranean communication made by the counselor includes the art of effective interpersonal communication. The counselor does not argue, blame, or criticize. He accepts the client and helps her look to the future. This approach strengthens the counseling relationship and constitutes behaviors that the client can adopt for herself.

Chapter 8
Reality Therapy FAQs

This chapter provides answers to some of the most frequently asked questions (FAQs) about reality therapy. After reading textbooks as well as entire books on the theory and practice of reality therapy and after witnessing live or recorded demonstrations, students, supervisors, and instructors often seek answers to the following questions.

What Is the Connection Between Reality Therapy and Spirituality?

The concepts of spirituality and mental health have always been interlocked. Because the purpose of counseling is to facilitate mental health and personal growth, it is logical to state that counseling and spirituality are connected. In fact, in some ways all counseling is spiritual in that it focuses on the immaterial rather than on creating a tangible manufactured product or a concrete touchable service such as repairing a computer, servicing an automobile, or functioning as a sales representative. Reality therapy as a counseling system assists people in satisfying their wants and needs and in evaluating their behavior. Thus it is logical that among the questions emerging from participants in training sessions and students studying counseling theories is, "What is the relationship between choice theory/reality therapy (CT/RT) and spirituality?"

Because of the nonmaterial nature of counseling, there is often a moral or ethical aspect to the counseling interaction. Counselors ask clients if their behavior involves morality or ethics and, more specifically, if their behavior is connected with human relationships. Often, the moral principles are based on spirituality or religion. "Thou shalt not kill" (the Hebrew word means "murder") is a moral principle that underlies civil society. "Religious faith, or some form of personal spirituality, can be a powerful source of meaning and purpose" (Corey & Corey, 2018), and "in the past couple of decades, increased attention has been given to religious values and goals in psychotherapy literature" (Harris, 2016, p. 452). More specifically, Tan (2011) has written about the close connection between psychological counseling and biblical theology. Harris (2016) adds that religious and spiritual psychotherapies have been shown to be effective in lessening psychological symptoms, and Nickles (2011) agrees that spirituality and religion are salient components for dealing with clients' behavior, beliefs, and experiences.

Some believe that CT/RT and spirituality and religion are incompatible. I believe it is incorrect to assert that choice theory stands against spiritual and religious values and accepts the human person as totally selfish, interested only in fulfilling his or her own needs regardless of others' needs. A more thorough knowledge of CT/RT clearly demonstrates the compatibility of Judeo-Christian traditions and choice theory as well as the interface with other religions. David Jackson (2015) has detailed the connection between serving others and need satisfaction, and he emphasizes the value of altruistic behaviors. While teaching training workshops in Kuwait, I was asked if I was a Muslim. Participants found the principles of Islam reflected in the principles of CT/RT. They continually stated that the theory and practice coincided with "the words of the Prophet." In fact, when teaching reality therapy in the Islamic world, the instructor should have at least some knowledge of Islam and connect it with CT/RT.

Japanese trainees in the certification process of reality therapy are often rooted in Buddhist thinking and Singaporeans in Confucian thinking. Similar to the assumptions underlying the great religions of the world, a cornerstone of CT/RT is personal responsibility for one's own behavior (Richey, n.d.). Masaki Kakitani, senior instructor with the William Glasser Institute, president of the Japan Association of Reality Therapy (JART), and a Christian minister, has trained Christians and Buddhists in Japan for decades and asserts that choice theory and reality therapy, with its foundational principle of personal responsibility as a cornerstone, is essential to successful counseling outcomes.

Similarly, Rhon Carleton, a Protestant minister, former U.S. Air

Force chaplain, and instructor with the William Glasser Institute, trains ministers and others using frequent references to the Hebrew and Christian scriptures. Having 9 years of experience in a Catholic seminary and 6 years as a Catholic priest, I believe that the principles of choice theory and Christian theology are totally compatible. Clinton and Hawkins (2011) state that "a Christian appraisal of this theory finds much to appreciate in Glasser's affirmation of the role of choice and responsibility for one's actions" (p. 453).

Another aspect of spirituality is inspired by the work of Victor Frankl (1963). He believed that the most basic human need is that of purpose and meaning. Though not strictly part of choice theory, it serves as an extension of the human need system described by Glasser. The advanced use of reality therapy includes assisting clients in finding an uplifting sense of purpose in their life regardless of their external circumstances. It is also possible to add the need for faith to the choice theory schema of motivational drives, or the need system. Finding something to believe in outside of one's self can be a framework for purpose and meaning. Faith could be a religious faith, a belief in the deity, or a belief in a loving God that asks us to see His (Her) hand in creation.

In the 21st century, many people live a lifestyle that can be characterized by the broad label of *secular humanism.* They are members of no organized religion but live totally for others. They are generous with their resources and work to better the lot of humankind and to lighten the burden of others. They are altruistic, philanthropic, law-abiding, and generous leaders or citizens. I am personally proud to have friends who subscribe to each of these groupings.

Counselors using reality therapy formulate an internal standard that often appeals to clients. Does their current behavior match, or is it incongruent with, their spiritual belief system, their religious values, their faith, and their sense of personal destiny or their humanistic/altruistic values?

Can You Summarize the Value of Learning WDEP?

The English acronym WDEP represents a wide range of counseling and managing techniques. W represents helping clients formulate and clarify their wants; the counselor asks: "What are you seeking?" "What are your hopes?" "What are your dreams about the immediate and distant future?" W also encompasses an exploration of clients' perceptions: "Where do you see your behavior originating, from inside of you or from a source external to you?" W can also represent helping clients determine and at times increase their level of commitment to behaviors that satisfy their needs in a more appropriate and efficient manner.

D stands for exploring what the client is doing, thinking, feeling, and "physiologizing." These four components, known as "total behavior," are present in all behaviors. Glasser (2005b) has described total behavior as analogous to an automobile with the front two wheels symbolizing action and thinking and the rear two wheels symbolizing feeling and physiology. People have more direct and immediate control over the front wheels (especially the action wheel) than the back wheels.

E symbolizes the many forms of self-evaluation that constitute the core of reality therapy. Wubbolding (2011) has extracted 22 types of self-evaluation from choice theory, many of which are presented in dialogue form in this book. Determining the effectiveness of current behaviors—Do they help or impede need satisfaction of both clients and their families?—constitutes the most significant element of need satisfaction.

Finally, P represents planning. Plans can focus on short-term benchmarks or satisfaction of long-term goals or strivings. The underlying principle, which is often implicit, is that clients can continuously improve their lives by making a plan, formulating a high level of commitment to the plan, and following through with implementation of the plan. Chapter 4 described the specific characteristics of effective planning. The result of effective planning is internal happiness. To paraphrase William James, "We do not sing because we are happy, we are happy because we sing"; and, as Glasser says, "We are always happy when we *choose* to sing."

The acronym WDEP, which I developed for pedagogical reasons, is a teaching tool for learning reality therapy. It is secondary to the principles and the skills summarized in each letter. In my experience, having a succinct and easily remembered outline for keeping detailed information in mind helps individuals and groups learn and retain the principles of reality therapy and its underlying theory. It incorporates an education psychology principle of learning: the art of "chunking." In her excellent book on learning mathematics and science, Barbara Oakley (2014) formulates a principle applicable to all learning: grouping ideas. She defines chunking as "mental leaps that unite separate bits of information through meaning" (p. 55). She adds:

> Chunking the information you deal with helps your brain run more efficiently. Once you chunk an idea or concept, you don't need to remember all the underlying details; you've got the main idea—the chunk—and that's enough. It's like getting dressed in

the morning. Usually you just think one simple thought—*I'll get dressed.* But it's amazing when you realize the complex swirl of underlying activities that take place with that one simple chunk of a thought. (p. 55)

The WDEP formulation of the procedures of reality therapy represents an easily remembered "chunk."

Glasser has emphasized that WDEP "is an eminently usable tool that can be learned by readers, used in agencies and schools, and taught in classrooms. I hope that this system will become a household phrase and used by therapists, counselors, teachers, and parents" (as cited in Wubbolding, 1991, p. xii).

How Does Reality Therapy Deal With Feelings?

A common misconception about reality therapy is that the system does not allow for the discussion of emotions, or "dealing with feelings." This misconception is based on the principle that feelings or emotions present personal dysfunctions that effective counseling can correct. From the perspective of CT/RT, emotions do not cause actions. They are not the source of problems. Rather they accompany actions, thinking, and even physiology. Feelings are analogous to the lights on the dashboard of an automobile. When they light up, they tell us something. Often they tell us something else needs attention. Sadness, shame, guilt, depression, or dozens of other feelings send a signal to the person that his or her life is not going well. Similarly, physical pain tells an individual that there is a physiological condition that requires medical attention. Because human emotions can be intense, it is easy to mistake them as being the problem. A skilled reality therapist sees emotions as *very important* signposts and assists clients in modifying their total behavior by adjusting the most easily altered component of total behavior—actions. When actions change, alterations in thinking, emotions, and even physiology occur. This view of total behavior is easily described, but the development of more satisfying behaviors often requires time, opportunity for change, and, most important, a commitment to alter one's choices with the belief that changed emotions will eventually follow.

The question still remains, "Does reality therapy allow for the explicit discussion of feelings?" I answer this question with a resounding "yes." Effective counseling using reality therapy includes the acknowledgment and elaboration of the most prominent component of total behavior. For example, if a client demonstrates feelings of shame, depression, or anger, it makes logical sense and is effective counseling to discuss these emotions: What purpose do they serve? Do they help the client satisfy human needs? Does the client wish to replace these emotions with other feelings that can facilitate better human relationships? As you read the brief dialogues in this book, you observed the counselor implementing these principles.

How Is Reality Therapy Connected With Ethical Principles?

In the dialogues presented in this book, the counselor does not emphasize issues that focus on ethical considerations such as informed consent, confidentiality and its limitations, duty to warn, professional disclosure, the need for consultation, and the many other issues described in various codes of ethics. These ethical principles, when applied to reality therapy, are no different than those applied in any counseling relationship or agency setting. The significance of maintaining ethical relationships is paramount, and resources abound for understanding various codes of ethics (Corey, Corey, Corey, & Callanan, 2015; Mitchell, 2007; Wilcoxon, Remley, Gladding, & Huber, 2007). This book focuses on the use of reality therapy and is not intended to be a source document for legal and ethical issues.

What Is the Evidence for the Effective Use of Reality Therapy?

The answer is twofold. First, in recent years the professional world has seen a deluge of articles and books published on the necessity of utilizing evidence-based theories and practices. Reed (2006) states, "The most widely cited definition of evidence-based practice (EBP) is one adapted from Sackett and colleagues . . . 'evidence-based practice is the integration of best research evidence with clinical expertise and patient values'" (p. 13). Reality therapy embraces these three components of evidence-based practice. A skilled, well-trained practitioner of reality therapy possesses tools for exploring client values, wants, and goals as well as behaviors. The third component of this definition is scientific studies that validate the theory and practice of reality therapy. After a 2-year effort by the research committee of the international reality therapy organization known as William Glasser International, the federal Substance Abuse and Mental Health Services Administration (SAMHSA) has not yet registered reality therapy as evidence-based.

A prestigious endorsement of reality therapy comes from the European Association for Psychotherapy (EAP). The EAP represents

120,000 members in 41 European countries, including 27 European Union countries. Wubbolding (2011) summarized the endorsement process followed by the European Association for Reality Therapy (EART): "The EAP recognized reality therapy as a scientifically validated psychotherapy" (p. 122). This approval solidifies reality therapy as an independent system that practitioners and the public can rely on as a scientifically established behavioral health intervention.

Second, studies that validate the practice of reality therapy have existed for decades. For example, Glasser and Wubbolding (1995) summarized the outcome research of a reality therapy program initiated by Glasser (1965) during his early career when he worked with long-term hospitalized psychotic patients in the Veterans Administration Neuropsychiatric Hospital in Los Angeles. They state that after 2 years of reality therapy treatment 100 of 210 patients whose "problems were categorized into paranoid schizophrenia, catatonic schizophrenia, hebephrenic schizophrenia . . . and undifferentiated schizophrenia" were released from the hospital (p. 310).

Use in Correctional Facilities

Leon Lojk (1986) conducted a follow-up study of former residents of a correctional institution over a 12-year period. The findings indicated complete rehabilitation for 69% of the former residents and partial rehabilitation for 15%. In his own words:

> We felt these results were very promising. Unfortunately, some influential people didn't share our opinion. They were very skeptical about the sincerity of the social workers who gathered the data for the follow up study, and about our objectivity. The skeptics acknowledged that the released residents were no longer stealing; they had abandoned promiscuity; they were earning money for themselves and their children; they didn't change jobs more often than usual; they had no trouble with the police; and they didn't need any psychological or psychiatric help. However, the skeptics challenged the results and methodology of our study with the following arguments and questions: "The former residents seem O.K. but who knows?" "Are they internally happy?" "Could it mean that these methods of correction had broken their will for life?" Here you can see major misunderstandings about total behavior. (p. 30)

The impact of teaching choice theory (inseparable from reality therapy) was studied by Grills et al. (2015), who stated that the program "significantly improved perceived stress, mindfulness, emotion regulation, impulsivity and wellbeing" (p. 757). They noted that the effects were stronger for an introductory group. They concluded that the program "can improve incarcerated women's wellbeing pre-release, a strong predictor of recidivism post-release" (p. 757).

Use With Clients With Serious Mental Disorders

Casstevens (2011, 2013) studied the effects of CT/RT in the context of health and wellness programs in community-based clubhouses that served adults with severe mental disorders. Surveys conducted 15 months after treatment showed that reality therapy provided relief for adults "in small non-profit organizations that serve adults diagnosed with serious mental disorders" (Casstevens, 2013, p. 50).

Hey Sook Kim (2016) of the Department of Social Welfare, Inje University in Pusan, South Korea, studied the effects of parenting stress for mothers of children with emotional/behavioral problems. The program, designed to promote well-being (self-acceptance, positive relationships with others, and other elements), consisted of 2-hour weekly sessions for 10 weeks and a booster session a month after completion of the program. The data from this experimental study were analyzed in a statistical package that included an analysis of variance. The results showed a significantly lower parenting stress level for the experimental group compared with the control group. This study illustrates two important truths. It illustrates the value of utilizing reality therapy in an Asian culture, and it shows that reality therapy can affect clients participating in a realistically brief program of 10 weeks.

Use in Couples Counseling

Though not experimental research, Robey, Wubbolding, and Carlson (2012) assembled examples illustrating the successful application of reality therapy to a wide variety of issues including recovery after infidelity, substance abuse, military concerns, interfaith issues, premarital counseling, and other topics. Dr. and Mrs. Glasser endorsed this book, stating the following:

> Contemporary issues in couples counseling is a practical and usable example of counseling at its best, one that will appeal to any counselor or therapist looking for an effective approach backed by sound theory. This book is a fascinating read and we recommend it enthusiastically for professionals or anyone wishing to improve their own relationships. (as cited in Robey et al., 2012, back cover)

In summary, research studies continue to enhance the credibility of reality therapy as an effective counseling system with worldwide appeal.

Self-Evaluation Applied to the Professional

The question arises: How does self-evaluation apply to me the professional person? If we ask our clients to evaluate their own behavior, we can expect that the same principles apply to us both in our personal lives and in our professional lives. If we teach mindfulness, it makes sense for us to practice mindfulness. We can ask clients to be congruent in their actions and feelings if we ourselves live congruent lives. Similarly, a teacher of such topics as driver education needs to drive effectively. Most tennis instructors are current or former tennis players. It follows that the skills we use with clients are skills that apply to us as well. Fundamentally, professional self-evaluation means possessing a working knowledge and commitment to the codes of ethics formulated by various professional organizations. The American Counseling Association and other associations continually update and even alter their ethical principles. The professional reality therapist uses these codes as standards for self-evaluation. Among the many self-evaluation questions for professionals are the following:

- Am I a member of my professional organization?
- How familiar am I with the current code of ethics? What part of the code do I need to study in more detail?
- How committed am I to the values contained in the code of ethics: autonomy, nonmaleficence, beneficence, justice, fidelity, and veracity?
- Am I aware of and do I implement the complex issue of informed consent?
- Do I follow the rules for accurate and complete documentation?
- Do I have a plan for establishing boundaries and dealing with the possibility of dual relationships?
- To what extent do I acknowledge and attempt to extend the limits of my skills?
- Do I have a plan for dealing with clients whose values conflict with my own?
- What is my attitude toward professional continuing education? Do I take advantage of opportunities to grow in my skill and worldview?

These questions focusing on professional self-evaluation constitute a partial list of standards, some minimal and some aspirational. I suggest that counselors review their profession's codes of ethics and use them as a guideline for professional self-evaluation.

Maintaining competence involves lifelong learning. "Learning never ceases: new clients present new challenges. New areas of knowledge and practice demand ongoing education. Even recent graduates may have significant gaps in their education that will require them to take workshops or courses in the future" (Corey et al., 2015, p. 331).

A Question for Your Consideration

Both neophyte counselors and seasoned veterans ponder this theoretical issue about reality therapy:

> At this point in my learning and in my practice, do I believe that reality therapy constitutes a subset of another theory and method? Or does it merit the label of "a free-standing theory and practice"?

Reflect on this question to determine whether your opinion has changed after reading this book. Please provide a brief rationale for your answer.

A. Free-standing: _____

B. Subset: _____

Brief rationale: _____

What Are the Criticisms of Reality Therapy, and How Do You Answer Them?

As with most counseling theories and practice, authors of textbooks perceive limitations in reality therapy. Corey (2017) states, "Reality therapy does not give adequate emphasis to the role of . . . insight, the unconscious, the power of the past, and the effect of traumatic experiences in early childhood, the therapeutic value of dreams and the place of transference" (p. 333). My response to these perceived limitations is that insight need not precede behavioral change. Often, it follows a change in actions. Also, insight does not always result in change. From the point of view of reality therapy, people can have a high level of insight and still maintain the same destructive behavior.

The lack of explicit emphasis on the unconscious seems to be an accurate observation about reality therapy. The advanced practitioner of reality therapy, however, realizes that uncovering the content of the unconscious is a convoluted journey that can require a time commitment unrealistic for many clients as well as beyond the bounds of managed care. This objection coincides with the limited use of dreams in reality therapy, although reality therapy does allow for a limited discussion of dreams that represent clients' wants and hopes of which they are often only marginally aware. Minimized in the practice of reality therapy is the place of transference. From my point of view, this is a valid criticism if transference and counter-transference are not seen as psychodynamic, that is, the transference of the client's feeling from another person to the counselor or the transference of the counselor's feelings from another person to the client. The reality therapist is well-advised to be in consultation with a supervisor or another professional person for the purpose of acknowledging and dealing with issues included under the umbrella term *transference*.

Another perceived criticism of reality therapy is that it can serve as an excuse for the authoritarian imposition of a counselor's agenda and values. I believe the structure of reality therapy can indeed lend itself to this possibility. Practitioners of genuine reality therapy are aware of the wider world of professional counseling and the responsibility of accepting clients and avoiding the whimsical imposition of values and plans.

Ivey, D'Andrea, and Ivey (2012) state that "reality therapy . . . stresses the need for the client to adapt to necessary environmental contingencies" (p. 358) and add that "although it is important that the client adapt to reality, such adaptation can result in clients returning to oppressive systems with the idea that the 'fault' is in them rather than in the environment" (p. 358). I believe this objection lacks evidence. Neither choice theory nor its implementation, reality therapy, include "blaming the victim." In fact, finding fault is a concept that is in direct opposition to the empathic and yet direct use of the WDEP system of reality therapy. Utilizing this system, counselors assist clients in evaluating their own behavior and seek ways to satisfy their needs and wants. This choice is often made in opposition to what is called "oppression." Reality therapy empowers clients rather than facilitating their adaptation to injustice.

Clearly there are limitations to the theory and practice of reality therapy, but I believe that many perceived drawbacks are due to misinterpretations or to the less than artful practice of reality therapy.

What Is an "As If" Plan?

To answer this question, let's consider the following case. Sam (Samuel or Samantha), 22, reluctantly seeks counseling to overcome shyness. After the counselor applies the principles of reality therapy—empathic relationship, therapeutic alliance, and the WDEP system—the client plans to attend the organizational kick-off party of Habitat for Humanity, which Sam recently joined. After discussing Sam's reluctance to approach people, the counselor helped Sam solidify the desire to become more outgoing and even assertive. The counselor also explored specific past instances when Sam shied away from speaking with people even to the point of avoiding them. The counselor asked Sam if the chosen behavior helped or impeded the attainment of the goal. Then together they formulated a plan: Sam would pretend to be outgoing in the following ways:

1. Nod to two people on the elevator as it rises to the floor of the party.
2. During a 10-minute period, smile at three volunteers for a couple of seconds.
3. Approach two volunteers and ask what prompted them to join the organization and what kind of work they do on the project.
4. Look at the individuals' eyes for a few seconds as they respond to these questions.

Comentary: The client need not be genuinely outgoing. Sam realizes that the plan is merely practice. Genuine outgoingness and assertiveness will happen at a future date. For now, Sam formulates an "as if" plan. Later, the counselor will ask Sam to make a simple evaluation of the plan by asking, "Sam, how did that work out for you?"

The "as if" plan parallels the use of *acting as if* in Adlerian counseling and is congruent with standard counseling practice. In describing Adlerian counseling, Sommers-Flanagan and Sommers-Flanagan (2012) state:

> Most people, at least occasionally, wish for traits they don't have. Some wish for self-confidence and others wish they were calm, instead of nervous and edgy. Still others wish they could focus, get organized, and follow through on a project. The **acting as if** technique is used when clients are wishing for behavioral change. (emphasis in original, p. 102)

Chapter 9

Conclusion

The purpose of this book is to describe the cornerstone of reality therapy in a specific way: helping clients conduct a searching self-evaluation of their behaviors, wants or goals, and perceptions. Each of these three elements contains many subsets. Behavior is composed of action, thinking, feelings, and physiology. The quality world, or mental picture album of each individual, contains a wide variety of wants or goals, which allows for a countless number of counseling interventions. Perception involves our worldview, our judgments, and the values we form regarding people, information, experiences, and objects.

For the most part, counseling has focused on helping clients change behavior. From the point of view of choice theory and reality therapy, no one changes a single behavior without evaluating its effectiveness. A motorist driving a car does not change directions without a prior evaluation that a different direction is more helpful in reaching the destination. The founder of reality therapy, William Glasser, repeatedly described self-evaluation as the core of the system. On an organizational basis, he insisted that a school wishing to become a Glasser Quality School would self-evaluate, determining that they deserved this status based on fulfilling various standards such as the significant lessening of discipline problems.

The dialogues contained in this book are intended to illustrate specific interventions that typify only one component of reality therapy: the use of self-evaluation. Self-evaluation does not occur without some connection to other components of reality therapy and to the entire process of counseling. For instance, a person defines and clarifies a specific want: "I want a college degree." "I want to be left alone." "I want a promotion at work." "I want my children to do what I tell them to do." Utilizing reality therapy, the counselor helps clients evaluate the realistic attainability of these wants. Similarly, the counselor assists clients in self-evaluating their behavior, especially actions, using interventions like these: "Describe how your actions are effective or ineffective." "Tell me how your actions/choices enhance or undermine your relationships." In schools and in many other agencies, counselors use an external standard to assist in the self-evaluation process. "Are your current actions against the rules of the organization, the law, the expectations of others, or cultural norms?"

Self-evaluation becomes even more important when counseling specific clients whose judgments are ineffective, dangerous, or harmful to themselves or others.

The purpose of the dialogues is not to communicate that there is only one way to respond to clients' statements. On the contrary, the purpose of the dialogues is to help you think about how you could assist your clients to be more skilled in this preeminent and compelling skill.

Finally, I wish you the best in every way. In choosing to work as a counselor, you have chosen one of the most noble professions devised by the human mind. My foremost wish is that you realize that when you help one single person you are helping not only that individual but his or her children and their children's children. The extraordinary and sublime work that you do as a counselor cascades down through history. Future generations will not know the good you have done, but be assured that your influence continues.

Resources for Further Study

Counselors, therapists, educators, and all who are interested in learning more about choice theory and reality therapy and its many applications can utilize the following resources.

Journal and Texts

International Journal of Choice Theory and Reality Therapy, Tom Parish, Editor. Semiannual online journal available free of charge. Includes current articles about applications and research studies.

Glasser, W. (1998). *Choice theory*. New York, NY: HarperCollins. This seminal book presents an overview of choice theory and applications to love and marriage, family, education, the workplace, and the quality community.

Glasser, W. (2011). *Take charge of your life*. Bloomington, IN: iUniverse. On the cover of the book Dr. Phil McGraw states, "This book is a 'game changer' for anyone ready to become the captain of their own ship. Going far beyond theory and philosophy this powerful book is a hands-on guide to creating rather than just observing one's own life."

Wubbolding, R. (2000). *Reality therapy for the 21st century*. Philadelphia, PA: Brunner Routledge. The most comprehensive book on reality therapy. Contains a detailed treatment of procedures, an interview with Dr. Glasser, extensive multicultural applications, and research studies. Recommendation: Begin reading with Chapter 9.

Wubbolding, R. (2011). *Reality therapy: Theories of psychotherapy series.* Arlington, VA: American Psychological Association. An overview of theory and practice with summaries of several research studies. Recommendation: Begin reading with Chapter 4.

Wubbolding, R. E., & Brickell, J. D. (2001). *A set of directions for putting and keeping yourself together.* Warminster, PA: Marco Products Inc. A manual for clients and others to use as a self-help resource. Contains practical exercises for dealing with excuses, establishing and exploring wants and goals, making plans, and the role of faith.

Wubbolding, R. E., & Brickell, J. D. (2015). *Counselling with reality therapy* (2nd ed.). London, United Kingdom: Speechmark Publishing. Emphasizes relationship counseling, group counseling, addictions counseling, and paradoxical techniques.

Websites

Center for Reality Therapy (Robert E. Wubbolding)
www.realitytherapywub.com

John Brickell, UK (instructor for Center for Reality Therapy)
www.real-choice.co.uk

International Journal of Choice Theory and Reality Therapy (Tom Parish, ed.)
http://www.wglasserinternational.org/publications/journals/

William Glasser Inc.
www.wglasserbooks.com

William Glasser International (quality schools)
http://wglasser.com/quality-schools

William Glasser International, Inc. (links to countries around the world)
www.wglasserinternational.org

References

Alfred Adler.org. (2016). *What is an Adlerian?* Retrieved from http://www.alfredadler.org/what-is-an-adlerian

American Counseling Association. (2014). *ACA code of ethics.* Alexandria, VA: Author.

American Psychiatric Association. (2013). *The diagnostic and statistical manual of mental disorders* (5th ed.). Arlington, VA: Author.

Arden, J. (2014). *The brain bible.* New York, NY: McGraw Hill.

Arkowitz, H., Westra, H. A., Miller, W. R., & Rollnick, S. (Eds.). (2008). *Motivational interviewing in the treatment of psychological problems.* New York, NY: Guilford Press.

Berman, M., & Brown, D. (2000). *The power of metaphor.* Norwalk, CT: Crown House.

Bray, B. (2014, February 18). A passion to serve: Veterans and counseling Q+A. *Counseling Today.* Retrieved from http://CT.counseling.org/category/online-exclusives

Burdenski, T., & Wubbolding, R. (2011). Extending reality therapy with focusing: A humanistic road for the choice theory total behavior car. *International Journal of Choice Theory and Reality Therapy, 31*(1), 14–30.

Capuzzi, D., & Stauffer, M. D. (2016). *Counseling and psychotherapy: Theories and interventions* (6th ed.). Alexandria, VA: American Counseling Association.

Carlson, J. (2012). Commentary from the editors. In P. Robey, R. Wubbolding, & J. Carlson (Eds.), *Contemporary issues in couples counseling* (pp. 225–233). New York, NY: Routledge Taylor & Francis.

Carson, B. (2012). *America the beautiful.* Grand Rapids, MI: Zondervan.

Casstevens, W. J. (2011). A pilot study of health and wellness development in an International Center for Clubhouse Development (ICCD): Procedures, implementations, and implications. *Psychiatric Rehabilitation Journal, 35*(1), 161–240.

Casstevens, W. J. (2013). Health and wellness at a clubhouse model program in North Carolina: A choice theory-based approach to program development and implementation. *International Journal of Choice Theory and Reality Therapy, 32*(2), 48–53.

Cherry, K. (2016). *Erikson's psychosocial stages summary chart.* Retrieved from http://psychology.about.com/library/bl_psychosocial_summary.htm

Clinton, T., & Hawkins, R. (2011). *The popular encyclopedia of Christian counseling.* Eugene, OR: Harvest House.

Corey, G. (2017). *Theory and practice of counseling and psychotherapy* (10th ed.). Boston, MA: Cengage Learning.

Corey, G., & Corey, M. (2018). *I never knew I had a choice: Explorations in personal growth* (11th ed.). Belmont, CA: Cengage Learning.

Corey, G., Corey, M., Corey C., & Callanan, P. (2015). *Issues and ethics in the helping professions* (9th ed.). Stamford, CT: Brooks/Cole Cengage Learning.

Daft, R., & Marcic, D. (2015). *Understanding management* (9th ed.). Stamford, CT: Cengage Learning.

Deming, W. E. (1986). *Out of the crisis.* Cambridge, MA: Massachusetts Institute of Technology.

Deming, W. E. (1993). *The new economics.* Cambridge, MA: Massachusetts Institute of Technology.

Ellis, A. (2008). Rational emotive behavior therapy. In R. Corsini (Ed.), *Current psychotherapies* (8th ed., pp. 187–222). Belmont, CA: Thomson Brooks/Cole.

Ellis, A., & Harper, R. (1997). *A guide to rational living.* North Hollywood, CA: Wilshire Books.

Ellis, D. (2012, December 5). *The brief, lasting and vigorous approach of rational emotive behavioral therapy.* Presentation at the Milton H. Erickson Brief Therapy Conference, San Francisco, CA.

Frankl, V. (1963). *Man's search for meaning.* Boston, MA: Beacon.

Fulkerson, M. H. (2014). *Treatment planning from a reality therapy perspective.* Owensboro, KY: Fulkerson.

Glasser, C. (1996). *The quality world activity set.* Northridge, CA: William Glasser, Inc.

Glasser, C. (2017). *My quality world workbook* (2nd ed.). Northridge, CA: William Glasser, Inc.

Glasser, W. (1965). *Reality therapy.* New York, NY: Harper & Row.

Glasser, W. (1968). *Schools without failure.* New York, NY: Harper & Row.

Glasser, W. (1972). *The identity society.* New York, NY: Harper & Row.

Glasser, W. (1981). *Stations of the mind.* New York, NY: Harper & Row.

Glasser, W. (1984). *Control theory.* New York, NY: HarperCollins.

Glasser, W. (1990). *The quality school.* New York, NY: HarperCollins.

Glasser, W. (1998). *Choice theory.* New York, NY: HarperCollins.

Glasser, W. (2000). *Reality therapy in action.* New York, NY: HarperCollins.

Glasser, W. (2003). *Warning: Psychiatry can be hazardous to your mental health.* New York, NY: HarperCollins.

Glasser, W. (2005a). *How the brain works.* Chatsworth, CA: The William Glasser Institute.

Glasser, W. (2005b). *Treating mental health as a public health issue.* Chatsworth, CA: The William Glasser Institute.

Glasser, W. (2011). *Take charge of your life.* Bloomington, IN: iUniverse.

Glasser, W., & Glasser, C. (2005). *Chart talk: The choice theory chart workbook.* Chatsworth, CA: The William Glasser Institute.

Glasser, W., & Glasser, C. (2008). Procedures: The cornerstone of institute training. *The William Glasser Institute Newsletter*, Summer. Chatsworth, CA: The William Glasser Institute.

Glasser, W., & Wubbolding, R. (1995). Reality therapy. In R. Corsini (Ed.), *Current psychotherapies* (pp. 293–321). Itasca, IL: Peacock.

Grills, C., Villanueva, S., Anderson, M., Corsbie-Massay, C., Smith, B., Johnson, L., & Owens, K. (2015). Effectiveness of choice theory connections: A cross-sectional and comparative analysis of California female inmates. *International Journal of Offender Therapy and Comparative Criminology, 59*(7), 757–771.

Gunaratana, H. (1992). *Mindfulness in plain English.* Somerville, MA: Wisdom.

Harder, A. F. (2012). The developmental stages of Erik Erikson. In *Healing relationships is an inside job.* Retrieved from www.support4change.com

Harris, J. (2016). Integrative theories of psychotherapy. In H. E. A. Tinsley, S. H. Lease, & N. S. Giffin Wiersma (Eds.), *Contemporary theory and practice in counseling and psychotherapy* (pp. 434–464). Los Angeles, CA: Sage.

Helzer, E. G. (2012). How much do intentions tell us about behavior? *The IACFP Newsletter, 44*(1), 20–21.

Herlihy, B., & Corey, G. (2015). *ACA ethical standards casebook* (7th ed.). Alexandria, VA: American Counseling Association.

Ivey, A. E., D'Andrea, M., & Ivey M. B. (2012). *Theories of counseling and psychotherapy: A multicultural perspective* (7th ed.). Thousand Oaks, CA: Sage.

Jackson, D. (2015). *Becoming a better good Samaritan.* Independence, MO: Aardvark.

Jacobs, E., & Schimmel, C. (2013). *Impact therapy: The courage to counsel.* Star City, WV: Impact Therapy Associates.

Jones-Smith, E. (2016). *Theories of counseling and psychotherapy.* Thousand Oaks, CA: Sage.

Kaku, M. (2011). *Physics of the future.* New York, NY: Anchor Books.

Kalodner, C. (2011). Cognitive-behavior theories. In D. Capuzzi & D. Gross (Eds.), *Counseling and psychotherapy theories and interventions* (pp. 193–214). Alexandria, VA: American Counseling Association.

Kim, H. S. (2016). *Development and effect of psychological well-being promoting program to reduce parenting stress for mothers of children with emotional behavioral problems* (Doctoral thesis, Inje University, Pusan, Korea).

Lojk, L. (1986). My experiences using reality therapy. *Journal of Reality Therapy, 5*(2), 28–35.

Marlatt, E. (2014). The neuropsychology behind choice theory: Five basic needs. *International Journal of Choice Theory and Reality Therapy, 34*(1), 16–21.

Mayo Clinic Staff. (n.d.). *When it comes to relieving stress, more giggles and guffaws are just what the doctor ordered. Here's why.* Retrieved from http://www.mayoclinic.org/healthy-lifestyle/stress-management/in-depth/stress-relief/art-20044456

Mitchell, R. (2007). *Documentation in counseling records* (3rd ed.). Alexandria, VA: American Counseling Association.

Myers, K. (2016). Member insights. *Counseling Today.* Retrieved from http://CT.counseling.org/category/member-insights/

Nickles, T. (2011). *The role of religion and spirituality in counseling.* Retrieved from http://digitalcommons.calpoly.edu

Nystul, M. (2011). *Introduction to counseling.* Upper Saddle River, NJ: Pearson.

Oakley, B. (2014). *A mind for numbers: How to excel at math and science even if you flunked algebra.* New York, NY: Tarcher Penguin.

Padesky, C., & Greenberger, D. (2012). *The clinician's guide to mind over mood.* New York, NY: Guilford Press.

Patterson, C. (1973). *Theories of counseling and psychotherapy.* New York, NY: Harper & Row.

Powers, W. (1973). *Behavior: The control of perception.* New York, NY: Aldine.

Reed, G. (2006). What qualifies as evidence-based practice? In J. Norcross, L. Beutler, & R. Levant (Eds.), *Evidence-based practices in mental health* (pp. 13–22). Arlington, VA: American Psychological Association.

Richardson, B. (2015). *Working with challenging youth* (2nd ed.) Philadelphia, PA: Brunner-Routledge.

Richey, J. (n.d.). *Principles of moral thought and action.* Retrieved from http://www.patheos.com/Library/Confucianism/Ethics-Morality-Community/Principles-of-Moral-Thought-and-Action.html

Robey, P., Wubbolding, R., & Carlson, J. (2012). *Contemporary issues in couples counseling.* New York, NY: Routledge Taylor & Francis.

Rogers, C. (1957). The necessary and sufficient conditions of therapeutic personality change. *Journal of Consulting Psychology, 21,* 95–103.

Rotter, J. B. (1954). *Social learning and clinical psychology.* New York, NY: Prentice-Hall.

Roy, J. (2014). *William Glasser: Champion of choice.* Phoenix, AZ: Zeig, Tucker & Theisen.

Satel, S., & Lilienfeld, S. O. (2013). *Brainwashed: The seductive appeal of mindless neuroscience.* New York, NY: Basic Books.

Short, D., Erickson, B., & Klein, R. (2005). *Hope and resiliency.* Norwalk, CT: Crown House.

Siegel, B. (2011, July 15). *A merry heart—Still the best medicine.* Retrieved from http://berniesiegelmd.com/2011/07/a-merry-heart—still-the-best-medicine/

Siegel, D. (2007). *The mindful brain.* New York, NY: Norton.

Siegel, D. (2010). *The mindful therapist.* New York, NY: Norton.

Siegel, D. (2012). *Pocket guide to interpersonal neurobiology.* New York, NY: Norton.

Siegel, D. (2015). *Brainstorm.* New York, NY: Tarcher.

Simpson, L. (2011). Dialectical behavior theory. In D. Capuzzi & D. Gross (Eds.), *Counseling and psychotherapy: Theories and interventions* (pp. 215–236). Alexandria, VA: American Counseling Association.

Sommers-Flanagan, J., & Sommers-Flanagan, R. (2012). *Counseling and psychotherapy theories in context and practice.* Hoboken, NJ: Wiley.

Sowell, T. (2013). *Intellectuals and race.* New York, NY: Basic Books.

Sowell, T. (2015). *Basic economics* (5th ed.). New York, NY: Basic Books.

Tan, S-Y. (2011). *Counseling and psychotherapy: A Christian perspective.* Grand Rapids, MI: Baker Academic.

Tinsley, H. E. A., Lease, S. H., & Wiersma, N. S. (2016). *Contemporary theory and practice in counseling and psychotherapy.* Los Angeles, CA: Sage.

Understanding military culture. (2016). *Good Practice,* Winter, 2–5.

Vernon, C. (2011). Rational emotive behavior therapy. In D. Capuzzi & D. Gross (Eds.), *Counseling and psychotherapy: Theories and interventions* (pp. 237–262). Alexandria, VA: American Counseling Association.

Wehrenberg, M. (2008). *The 10 best anxiety managing techniques.* New York, NY: Norton.

Wiener, N. (1948). *Cybernetics.* New York, NY: Wiley.

Wiener, N. (1952). *Nonlinear problems in random theory.* New York, NY: Technology Press of MIT & Wiley.

Wilcoxon, S., Remley, T., Gladding, S., & Huber, C. (2007). *Ethical, legal, and professional issues in the practice of marriage and family therapy* (4th ed.). Upper Saddle River, NJ: Pearson Education.

Williams, P., & Davis, D. (2007). *Therapist as life coach.* New York, NY: Norton.

Wubbolding, R. (1991). *Understanding reality therapy.* New York, NY: HarperCollins.

Wubbolding, R. (1997). *Reality therapy: Psychotherapy with the experts series* [DVD]. Available from http://psychotherapy.net

Wubbolding, R. (2000a). Brief reality therapy. In J. Carlson & L. Sperry (Eds.), *Brief therapy with individuals and couples* (pp. 264–286). Phoenix, AZ: Zeig, Tucker & Theisen.

Wubbolding, R. (2000b). *Reality therapy for the 21st century.* Philadelphia, PA: Brunner Routledge.

Wubbolding, R. (2007). Glasser quality school. *Group Dynamics: Theory, Research, and Practice, 11*(4), 253–261.

Wubbolding, R. (2011). *Reality therapy: Theories of psychotherapy series.* Arlington, VA: American Psychological Association.

Wubbolding, R. (2013). Reality therapy. In J. Frew & M. Spiegler (Eds.), *Contemporary psychotherapies for a diverse world* (2nd ed., pp. 339–372). New York, NY: Routledge Taylor & Francis.

Wubbolding, R. (2014). Reality therapy. In. G. R. Vanderbos, E. Meidenbauer, & J. Frank-McNeil (Eds.), *Psychotherapy theories and techniques* (pp. 307–315). Arlington, VA: American Psychological Association.

Wubbolding, R. (2015a). Acronyms and abbreviations in CT/RT. *International Journal of Choice Theory, 35*(1), 14–17.

Wubbolding, R. (2015b). Reality therapy and school practice. In R. Witte & G. S. Mosley-Howard (Eds.), *Mental health practice in today's schools* (pp. 169–192). New York, NY: Springer.

Wubbolding, R. (2015c). *Reality therapy training manual* (16th ed.). Cincinnati, OH: Center for Reality Therapy.

Wubbolding, R. (2016). Reality therapy. In H. E. A. Tinsley, S. H. Lease, & N. S. Giffin Wiersma (Eds.), *Contemporary theory and practice in counseling and psychotherapy* (pp. 173–200). Los Angeles, CA: Sage.

Wubbolding, R. (2017). *Cycle of counseling, coaching, managing, supervising, and parenting* [chart] (20th ed.). Cincinnati, OH: Center for Reality Therapy.

Wubbolding, R., & Brickell, J. (2005a). Purpose of behavior: Language and levels of commitment. *International Journal of Reality Therapy, 25*(1), 39–41.

Wubbolding, R., & Brickell, J. (2005b). Reality therapy in recovery. In *Directions in addiction treatment and prevention* (Vol. 9, Lesson 1, pp. 1–10). New York, NY: Hatherleigh.

Wubbolding, R. E., & Brickell, J. D. (2015). *Counselling with reality therapy* (2nd ed.). London, UK: Speechmark.

Zeig, J. K. (2006). *Confluence: The selected papers of Jeffrey K. Zeig.* Phoenix, AZ: Zeig, Tucker, & Theisen.

Index

Figures are indicated by "f" following the page numbers.

A

219

Z